Raising Our Children's Children

Deborah Doucette

Raising Our Children's Children

Deborah Doucette-Dudman
with Jeffrey R. LaCure

Fairview Press
Minneapolis

Alternative Cataloging-in-Publication Data
Doucette-Dudman, Deborah.
      Raising our children's children. By Deborah Doucette-Dudman, with Jeffrey R. LaCure. Minneapolis, MN: Fairview Press, copyright 1996.
      PARTIAL CONTENTS: The "bad" parent. -Family secrets. -When grandparents don't agree. -Healing the wounds. -Integrating the birth parent. -Mothers in prison. -Guardianship—adoption—letting go. -Grandchildren—having their say.
      1. Parenting by grandparents. 2. Family secrets. 3. Grandparents—Personal narratives. 4. Children of prisoners—Development and guidance. 5. Adoption by grandparents. 6. Guardian and ward. 7. Grandchildren—Personal narratives. I. Title. II. Title: Our children's children. III. LaCure, Jeffrey R. IV. Fairview Press

301.427 or 649.1

ISBN 0-925190-91-8 : $19.95

First Printing: March 1996 • Printed in the United States of America
00 99 98 97 96   7 6 5 4 3 2 1

Jacket design and illustration: Circus Design
Photo of Deborah Doucette-Dudman: Loren Sklar Photography

Publisher's Note: Fairview Press publishes books and other materials related to the subjects of family and social issues. Its publications, including *Raising Our Children's Children* do not necessarily reflect the philosophy of Fairview Hospital and Healthcare Services or their treatment programs. For a free current catalog of Fairview Press titles, please call this toll-free number: 1-800-544-8207.

Excerpt on page 5 from "The Bad Mother" from *Unremembered Country* © 1987 by Susan Griffin. Reprinted by permission of Copper Canyon Press, PO Box 271, Port Townsend, WA 98368. • Excerpt on page 23 from "Two Headed Poems" from *Selected Poems II: Poems Selected and New 1976-1986* © 1987 Margaret Atwood, published in the U.S. by Houghton Mifflin. Reprinted by permission of the author, Houghton Mifflin Co., and Oxford University Press, Canada. All rights reserved. • Excerpt on page 113 from the poem "Crazy Quilt" by Jane Wilson Joyce from the book *Quilt Pieces* is reprinted by permission of Gnomon Press. • Excerpt on page 141 from "Who Am I" by Felice Holman from *At the Top of My Voice and Other Poems* © 1971 Charles Scribner's Sons. Reprinted by permission of the author. • Excerpt on page 151 from "29" by ALTA from *Theme and Variations* © 1975, 1995 ALTA. • Excerpt on page 165 from "The Network of the Imaginary Mother 4 the Child" from *Upstairs in the Garden: Poems Selected and New, 1968-1988* by Robin Morgan copyright © 1990 by Robin Morgan. By permission of Edite Kroll Literary Agency.

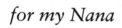

for my Nana

Contents

Acknowledgments

First and foremost, I wish to thank my daughter, Tyra, for her unflagging support and encouragement of my work on this book. I am grateful to my husband, Richard, for always being there for the kids, and I am deeply appreciative of my loving family—my source of strength and inspiration—including *all* my beautiful babies: Tyra, Tasha, Dane, and Sabra.

I would like to thank Jeffrey LaCure for his expertise, and the staff at Fairview Press for their patience. A special salute goes to the members of the Massachusetts Grandparent Support Group Network, and to the Massachusetts Executive Office of Elder Affairs who have worked so hard, and done so much for caregiving grandparents.

And, finally, I want to thank and praise each of the grandparents, children, grandchildren, and all of those caring individuals who participated in this project. Without their generosity, strength, wisdom, and love, this book could not have been written.

Preface

" Where there is room in the heart, there is always room on the hearth."
—Elisabeth Marbury, *My Crystal Ball*

"Mom, I'm pregnant." One of the most dreaded phone calls parents of a teenager can receive.

I was in my office when I got the call. At that time, I was a real estate broker in a country-style suburb about thirty minutes west of Boston, Massachusetts—a bedroom community of daffodil trails and bridle paths, with a one-gas-station, volunteer-fire-department, don't-blink-because-you'll-miss-it center. My husband Richard and I settled on this little town for the acre minimum zoning, the best-in-the-state school system, and because maybe, if you pay enough money, it will only rain after sundown.

We had three children: Tyra, 19, and a sophomore in college; Tasha, 16; and a little boy—our surprise package—Dane, who was three years old. Now, this phone call had brought me more than just another surprise, a mere bump in the road; this was more akin to a cement wall on the highway—a crack in the sky. It was a dizzying shock—the kind that spins you around until you are facing in a totally different direction, forever altered, and the very next step you take is a journey into foreign territories, unfamiliar landscapes.

Tyra's voice held a faint tremor of panic. I pictured her hunched over, sitting on the edge of her bed, gripping the phone as if she could squeeze some comfort from it. My heart hurt for her at the same time I was thinking, "Stupid, stupid, stupid!" I blurted out an "Oh my God!" before managing to get a grip on myself. I told her everything would be okay. We would work things out. Don't worry, I told her—and myself—then drove out to Connecticut to be with her and make some short-term plans.

Tyra was too far along in her pregnancy for a safe abortion. (A combination of the effects of birth control pills, antibiotics, and bronchitis had masked the pregnancy.) Having already gone through a painful break-up with her boyfriend months before, she was feeling more and more defeated, depressed, and angry. Tyra dropped out of school and came home to have her baby. She talked about putting the child up for adoption.

I let her talk and said nothing. I knew, though, we would never let that happen. At first, I hoped, fantasized that she would become an entirely different Tyra and actually want to raise a child. But I also knew that she wasn't ready for that and, in fact, might never be interested in raising children. She had never liked babies, never played with dolls, and never harbored any wish to be a mother. Tyra, bright and artistic, definitely marched to the tune of a different drummer. We always accepted that. We still accept it—celebrate it—even now. However, she was feeling so trapped, so sad, that I didn't want to agitate her any further; I kept my thoughts and feelings to myself for a while.

She asked me to find her a woman doctor, and I made an appointment with a very well regarded Ob/Gyn group in the area. I then made a call to speak to the doctor personally so that I could explain Tyra's situation to her. I began to tell her that although Tyra might want to talk about adoption with her that, in fact, we would never allow that to happen. I didn't want any action taken to hook her up with prospective adoptive parents. Among other things, I still held out a small kernel of hope that she might bond with her baby during the process of pregnancy, and I certainly didn't want that potential severed prematurely.

But I no sooner got the words out of my mouth, "Tyra will want to talk about adoption ... ," than she cut in on me, telling me effusively that she had "many wonderful couples in my practice waiting to adopt."

I interrupted her. "Wait a minute, I just wanted to let you know that it will never happen, that my husband and I would adopt the baby before we would allow the child to be adopted out."

"Because that's the way *you* want it to be!" she spat out at me indignantly. I believed I could hear her salivating over the phone lines, licking her chops over my grandchild.

Angered, I replied, "Because that's the way it *will* be."

I wondered then about society's well-meaning rush to sever those tenuous bonds with other young women brought to their knees by the uncertainty, fear, and desperation of an unexpected pregnancy. I am uncomfortable with the blanket of moral certitude under which these decisions are made by those in authority. Attaching young pregnant women who are often alone, unhappy, and impoverished to eager, happily married couples who are more financially stable may force the beleaguered birth mother's life-altering decision into a too-early fait accompli. I wonder about this still.

The doctor made me her adversary from that moment on. She never understood that, for us, this was a *family* decision. Tyra was young, panicked, and confused. At this point, all she wanted was to have her pain erased. We needed time over the next few months to help her sort out her feelings and goals and make plans for the future—hers and the baby's.

I wanted this doctor to be an advocate for the family as a whole, but she couldn't get past her bias. Ironically, society as a whole embraces the concept of traditional adoption, but adoption within families is still regarded as odd. I have come across this attitude time and time again over these last few years, the attitude that although there is something inherently good and noble about traditional adoption, there is, on the other hand, something unseemly or unfortunate about interfamilial adoptions.

When I made a second call to Tyra's doctor in later weeks because of my concern that Tyra wasn't eating, she responded, "I'm going to tell Tyra that you called." She said it like a threat. And while I fully realized that she had to share this information with Tyra, she couched it in such a way as to portray me as interfering, my call as unacceptable.

Over the next few months, the doctor and her staff managed to convey to Tyra that the idea of grandparents adopting a baby was peculiar. Fortunately, Tyra has never felt the need to be conventional or feared things that were "different." Nonetheless, their attitudes made our family decision-making process that much more difficult at a time when we would have welcomed any constructive input.

In time, Tyra came to see the good in keeping the baby within the family. Frankly, though, their relationship did have a slow start. Two days after the baby was born, my daughter left to go back to college. She fled. She could not cope with the baby at all. Back at school, she went into a depressive tail spin. Tyra had difficulty coming to terms with the fact that she had a daughter back in Massachusetts. I spent a lot of time explaining to her that even though she wouldn't be a "mother" to her baby, she needed to establish a caring relationship with her. She was so traumatized by the whole experience that it took her some time to reconnect with the bonds of love that were buried under her personal pain.

Tyra did lift herself out of that well of despair, but it took months. It took phone calls and visits and talks and threats and tears. Slowly, her depression lifted. Her negativity evaporated as if a bad fever had finally broken and she was herself again. Even during those most difficult days, I had some confidence that Tyra would eventually work her way through her pain and ambivalence.

During those bad days—the ones that I swam through in lethargic slow motion as if in a river of molasses, and after several weeks of getting up at night for feedings and changing what seemed like hundreds of diapers a day, I was feeling quite sorry for myself. We never regretted our decision—not ever! But that never stopped me from rolling in self-pity now and then. Occasionally, I tried to look on the bright side; at least I didn't have cracked nipples this time around.

Here was our little Sabra—all seven and a half pounds of her. I had watched her slip quietly into the world—into our family—and I recognized her instantly. She was ours. The fourth in a line of first-born daughters, connecting us to generations past, leading us to our future. It was inconceivable that our sweet, bald-headed baby girl could be anywhere else. The absence of her, the loss would be unimaginable. I never lost sight of that.

Meanwhile, because of the added work load, I not only left my job at the real estate office, but also totally abandoned any hope of continuing my fledgling career as a freelance journalist. While I am sure there are women out there who are able to combine teenagers, toddlers, and infants with a writing career, I knew that I was not one of them.

In addition, this was the second time in my life that I had to deal with the combination of a teenager in high school and an infant in diapers. (Tyra was in high school when my son Dane was born.) It seemed a weird and incompatible mix. There I was, waiting up at night for one child to come home and getting up an hour later to feed the other. For the second time in my life, I was grappling with a teenager (Tasha this time) over schoolwork, dating, drinking, and birth control, while adjusting formula, worrying about colic, and trying to work out naps with an infant. In the meantime there were nursery school carpools, karate lessons, and play dates for Dane. All of which I experienced through a numbing haze of sleep deprivation. A friend pointed out that I must be working out some mighty strange karma. This is not what I had envisioned my forties to be like.

One morning, while sitting on the couch still in my pajamas, my hair uncombed, the baby lying against my chest so she would finally—Please God!—sleep, I tuned in to a local TV talk show. There were two older women talking about their support group, Grandparents As Parents. I remember clearly one of the women saying to the host, "We haven't even had time to roll over." The host didn't have the slightest clue what the woman meant by that, but I knew. No chance to ever think of yourself. No time when you don't have to get up in the morning for someone else. No time that you could just roll over and go back to sleep if you choose.

I managed to write down the telephone number that flashed on the screen without—Thank you God!—waking the baby. Later that month I traveled the 30 miles one rainy night to attend their monthly meeting.

That meeting—with over 50 other grandparents, mostly women—was a tremendous eye-opener for me. At the age of 42, I was by far the youngest there. As the others talked, they revealed concerns and problems ranging from custody battles to losing elderly housing because of grandchildren in their home to finding child care while they went into the hospital for hip replacement surgery. Some were so old that they had trouble making it down the steep stairs to the basement meeting room of the Council on Aging building. Hearing about their experiences really put things in perspective for me. I stopped feeling sorry for myself and came to see myself and my family as quite blessed.

Yet we still had some kinks to iron out with regard to the newest member of our family. Because Tyra had left so soon after Sabra's birth to go back to school, I was concerned that she did not have time to bond with her baby. I knew their relationship would need to be encouraged and nurtured for it to grow. It would take patience and time and work.

Their relationship has blossomed. Tyra and Sabra have grown to love one another and have became connected in a very special way. Sabra's birth father and his family are an essential part of Sabra's life as well. We have been successful, I think, in integrating both birth parents into Sabra's life and ours. It takes work. It takes a commitment to family—immediate and extended—and to the good of the child. We have always believed that there is room for everyone in Sabra's life and that it is healthy and, in fact, quite normal to be so inclusive.

Our story is not the norm, however. In most cases many destructive forces have come into play leading to the necessity of grandparents stepping into the breach. We have been very fortunate. We did not have to deal with any of those negative elements, and so it was relatively easy for us to open our arms in welcome to everyone involved.

Other grandparents do not find their lot so easy. They may be elderly and coping with ill health and fixed incomes. They may have several grandchildren to house, clothe, and feed. They may be dealing with birth parents who are abusing drugs, are alcoholic, violent or in jail. And they may be dealing with grandchildren suffering the effects of years of abuse and neglect, children with serious special needs. Some grandparents must scrape by at poverty level, receiving little or no assistance from state agencies for their grandchildren. Or they may be embroiled in an emotionally and financially draining battle with birth parents over custody of the children.

These are the grandparents for whom this book is written: for the grandparents who hesitate to step forward to ask for help because they are too filled with guilt or shame; for grandparents who feel their situation is unique; for grandparents who need to know that others have been there too and that there are ways to cope, opportunities to heal, and help available.

In gathering material for this book, I met with family members—grandparents, adult children and grandchildren—over the course of a year. Seasons changed as I got to know each of them, the remarkable people that speak to you now from these pages. Their stories are harrowing, touching, and true. With few exceptions, names have been changed, and in some cases, locations and other identifying markers have been altered to provide some measure of privacy. But I have tried to capture the essence of each person, each family, each experience, and to share with you their feelings and mine in the hopes that you can feel you know them as well as I do.

Additionally, family therapist Jeffrey LaCure provides guidelines for coping with situations described in each chapter. Questions that arise about adoption, birth parents, sibling rivalry, and the like are answered by LaCure, and also by the successful experiences of the grandparents themselves.

The people interviewed for this book came forward out of a desire to help others. They opened their generous hearts to me, often revealing painful wounds and unspeakable hurts. And, even though some grandparents' stories have been utilized to show examples of problem areas, they *all* have one thing in common; they are raising grandchildren who have thrived under their care.

Here now are the intimate portraits of families who have survived cataclysmic rifts in their family structure. Their backgrounds vary; they have differing religions and beliefs, come from various ethnic and economic groups, and function within a set of circumstances that is, at once, specific to them as well as universal to families everywhere. But at their very core, they share the same goals—children that are healed, families that are whole.

Introduction

There are 3.2 million children in the United States living with their grandparents or other kin, a 40 percent increase since 1980.[1]

Influencing the shift of custody from birth parents to grandparents are these factors: More than 500,000 children live in some form of alternate, funded care arrangement, i.e., foster care, group homes or institutional care;[2] Over half a million babies are born to teenage mothers every year;[3] At least 80% of incarcerated women are mothers;[4] Within five years, it is estimated that 125,000 children and teenagers will be orphaned by the AIDS epidemic.[5] Many of these children will be taken in by grandparents or other extended family members. Many more *would* be if their extended families, grandparents in particular, could count on the help they need from social service agencies.

Situations where grandparents have informal custody of grandchildren remain grossly underreported. Some grandparents conceal the fact that they have children in their care because they are afraid to lose their "elderly housing." Some fear interference by social service agencies that may take their grandchildren from them. Some fear reprisals from drug-involved children and keep a low profile while doing their best to keep grandchildren out of harm's way. Grandparents who don't want to rock the boat don't tell.

Grandparents stepping in to take care of grandchildren when parents cannot do so is nothing new. However, the exploding epidemic of drug and alcohol abuse in our younger population has forced more and more grandparents to rescue their grandchildren from the devastation of a life poisoned by addicted birth parents. Factors emanating from a home ruled by addicts such as poverty, chaos, and parents incapacitated by AIDS or absent through incarceration add to the problems the grandchildren bring with them.

Many grandchildren coming into the care of our elders are hurt, deprived, needy. They may be affected by attention deficit disorder and fetal alcohol syndrome, learning disabilities and hyperactivity. They have suffered the mind-numbing wounds of neglect and a terrifying array of abuses—physical, sexual, and emotional.

Frequently, grandparents are forced to struggle with birth parents and/or social service departments in costly and protracted custody battles. Too often social service systems under the mandate of "family reunification," squander the childhoods of the children involved, condemning them to years of being jerked from foster care to failed birth parents and back into foster care again. All this shuffling is done for the sake of "parental rights" and a narrowly defined policy of reunification of the family.

Sometimes a family is *not* a family when birth parents cannot, do not, and will not parent. Obviously the function of giving birth does not automatically lead to healthy child rearing; many obstacles may stand in the way. Meanwhile, the concept of family reunification, so strictly adhered to, may prevent children from living with loving members of that same *extended* family.

Social service agencies need to redirect their "prime directive" to read, "in the best interest of the child." The mandate toward family reunification must be secondary to what is best for the child, always. That mandate should be altered to fall under the broader heading of "family preservation," while expanded to include extended family such as grandparents and the strengthening of those preexisting bonds. It takes work to preserve a family in the larger sense, to strengthen families. And it will take a more encompassing outlook by society at large as well as social service agencies. "It takes a village to raise a child" is an old proverb that rings especially true today.

But the battle cry of the day is welfare reform, and it would be tragic if that reform translated to fewer services and less help to children in need. Now there is even talk of bringing back orphanages. Ironically, this solution is most often spoken by those who wave the banner of "family values." To those men and women, one might ask: On your watch, is this the best you can do for the children under your guard?

In a recent article about orphanages, a boy named Jimmy was profiled. Born of alcoholic, drug-abusing parents, he was bounced around between foster care and group homes. When he was 13, Jimmy was finally placed with his grandmother whom he loved. But her poverty, and the rough neighborhood she was consigned to live in because of it, made their situation unworkable. Jimmy was taken from his grandmother and placed in a group home for teens. Group homes and similar institutional care for kids like Jimmy can cost up to $59,000 per child per year.[6] It would have taken a lot less to allow Jimmy and his grandmother to stay together as a family in a safe environment.

However (grandparent's catch-22 number one), grandparents do not receive the same services or the same financial assistance as foster care parents. Although "kinship care"[7] is a concept that is beginning to be considered today, for the most part, the attitude of social service agencies seems to be that extended families should care for their related children solely out of the goodness of their hearts. But one can't eat goodness, or buy clothes with it, or use it to obtain counseling or better housing. Grandparents willing to relinquish hard-won custody over to the local department of social services *may* qualify as foster parents or (grandparent's catch-22 number two) they may *not*. But (grandparent's catch-22 number three), these grandparents do not want to give their grandchildren back to the foster care system from which they probably fought to free them!

What are the answers? Defining families to include kin would be a start, then it's necessary to provide them with the means to care for damaged and needy children and also recognize grandparents as a resource gold mine, while respecting *their* special needs as elders.

Grandparents raising their grandchildren, contrary to what most people believe, is not only an urban problem, a minority problem, or a problem restricted to the poor. This is an exploding sociological trend with far-reaching implications for our future. It spans every segment of society—rich and poor, black and white, Asian and Hispanic, urban and suburban. Whenever and wherever drug or alcohol addiction, domestic violence, or child abuse touch a family, the specter of hurt and abandoned children haunts us all. The measure of a culture is how well it treats its most vulnerable—its children. The strength of a culture is determined by what those children become. How are we measuring up?

This is a book of windows—windows and doors. Each chapter becomes a window on the private lives of those grandparents, birth parents, and children who are at the core of this alarming trend. Within each interview are examples of the many challenges that face grandparents who are drawn into the fray to protect their grandchildren. As you read their stories, you can see for yourself how well we measure up.

Look in one window and find a court system fumbling its way through a child rape trial, another affords a view into a troubled social service system riddled with inconsistency. Another shows us a drug war focusing on an ineffective cops and robbers game while overlooking the children caught in the crossfire and politicians who just don't get it. One window clearly shows a prison system filled by the rules of gender politics, and still another shows school systems inadequately prepared to deal with the influx of special needs students.

For grandparents, these windows offer ways of coping and methods of healing. There are views onto what has worked for others and what has not, as well as a look at the skills used to navigate the minefield of challenges that confront grandparent caregivers.

My hope is that these windows will become doors to finding help for grandparents: doors to raising awareness; doors to changing our views about parental rights, the nature of family, and what is in the "best interest of the child." Ultimately, I hope these doors lead to a better understanding of the complex issues involved when we must raise our children's children.

—Deborah Doucette-Dudman

Note from the Therapist

While working as a counselor and coordinator for a family services agency in Roxbury, Massachusetts, I learned that while there were many skilled and competent mental health professionals, there were, however, very few who truly understood and appreciated the variety of issues that occur in foster, adoptive, and custodial families. I am an adoptee and know firsthand what it is like to be raised by someone other than a birth parent. I empathize with the struggles and joys of the families highlighted in this book. If a grandparent is willing, loving, and available to parent his or her grandchild, it can be a win-win arrangement for all involved, particularly the child.

My commentary, liberally sprinkled (in smaller type and indented) throughout the book offers my professional advice on issues with which each family must contend. I have addressed challenges that face grandparents every day from dealing with a troubled grown child, to family secrets, to guilt. I hope that the advice I offer, combined with the experiences of the grandparents interviewed, will help others successfully deal with their own family situations as they work together for the sake of their grandchild. There is no better motivation.

—Jeffrey R. LaCure

1

The "Bad" Parent

"... she drives with all her magic down a
different route to darkness ..."
                    —Susan Griffin, "The Bad Mother"

"He hates his mother." One grandmother was telling me about the teenage grandson she was raising. "He told me he'd like to kill her!" Her eyes glittered with self-righteous satisfaction. I winced and thought, here is the next generation of men who hate women.

We were at a monthly meeting of Grandparents As Parents (GAP), a support group for grandparents raising their grandchildren. GAP has chapters nationwide, as do other grassroots organizations formed over the last few years to fill the need for information and for connecting with others trying to cope with similar issues and concerns—groups such as Grandparents Offering Love and Devotion (GOLD), Raising Our Children's Kids; an Intergenerational Network of Grandparenting (ROCKING), and Grandparents of the Nineties. I began a support group in my area when I realized how many grandparents were struggling in this situation with nowhere to turn.

Clearly, the self-righteous grandmother attending our little group disliked her daughter-in-law, despised her in fact. There are toxic birth parents to be sure, and perhaps this was one. But we as grandparents must be so careful with the delicate balance between what we know and what we convey to the grandchildren involved. We should not conceal truths, but rather explain faults.

Working to preserve a relationship between birth parent and child is one of the caregiving grandparent's most critical tasks. Grandparents need to find ways of dealing with the questions and concerns children have that help them to turn anger into understanding.

Many grandparents harbor hard feelings toward the birth parents who left them struggling with the care of their grandchildren—parents who may even have neglected or abused the children. It's a difficult job to check back that anger and talk about the birth parents calmly with such a bitter taste in your mouth. But the children deserve to see their world with clear eyes, unclouded by hatred.

I wince again every time I think about that teenage boy and how the hatred he harbors will infect his life. I would be willing to bet that he will grow up not just hating his mother, he will hate himself, and he'll feel he is worth nothing because he believes his own mother was worthless. Perhaps he will be fearful and suspicious of women in general. He will probably have low self-esteem and the poor judgment that grows out of it, and the cycle of addiction, abuse, and neglect will come full circle.

Certainly grandparents do not intentionally plant the seeds of doubt and self-loathing in their grandchildren. They may do it inadvertently, however, with the unchecked remark, the conversation overheard, the stony silence when the birth parent is mentioned.

Healthy children is what we grandparents are all after. Sometimes the road to achieving that is so hard that we have to leave all the negative feelings behind—like so much dead weight—or we won't get to that good place.

The Donaldsons

Marci and Pete Donaldson are a caring, thoughtful couple in the midst of a custody battle with their daughter. They often talk about her and her boyfriend with angry voices as they churn over and over again the events of the last few months. The challenges they face on a daily basis with the care of their grandsons, the court battles, and their disappointments naturally fuel the fire of their anger. They may believe the boys are too young to understand. But they understand all too well, and they quietly store their feelings up. They will let them out later.

Cranberry Court is quite nice, not what I expected at all. Here the trailers are laid out on comfortable little tracts of land just like any other neighborhood. The small homes, looking very much like ranch houses, sit on landscaped lawns dotted with trees, gardens, and shrubs. At the edges of each of the lawns is a rim of sand that fans into the street—a reminder that the ocean isn't far away, an explanation for the scrub oak and gnarled pine and the flirting breeze that ruffles the leaves in defiance of the white hot air. Some yards are neat and orderly, and some are scruffier, scattered with flung down toys, Barbie carcasses, and large, plastic, turtle-shaped sandboxes. The Donaldsons' yard is clearly the latter variety. Two orange and yellow "crazy coupes" dominate the front walk. A big, blue Oldsmobile has been carefully parked across the lower end of the drive so that rambunctious little feet can't paddle into the road.

Matthew is the first to greet me. At five years old, he is close to the same height as his three-year-old brother Joshua. Matthew has a sweet, pixie look with sparkly blue eyes and a freshly "buzzed" head ready for the summer heat wave we are swimming in. His face has the flattened appearance typical of children with fetal alcohol syndrome.

Joshua is stockier than his older brother. His square little body charges around the small house and enclosed porch demanding attention. He runs up to me and shouts "Hi!" He has a sturdy look about him, from his full, round face to his solid shoulders, a direct contrast to his older brother. I become instantly confused as to which is the older and which is the younger brother, a problem which plagues me throughout the interview.

Their speech is difficult to understand. It is essentially baby talk, but in Matthew's case the sounds he makes are also affected. They are muffled and monotone, like the speech attempts of someone hard of hearing. Marci and Pete alternate translations.

Marci and Pete are an average couple—middle-class, middle-aged, working Americans, young as grandparents go, fortysomething. Pete is compact, wiry, energetic, with a careworn, mustached face, and brown eyes underneath expressive dark eyebrows. Marci, a bit taller than Pete, has neatly coifed, short, blonde hair; flawless, alabaster skin; and nearly transparent blue eyes that flash with anger as she speaks.

Matthew and Joshua are the children of Marci's 25-year-old daughter Jennifer. Pete is Jennifer's step-father. Marci's back goes rigid as we sit around the dining table and she begins to talk. "From the beginning when they were born, we were very concerned about their well-being," she says. "Jenny's boyfriend, Mark, had always been very abusive with us, very hostile and violent, and it made me wonder what kind of man was this to be around children. And, of course we can't prove it, but we think he also abuses her."

Pete leans forward and adds, "He is abusive to her but she doesn't admit it—she's battered, but she doesn't recognize it. He has pulled her by the hair and dragged her around by the hair. He has verbally abused her, and he has taken some swats at her, but she excuses it. She says, 'Oh, he's got problems, he's a schizo.'

"We began to see the signs before Matthew was born, Marci had brought vitamins for Jenny to take while she was pregnant. Mark told Jenny, 'You don't need vitamins. My mother never took vitamins and you don't need them either.'

"Sometimes after we'd spoken to Jenny, and maybe we might have argued with her or told her she should be doing this or that, he would call us up and threaten us, tell us he was going to cut our heads off or put me in cement shoes and drop me into the water." Pete relays this information calmly, leaning forward, elbows on the table and stroking his mustache. His voice is even, his speech slow and measured.

"When I went in to see Jenny while she was in labor with Matthew, there he was slapping her on the thighs and saying 'It don't hurt, don't be a baby!' Pete's eyebrows shoot upward and he shakes his head. "And I mean, if you've had a child, you know what the pain is. So I encouraged her and I helped her through it. He left. After a while he came back, but he was more out of the room than he was in. The doctor came in and said to me, 'You're coming in with her.' Well, I had never done that before, but I went in and the baby was born.

"Two or three days later we went back to the hospital," Pete continues, "and we told her we would come back in the morning and she could come home with us for a couple of days. We were concerned because she was young and inexperienced, and we wanted to help out. When we came back the next morning, Mark yelled at me, 'You're not taking her anywhere!' and he pushed me against the wall. I tried to calm him down and told him, 'All she wants to do is come down with her mother for a few days. She's never taken care of a little infant before.'

" 'That baby's not going anywhere!' Mark said. Well, I got really angry and told him, 'If you are so concerned, why don't you go put your name on the birth certificate.' He wouldn't do it. But a nurse came over to us quietly and said, 'It's best that he doesn't do that. Let that lie. Someday, if you ever want custody of the child, you can just ignore him.'

Marci is sitting at sharp attention, focusing intensely on Pete's recollections. She jumps in with some memories of her own, "When Matthew was born, and later too, he had all the classic symptoms of fetal alcohol syndrome—not sleeping, hyperactivity, short attention span." She adds, "Of course we didn't realize what it was at the time."

"Things became more and more difficult between Jenny and us. From time to time they would come down here for visits, but mostly they would hold Matthew over our heads, not allow us to see him. After a while, it got to a point where I just gave up. I didn't call anymore." Marci continues in a thoroughly disgusted tone, "Jenny got pregnant a couple of more times and had abortions and then she finally got pregnant again and had Joshua."

The children have been playing in a screened porch filled with toys adjacent to the dining area where we sit talking. I look behind me to see brown eyes, round as stones, peering back over a huge yellow dump truck.

> "Bad-mouthing" birth parents in the presence of grandchildren will only serve to build a false, fragile allegiance between themselves and the children that will, in all probability, backfire down the road. More important, it may cause the children to feel that, If my birth parents are "no good," then I must be "no good." Grandparents need to be mindful of the whereabouts of their grandchildren, no matter how young or old, as they discuss the shortcomings of their birth parents.

At this point Matthew runs over to Pete and says, "Papa, Papa, more," and holds up a sippy cup with a few drops of apple juice still left in it. Pete bends to him and says slowly, patiently, "More? In a little while I can get you more, Okay?" Then he asks Matt, "Did you say Hi?" and nods in my direction.

"Hello," I say to the little boy. Again I ask of Pete, "Which one is this?"

"Matthew," Pete answers in the same patient tone he uses with the boys.

"This Papa Pete!" Matthew says to me proudly, pointing at Pete. Marci and Pete burst out laughing. Pete rubs the spikes of hair at the top of Matt's head, and Matt fairly sizzles with delight at the attention his grandparents are focusing on him.

Pete tells me that after Joshua was born the child had some difficulties breathing. "Well, she smoked real heavy during both of the pregnancies. We didn't see Joshua that much at first. We hadn't seen either of the children for a while. It was so difficult. We would try to visit them down there at their apartment, but Mark would turn the stereo on so loud while we were there that you couldn't even think. We would try to ignore him, because we didn't want any fighting or anything like that in front of the kids. Then Jenny started coming here to visit. We noticed that the children had bruises on them. That was just a couple of years ago. Matthew was two and a half and. ..."

"*Matthew* is the oldest?" I interrupt Pete, confused again. "I'm sorry, I have to write this down. I can never keep track of names," I say in apology. In fact, I am mortified because I realize every time I make this mistake, I am inadvertently pointing out that there is something very wrong with Matthew, that the reason I cannot keep straight which is the older and which is the younger brother is because Matthew is underdeveloped and so very delayed. I am horrified with myself. I open my notebook and in large print I write down that MATTHEW IS THE OLDEST = HE JUST TURNED FIVE, and I keep the book open in front of me.

Marci tells me that Jenny started to allow them to take the children for extended visits. "But when we started noticing more bruises on Mattie, we took them both to a doctor here in Plymouth. He said it looked like someone had grabbed Matthew's arm like this." Marci grabs her upper arm and squeezes hard. "The doctor said Matt had failure to thrive and was malnourished. And they both had very high lead levels. That was when we first heard about fetal alcohol syndrome and the shape of Mattie's face being abnormal. The doctor reported all this to the Department of Social Services (DSS) where she lives. They went and investigated, but they said they found nothing wrong."

Professionals that work with children, such as doctors, nurses, teachers, counselors, and the police are mandated to report any suspicions of abuse to the Department of Social Services. This report is referred to as a 51A and is simply a claim alleging abuse or neglect of a child by a caretaker. Anyone can, and should, file a 51A when abuse is suspected.

> Although abuse and poor parenting are a significant part of the boy's relationship with their parents, the boys will struggle with loyalty issues between their birth parents and grandparents. Even when children suffer from traumatic abuse at the hands of their parents, most children still want to "protect" their parents and continue a relationship with them.

It is critical that Pete and Marci foster the children's need for connection with their birth parents. Speaking accurately, honestly and using appropriate language with the children when discussing Jenny and Mark will give Pete and Marci great mileage and actually serve to strengthen their own relationship with the boys.

"DSS has done nothing," Marci continues. "The man I spoke to there was very rude to me on the phone. Refused to talk about it with me. I have a file this thick." She spread her index finger and thumb apart about three inches. "All the paperwork, everything. I have the doctor's report that says that he spoke to them. They were supposed to look into it but. ..." Marci shrugs and then stares at her hands folded on the table in front of her, shaking her head.

Documentation is critical for grandparents embroiled in custody battles with their children. Keeping a daily journal chronicling the amount of contact, telephone calls, missed visits, and conversations between birth parent and child is important for drawing a picture of the kind of relationship the birth parent is capable of sustaining. This information is particularly useful in court if birth parents attempt to portray an entirely different view of events. Written details, dates, and times lend credibility to an account brought forth by grandparents.

Marci looks up and says tightly, "We were supposed to have the kids all that week, but when Jenny found out we took them to the doctor, she called up and said, "I'm coming down to get those kids and don't try to stop me or I'll get the police." She'd done it before, so I said, 'Well, come down and get them then.' The visits after that were very sporadic."

"Then came last August," Pete says. "We pulled up in front of the office building where Jenny works to pick the kids up. Matthew had no underwear on and pants that were way too big for him, hanging down and filthy. He stank of urine. Joshua stank of urine, and they were very, very dirty. Jenny was inside working. Mark was outside sitting on a truck with a bunch of other people drinking beer. Mark was the one who took care of them while Jenny was working."

Marci interrupted, "We have reason to believe that the children were left alone. We can't prove it but, ..."

"That's right," Pete continues. "When we moved the kids into their bedroom, I had to take the door off the hinges before they would go inside, they were so afraid. They are terrified of closed doors. After I took the door off, they were so happy about their new room and they laughed. But it's funny, they have a laugh that has a cry in it too—it's a laugh with a cry ... ," Pete trails off reflectively.

"Anyway, when we were at the office building to pick up the children that day, Mark picked up Joshua and threw him, literally threw him at me saying, 'Here, take 'em!'"

> When Matthew and Joshua begin to ask questions, such as why they are not with their birth father, I would suggest the grandparents respond with something as follows: "Your father left you alone a lot, and sometimes he didn't treat you as well as a father should treat his sons, as well as you deserve to be treated."
>
> And I would encourage Pete and Marci, when talking to the children about their mother, to use clear, age-appropriate language such as: "Your mother drank too much and she did not take as good care of you as she could have," rather than something like "Your Mom is a drunk who isn't worth a damn." While many grandparents may be tempted to go with the latter, they will find that their grandchildren's self-esteem will benefit from the former.
>
> Sharing information needs to be at age-appropriate times. As the children approach the ages of nine or ten, they will be old enough to hear and understand the specific details of their father's behaviors and lack of parenting skills. Before the children are teenagers, they will need to know the rest of their story, including their parents' chaotic past.

"They smelled so bad and they were so dirty. We had to take them somewhere and get clothes for them and wash them up before we could even continue on."

Marci adds, "Matthew had a gash right here." She rubs her finger across a spot over her eyebrow.

Pete says, "I asked Matthew, 'What happened?' He said 'Daddy, boo-boo.' I said to Marci, 'These kids are not going back.' She said, 'Well, what are we going to do?' I said, 'We'll just stall for time.' So we kept them.

"I said, 'Come on, we are going up to the courthouse and we will get in front of a judge today, because these children aren't going back.'" Jenny called us and said, 'Are you bringing the children back?' and I said, 'Oh yes, we'll be up there.' I lied to her. Then I called back and said, 'The car broke down and we won't be there until later.'

"So we went to the courthouse and waited there with the children from nine o'clock in the morning until five o'clock in the afternoon to get in to see the judge. We finally saw the judge and he granted us temporary custody for one week until we could get her into court. The judge told us we had to go serve her with a paper that explained it.

"We drove back up to Saugus and Jenny started off 'Okay, c'mon kids.'

I told her, 'Wait a minute Jenny, we went and got custody of these children today because you're not taking care of them.' She said, 'You can't do that!' then she ran back into the building and came back out with Mark's mother who works in the same building.

"I told her again, 'These children aren't being taken care of, they are neglected, and until we get this straightened out, we will keep them.' She said, 'You can't do that.' I said to her, 'Jennifer, get in this car and come home with us if you don't want to be separated from them.' She said, 'You can't control my life, you're not telling me what to do!' I said, 'But you aren't taking care of these children and we have a right.' "

"We got into court a week later," Pete goes on. "We saw Mark come in. He had gotten a haircut, he was all cleaned up, and he said to us, 'We'll see what goes on today.' While we were sitting there, he kept taunting me, and his father who was also there kept going like this," Pete slices across his throat with his fingers. "I just ignored it.

"We all went into an office with the court officer who was trying to straighten things out. We sat down and Mark started ranting and raving, and finally the court officer said, 'Wait a minute, I am getting a little nervous sitting here with you. I can imagine how these kids feel living with you.' Mark went off the wall. Then the court officer said, 'I ran your rap sheet and you have quite a few warrants out for your arrest, and I have called and they are coming to arrest you right now.'

"One of the warrants was for rape. They came and arrested him, took him away, and we didn't have to deal with him that day; we had to deal with Jennifer."

Matthew comes running, full tilt, up to Pete again.

"Wan more!" he says and plunks his juice cup down on the table.

"You want more?" Pete says looking into Matthew's eyes. "How would you like me to put the sprinkler on?"

"Yeah!" shouts Matthew.

Pete smiles into Matt's face, pleased at the delight he sees there. The heat has steadily risen and is well over 90 degrees now, humid and stifling.

"These trailers really hold the heat," Marci tells me. A fine veil of perspiration glistens on her upper lip.

The boys have been very patient, and we take a break so Pete can turn on the hose and help Matt and Josh into their bathing suits. Marci and I chat awhile with the tape recorder off as we sip on tall glasses of ice water. She grows quiet, at loose ends without Pete by her side.

Their home is small but comfortable, neatly kept and jam-packed with mementos, photos, and knickknacks carefully arranged about the room. A waist-high stack of children's videos fill one corner near the TV. Another corner holds a bookcase overflowing with volumes, with Danielle Steele featured heavily. Marci tells me they really need more space now and are looking for a larger home.

Marci asks me about my own situation and how I came to be writing a book about grandparents. She seems to relax as I talk on, and I realize how tense she's been, not from nervousness, not because of the tape recorder, but from the angry feelings she harbors for her daughter, the situation, and the reliving of it.

Marci began to tell me that in early 1993 when they were having difficulty obtaining access to their grandchildren, she went to court to petition for visitation rights. At probate court she was given forms to fill in, but her situation did not fit in any of the categories required for completion of the form. There were provisions for divorced birth parents, or a parent with a deceased partner, couples who had moved out of state, but none that fit their particular situation. Grandparents' rights are sketchily drawn and vary from state to state. For the most part, when there is an intact marriage and one or both partners feel the need to exclude grandparents from the children's lives, they have that right and power. In other words, grandparents have little or no legal recourse. Marci asked if she could just fill in "other" and leave it at that, but the clerk said, "You better get a lawyer." "But I don't want a lawyer," Marci replied "I shouldn't have to have a lawyer to fill out a paper!"

Marci says that Pete eventually went back to probate court to see the lawyer they have on hand to answer questions. He waited all day, but there were so many people still ahead of him, he finally left. "It was just a month later that this other stuff came up, and we didn't need to go that route," Marci confides.

Pete comes back and settles into his chair, out of breath, and picks up where he left off. "Mark had been scheduled for a rape trial and had never shown up. The rape supposedly took place just before he started seeing my daughter. So that was hanging over his head and they arrested him right there. But he only got fined and then let out on the street."

"Ha!" Marci blurts out angrily. "That didn't surprise me!"

Pete talks a little more about Mark, "He is a very nice-looking young man, very well spoken. But he is like Jekyll and Hyde. He sounds very nice over the phone though, that's how Jenny met him, on a Talk Line. She was only 18."

"He collects SSI (Supplemental Security Income) because he is supposed-ly an epileptic. And that's the reason for being the way he is, according to my daughter. 'He can't help it, he is an epileptic,' she would say, or, 'It's a reaction from his drugs.'

"Anyway, when we got back into court with Jenny after the week of temporary custody was up, the Judge told Jenny to set up day-care for the two kids while she worked. But when we went to back to court, she hadn't done it. So the judge ordered her to see a psychologist and come back with an evaluation. But when we went back to court again, she hadn't done that either."

"We have a family services court officer that has been working with us," Marci explains. "That court officer was trying to help Jennifer to get the children enrolled into day-care, but Jenny wanted Mark's sister to take care of them. I told the court officer, "Do you think *I'm* crazy? I don't want them around anyone in that family, because I don't want Mark around the children. If they are with his sister, I don't trust that situation. The first piece of paper we got from the court says that he is not supposed to have any contact with the children.

"The court has been very good to us. We did this totally without lawyers. The family service investigator has been very cooperative; we can call her at a moment's notice."

In a custody dispute a judge may assign a court officer to assist in the investigation process. The court-assigned investigator is not an advocate for any of the parties involved. He or she is required to be an impartial finder of facts only. In some cases, a judge may assign a Guardian Ad Litem (GAL) to assist in the investigatory process, or attorneys for either side may also request a GAL for that purpose.

A GAL may also be enlisted by the court to represent the interests of a child involved in a difficult custody dispute. The level of commitment and care each GAL brings to a case varies from person to person. However, in the vast majority of cases about which I have heard, when there has been a GAL advocate to stand up for the child, the GAL has been an invaluable help in determining what is best for the child. Sometimes the only voice to speak for the child is that of the GAL.

"When the case worker came here to do a home study, she was here almost all day talking," Marci continues. "We had a very nice visit. She went that very same week to Jen and Mark's apartment. He threatened her; he was going to throw her down the stairs. And when we went back to court in October, the court officer told the judge 'I refuse to go anywhere near him. I refuse to go to the apartment, and if I have to meet with her (Jennifer), it will be in my office.' And every time she would ask Mattie about his Daddy, he would go like this." Marci balls one of her fists up and strikes her outstretched palm with it with a loud smack. "She said to the judge 'Mark Harrold is abusive and violent with me. Imagine what he is like with little children.'

"I don't know whether it's because of drinking or she just wasn't cut out to be a mother, Marci goes on. "She has only been here five times to see the kids since last August when this whole thing began. She is supposed to come every Monday on her day off, but she doesn't. We'll tell her, 'Come down and spend the weekend with them.' She'll come down and spend one night or one afternoon, and then she'll call one of them (Mark's family) and then say she has to go right back. It's like someone who is in a cult and her brain is programmed and they are controlling her. She hardly talks to the kids on the phone."

"She talks to Mattie," Pete says. "She'll always talk to Mattie. But if Josh doesn't speak to her first, she doesn't care. Jenny would call on the phone and Josh would say "I huv you, I huv you." And she would say, 'What's he saying? I don't understand what he's talking about.' I would tell her, 'He's saying, I love you.'

> The children will need to receive support and information about the disease of alcoholism to help them to understand that their mother has a disease that she cannot, at this point, control. At some point, Alanon or Alateen will be a useful resource for the children when they are older to help them understand that they are not alone and to validate that they did not cause their mother's drinking problem.

"It bothers me," says Pete, "and I think it bothers me more than it bothers Marci, that Jenny is not a mother to these kids. As time goes on, it bothers her less and less that she doesn't have them.

"Both the children are going to a special needs school where they get occupational therapy, counseling, speech therapy. They could barely speak at all when we first got them. The only thing they could tell us was who gave them the boo-boo. When Matthew can't say something and he gets frustrated, he slaps himself in the face."

> Anger is a very normal emotional response for children who have been abandoned and neglected. This anger will be released in the only place the children feel safe, in this case, with their grandparents. Understanding that

this anger may sometimes surface in inappropriate ways allows caregivers to be more patient and consistent with the children. If grandparents can provide an environment that doesn't attempt to take away a child's anger, and instead allows the anger to unfold, they will be providing an environment that encourages healing.

Pete says, "Mark now claims that we 'ripped Matthew off' and that we only wanted the children because Matthew was collecting SSI." Pete explains, "Matthew had just started getting SSI checks because of his learning disability."

Jennifer and Mark had received a retroactive SSI check in the amount of approximately $2000 for Matt before the monthly checks of nearly $400 started to be rerouted to the Donaldsons. Pete asked Jennifer if she would send some of the money for the care of the boys, but she angrily refused.

Jenny and Mark eventually lost their apartment and moved in with Mark's mother. Jenny became pregnant again. Pete says, 'My heart goes out to the child.' But Pete and Marci feel they could not take in another child, 'Because next year she's going to have another one, and she's going to have another one,' Pete laments. 'I have offered for her to go to have the implant (Norplant) so she wouldn't have any more children, I told her I'd pay for it. She won't do that. She says we are trying to control her.

"I have told her anytime you want to get your act straightened out and you want to come down here, we will help you with these children to straighten out your life, but until you do, you will never get them back."

Marci adds, "Not while he is in the picture. A while ago, when my other daughter Judi was living here temporarily, Jenny called and Judi put Mattie on the phone to talk with her. Next thing Judi knows he's hysterical and crying, so she picked up the other phone and listened. Mark was on the phone saying, 'I'm coming down there to get you. You are not going to go to school there.' So Judi told him off. Then he got verbally abusive and threatening, 'I am coming down there to wipe all of you out!'

"When I got home and learned about this, we went right up to the District Court to get a restraining order. I was afraid he was going to do something to us. The woman at the court said, 'Is this man related to you?' I said No. She said, 'Well, I can't give you a restraining order.' "

"But," says Pete, "we were able to get him on violating his court order to not have contact with the children. Now we have a speaker phone so we can hear what's being said to these boys."

"For a while, Matthew wasn't sleeping," Marci says. "He was afraid his father was going to come and take him. His therapist said he had never seen him so upset. And now when you mention Daddy he says, (here Marci sticks out her tongue and blows raspberries—a short, emphatic blast).

"The therapist has given a report to the court which says he would be strongly opposed to the children going back to their birth parents and recommends that they stay where they are. He has found evidence of sexual abuse, nothing done directly to them, but they have witnessed things they shouldn't have seen, they know things they shouldn't know. To have that in writing from a man who knows what he is talking about ... I would hope a judge would not even *consider* giving them back."

There is a sharp and desperate edge to Marci's words that escape through clenched teeth as if she's trying to hold them back, swallow down her fear. This fear seems to be always just beneath the surface as she speaks. A lot of effort is expended to keep it from bubbling up and taking control.

The Donaldsons haven't heard anything from the courts in over nine months, and although Marci says, "No news is good news, I guess," she shifts uneasily in her chair. The uncertainty is wearing them down. Thus far, the court has awarded them temporary custody only, and although they are afraid to press for more for fear of "rocking the boat," their real goal is to gain permanent legal custody of Matthew and Joshua.

"During that time when Judi was staying with us," Pete explains, "the kids were sleeping out here." He gestures to a nook beyond the dining area that holds a bookcase and small table now. "Jenny called DSS about us. She had told them it wasn't a suitable place to be sleeping. I said, 'Well, Jennifer, when they were sleeping on a mattress on the floor that was all dirty and there were cockroaches and bugs running all over it, do you think that was suitable for them?' And she replied, 'Material things are nothing; they don't need material things.' I said, 'They don't? They don't need things like clean clothes and food?' She said, 'Everybody's not rich like you!' I told her we were far from rich.

"Another time she called and said, 'I've got a little bit of news for you,' and I said, 'What's that?' She said 'I am going to court tomorrow and I'm going to swear out a warrant for your arrest.' I said, 'Why?' and she said, 'You sexually abused me.' I said, 'I did? Well let me tell you something. I will get a lawyer and when they find out you are lying, I will sue you and you will end up in jail.' Well, I never heard anything more about it. It was just a threat to try and scare me into giving up the children.

"I told her if I thought I had to go to jail or give up these children, I'd go to jail, but I wouldn't give them up.

"We still love Jenny, and we pray that she straightens out. But I am afraid that's not going to happen."

"Not yet," Marci interjects. "She is really going to have to hit bottom first. We thought that when her grandfather died—she was very close to him—that would maybe do it. That was just a month ago.

"He was my father and I was very close to him too. Jenny is the first grandchild in the family and almost every picture I have of her when she was little has my father in it too. He was so heartbroken when she hooked up with this guy. The day that Jenny went over to my parents' house to show them the baby, Mark started some argument and almost hit my father. My father stood right up to him, and Jenny stood right there and watched and was almost going to let Mark strike the grandfather that she loved so much!"

Marci shakes her head with a mixture of anger and sadness and becomes quiet, lost in thought. When she continues, she looks over to Pete for encouragement.

"Pete and I are going to marriage counseling. About three years ago we got a divorce. We are not married now. Jenny brought that up in court, but we had already told them. I told them they could have the records from our counselor; we have nothing to hide."

I wonder out loud if the stress of this unfolding situation was a contributing factor in their break-up.

"It didn't help," Marci exclaims. "All the tension. That was on my mind all the time. You get stressed out. Now we are getting just a little back to normal."

Pete says quietly, almost inaudibly, "I'll always wonder if we waited too long to get the children. So many things have happened to them."

"But when they're babies you can't prove anything," Marci bursts in frantically, her voice rising. "I didn't want Mattie to go home with him (Mark) the very day he was born! If I could've kidnapped that child and gone away with him I would have. Because I could see it!" The desperation is clear and present on her face. Her lips tighten as she continues, "There is something wrong with this guy. I don't know what this child is going to grow up to be like. Every day of my waking hours until he came to live with me, I was petrified that something was going to happen to him.'

"We went up to visit them and there were no screens on the windows on a third floor apartment," Pete adds in a disbelieving tone. "Even though it is very stressful to raise children at this age, at least you know they are taken care of and you can go to sleep at night and not worry, Are they falling out of a window? *Are* they being abused?"

Marci says, "Exactly, I'd rather have them under my roof."

"And as much as it would be rough for Jenny to come here to live and straighten out her life, it would be well worth it," Pete says.

"My advice," says Marci choosing her words carefully, "to anybody who is going to do this is: Make sure you have help. If Pete were still working, I don't know how we would be able to take care of them." Pete is a fireman with a permanent disability. He takes care of the children while Marci works full time. "I have often thought of switching to something more part-time to be home with them more, but we need the money and they are on my insurance."

The boys run in, soaking wet from the sprinkler. Matthew runs off to the bathroom with Marci. Joshua begins climbing on Pete, monkey fashion, clamoring for attention. Pete says playfully "You're soaking wet! What are you doing in *here*? Moo-Moo will be mad." They laugh together, knowing he's just kidding. "Who's baby are you?" says Pete with great affection, as he strokes the side of the little boy's face.

Joshua says, "Papa!" happily.

"What happened to your face?" asks Pete concerned over some minor scratches.

Josh, of course, doesn't know what he is talking about and just replies, "I all wet."

Pete excuses himself to help Marci, who is busy tending to the children—drying them off and dressing them.

The boys come charging back into the room, whooping and laughing. They are dressed in shorts, tee shirts, and blue-and-white, jacquard towels flying behind them, secured around their shoulders with wooden clothes pins. Two tiny Batmen.

Marci, the disciplinarian, marches behind them. "Get your sandals. No puzzles now. Get off the couch. No jumping!" she orders. She settles them down at the table with us. They are kept busy with individual plastic bowls of animal crackers.

Meanwhile, Pete continues on, "There has been no mention from Jenny of straightening out her life to get her children all under one roof. We had told the court we wanted Mark to get some psychiatric help or just be evaluated, but the court can't force him to do that unless he wants to be adjudicated the father. And I'll bet you when this next baby is born, the birth record will read 'Father Unknown.'

"I didn't know men were that scarce in this world that a woman would have to put up with what she puts up with from him. She is a perfect example of a battered woman. We called a battered women's hot line, and someone called her from there and Jenny told them to mind their own business.

"She says to me, 'I am fat, who would want me,' and I tell her, 'Someone who would see the good in you.' But you can't get that through to her.

"Now, here is a girl that was very kind hearted. She used to cry at *Little House on the Prairie*. Marci and I married when the girls were quite small, and I am the only father they have ever known. They never went without. I don't know where she went wrong.

"She started drinking—sneaking from a liquor cabinet we kept locked— at around 13 or 14. She hit a certain age and she went bananas, climbing out the window, staying out all night, smoking. At 15, she stole some stuff out of the house."

Marci explains, "She is a follower. She still, to this day, will not admit the damage that has been done to him," and she points to Matthew. He lifts his eyes from his bowl of crackers briefly—his long eyelashes flick up, then down—aware that he is being discussed. Marci plows forward, "With Joshua it's not too bad, it's been mostly aimed at Matthew. I don't know why. And yet, Matthew is the one they want to talk to on the phone; he is the favorite. I think if I told them (Jenny and Mark) that I am keeping Josh and sending Matt back, she wouldn't care." The two boys stand like little sentries by the table biting off zebra heads and elephant legs, munching away quietly.

> It is a mistake to state in front of children that parents have a "favorite" child. This can be very damaging to both children's self-esteem. The favorite child may believe that he has to live up to the expectations of being the favorite, while his sibling may feel that he must "live down" to the low-ered expectations. A self-fulfilling prophecy may develop for the less-than-favorite child and may, as often happens, result in difficult-to-manage behaviors, tantrums, and poor self-esteem.

Pete says, "Jennifer says to us all the time 'You can't run my life!' and I say to her, 'But you can't abuse these children,' and she answers, 'But they are *my* children!'"

"I just want this settled through the courts, so I know she can't come and take them out of here," says Marci.

"It's a horrible feeling to know it might happen. What would it do to them?" Pete says.

Marci adds, "If someone came in today and said I had to send them back, I couldn't live with it, knowing the life they had. If that life changed and things got better, it would be different. How could she stand back and allow her children to be abused? They are terrified of having a door closed. They are terrified of having bath water run into a tub. Why? Jenny's response is, 'Oh well, that can't be anything too serious.' It took a long time before I could put them into a tub to bathe them!" Marci is leaning forward in her chair. Her eyes are locked onto mine. They are wide and questioning, alarmed.

On the wall across from the dining area where we have been sitting is a large framed picture that stands out from the many others arranged around the room. There is a girl of about nine years old, wearing a crew neck sweater and looking like she just came in from picking apples—pink cheeks, slight smile, and a direct, firm gaze from clear blue eyes. She shares those eyes with her mother and has passed them on to Matthew. Her face is lovely, full of promise, and perfectly formed.

Just then, Matthew, who now has his towel draped over his head and pinned under his chin like a little sheik or saint, stands beside his Moo-Moo, points a tiny finger at me, and says, "You go home? You go home?"

Marci and Pete laugh, slightly embarrassed by his directness.

I take hold of his little extended finger and repeat, "Am I going home? Yes! Are you sick of me being here? I don't blame you." I have taken up most of this blazing hot and humid afternoon monopolizing the attention of his grandparents, and he has had enough. There are games to be played, toy stores to visit, and ice cream to be licked. It's time to go.

As I am leaving, Marci shows me an old black-and-white snapshot which had been blown up to 8 by 10 size. It is a grainy photograph of her father as a boy of about six or seven. Familiar dark eyes look out of a full, round face.

"Look at that." Marci exclaims. "Doesn't Josh look just like my father?" she says with pride and full of hope.

> Matthew and Joshua will need support and guidance to understand why their parents made the decisions they did and to be reassured that those decisions are the parents' responsibility and not their fault. As they continue to help their grandchildren understand their birth parents' behavior and help Matt and Josh feel good about who they are, Pete and Marci need to work on feeling good about who they are as well.
>
> If grandparents can overcome the temptation to talk negatively about the birth parents in front of the children, they will strengthen the relationship with their grandchildren while moving toward the healing and recovery process.

2
Family Secrets

"... her mouth closed on a pain
that could neither be told nor ignored ..."
　　　　　　—Margaret Atwood, "Five Poems for Grandmothers"

Secrecy is seductive. It can creep up on you and before you know it, you're caught in its web. Or it can be comforting, like a big blanket that can be pulled up over your head—a hiding place. It can have a life of its own. Secrecy requires the layering of more and more secrets upon itself to maintain its existence; and so it grows, fragile but suffocating, like a house of sand.

Grandparents are driven to keep secrets out of the desire to protect their grandchildren. They fear their grandchildren will be hurt or damaged by the knowledge of the sometimes painful details of their former lives and/or separation from birth parents, even from knowing who those birth parents are.

The younger the children are when they come to live with grandparents, the easier it is to slide them under a blanket of concealment. Most often the cover-up is not planned or even thought about at all. Secrecy can be a passive thing, an omission of telling.

At first it may seem that the child is just too young to understand. Stories of abandonment, neglect, or abuse seem too complex and awful to broach to a little one. Grandparents are loath to inject even the hint of the former turmoil from which the child has come, into the hard-won, peaceful existence they have painstakingly fashioned for him or her. Later, it may become more and more difficult to open up such an enormous can of worms. Where does one begin? What age is the *right* age?

An abundance of literature deals with questions such as these for the traditional adoptive parent. But for caregiving grandparents, whether adoptive parents or not, the questions take on a wholly different spin.

Family dynamics come into play. This makes for an array of variables not charted in the adoption manuals. Hurt feelings, betrayals, disappointment, anger, frustration, bitterness, shame, and resentment—the list goes on—all play a part in making a difficult situation seem overwhelming.

Grandparents deal with a mass of conflicting emotions always. The task of weeding out their bad feelings to bring up the subject of birth parents with a small child is daunting.

Just as difficult is talking with an older child or adolescent about the weaknesses in their birth parents that have caused him or her distress and upheaval.

Caregiving grandparents, in fact, rarely see themselves in the traditional adoptive parent role, even when they have legally adopted. They seldom seek out adoption literature to help them deal with issues that come up while raising grandchildren. They simply see themselves in an entirely different role, one for which there is no definition, and for which there are no hard and fast rules.

Grandparents need to know that there are methods of dealing with questions children ask about their past, about birth parents, and about their place in the family. Grandparents should be mindful of explaining faults without assessing blame when talking about birth parents. They should give simple, age-appropriate answers in much the same way one does when asked "Where do babies come from?" Obviously, how much you tell children depends on their age and maturity level. Often they are looking for only the simplest of answers. And, like the answer to the "babies" question, appropriate information should be spooned out over time. Waiting to have that "Big Talk" when the child is "older" is a mistake. Very often the child will have formulated his or her own distorted theories by then.

Although I often recommend author Lois Melina's book, *Making Sense of Adoption,* to grandparents, they seldom take up my suggestion, and when they do, they have difficulty correlating the author's advice with their specific situations, particularly when they have not adopted. Additionally, negative feelings toward birth parents ultimately cloud the picture. While it is true that each grandparent caregiver does function with a set of circumstances unique only to them, much of the advice given to adoptive parents can be extrapolated to fit grandparents in most caregiving situations.

I often hear, "Why does he have to know now?" The answers to that question are many: Because children have a right to know how they came to be here; Because even though they aren't asking the questions, they are wondering; Because when children wonder they imagine all sorts of things; Because the longer you wait, the more difficult is the telling and the more telling the blow.

When our Sabra was barely three years old, she muttered something to me as I was dressing her. I couldn't hear or understand what she was saying, but she was looking at me out of the corners of her eyes with her head down while she said it. She was definitely waiting for my response to what she had just whispered. I bent my head near to hers and asked her to repeat what she had said.

"The princess was adopted," she said a little louder, while keeping her head down and looking up at me through her lashes.

Where had that phrase come from? It was as if she had made up a story in her head and just told me the punch line. We had not as yet directed talk of "adoption" toward Sabra; I was astonished that she knew the word. And yet, she clearly knew that it had something to do with her. What must she have been thinking? What baby fantasy had she concocted in her head until she had the courage to blurt out the word to me and watch carefully for my reaction?

Sabra and I talked a bit that day about what it means to be adopted. It wasn't too difficult, because she already knew that her birth mother, Tyra, was the one who had "carried her in her tummy" before she was born. She already knew her birth story and how she came to live with us. But I had neglected to bring her up to snuff on the legal formalities. (Who could have guessed that this child, barely out of diapers, would need to know!)

It gives me chills when grandparents tell me that their grandchildren haven't asked questions, so they don't offer answers—grandchildren who are 5, 8, 10 years old. Who knows what may be churning around in their imaginations?

Additionally, family secrets are nearly impossible to keep. Someone usually spills the beans. When this happens in adolescence or young adulthood, the results can be disastrous.

Children of any age are better able to cope with the story of how they came to join their grandparents than they are able to recover from years of deception from those they trust. Adults who have inadvertently discovered the truth about their adoption or have been told late in life that their sister is really their mother, frequently feel that the very foundation on which they have built their lives is not solid, but rather, like a house of sand.

The Winetraubs

The Winetraubs have been bitterly disappointed by their daughter's abandonment of her young son, as well as what they refer to as her "lifestyle."

They are a solidly upper-middle-class couple just entering retirement age and living within a pencil's throw of a prestigious college. They are deeply religious, kind, intelligent people who have spent a lifetime teaching and helping others.

Irene welcomes me to their home between pale admonitions to their cocker spaniel who barks maniacally, skittering backwards, her nails scratching against the polished oak floors.

Irene Winetraub is pleasant, gray haired, and grandmotherly. She leads me to the kitchen, (where I always seem to wind up) and introduces me to her husband Bernard. Bernie is a short, bear of a man wearing a yarmulke and working amidst a pile of papers.

There are birds in a covered cage by the window and a very old and coddled cat sleeping under a square of sunlight. He has diabetes, they tell me, and is given daily injections by the Winetraubs. The ancient, gray black tabby is lying on the kitchen table. Irene laughs, a little embarrassed, while proclaiming, "You do not see a cat on the kitchen table." He stands up from his indulged spot and hobbles stiffly across the table to greet me. When he nearly reaches my nose, Irene scolds him mildly and scoops him down.

They begin to tell me a rather typical story of a troubled young woman, their middle child out of three daughters. They try to be positive at first. Irene begins, "She was very vivacious, she had everything going for her." But, as a teenager, things began to change. "There was tremendous dissension always. As far as we know, she was never on drugs. Alcohol was never a question. Just the idea of any kind of responsibility was completely overwhelming to her. She was extremely, extremely rebellious. My husband and I went through a tremendous period of tension and stress. Nightly phone calls ... different worries ... *where* is she? ... *is* she coming home? Three months before she was to graduate, she left school." As their daughter Susan got older, Irene tells me, "We took her in several times back into the house. We tried everything possible. We tried counseling. She would stop going." When Susan was in her midtwenties she came back into their lives. "She begged us and promised that everything would be fine and we took her back into the house. Then we found out she had a boyfriend and she was pregnant."

The Winetraubs supported them both "financially, emotionally, every which way." says Irene. But eventually the boyfriend "wanted out" and Susan followed suit. She left her infant son with her parents and disappeared.

Irene continues, "She knew the child would be taken care of and there would be no problems. We gave her every opportunity, we gave her everything. Everything you could possibly do for a child, we tried to do. We decided, when she did leave, to obtain legal custody."

"Someone said when we were going through the adoption, it was like a divorce, a bad divorce," Bernie tells me, head in hand. There is a hint of his old New York neighborhood in his speech.

"She contested it," Irene says. "By this time she was already living with another man. She didn't want the adoption, and yet she didn't want the child. So what do you do?" She shrugs. "We fought it. It cost us a fortune both emotionally and financially."

In a contested action, the birth parent is usually eligible for free legal assistance. In fact, the more troubled, down and out, and destitute they are, the more likely they are to be assured of free counsel. Grandparents fighting for the welfare of grandchildren must go into debt, lay down life savings, and secure second mortgages on their homes in order to gain legal custody. As in other types of legal battles over the best interests of a child, the rights of the birth parent are paramount and often conflict with what is in the child's best interest. Grandparents have few rights; children have none.

"She didn't want to assume any responsibility, she wanted to be like the divorced father," Irene tells me heatedly. "And finally I said 'Forget this! I don't want it!' Why should the child be so completely confused? She doesn't want any part of his upbringing."

Aaron is now nine years old. At the time adoption proceedings began, he was two, and became three before it was finalized.

"She has visitation rights which she stopped on her own," Bernie tells me. "She hasn't seen him for over three years."

Irene's eyebrows arch high above her wide eyes. Her hand lightly cradles her coffee cup as she sits, turned sideways on her chair, her feet locked side by side in front of her, so she fully faces me as she talks. We munch on homemade oatmeal raisin cookies big enough for a meal and coffee too strong for me. The gallon of milk is on the table where the cat was sitting a few minutes before. Mitsy, the cocker spaniel, barks loudly at the mailman, the neighbor's car, the wind. She has a pretty face, puckered with anxiety, and a shrieking bark. We all do our best to ignore Mitsy and Irene continues, her voice weighted with concern, "Maybe it sounds as if we are portraying her—especially me—as an ogre. She isn't. You say a million times, 'Where did we go wrong?' and yet, we feel we didn't do anything wrong.

"I don't know what kind of life she leads, I really don't want to know. I appreciate the fact, for whatever reason, she does not come around. Because I don't feel that the child should ... I think it would be confusing for the child."

Bernie interrupts, "It was her responsibility—if she was not coming—to tell him. Or sometimes she was late. Or she would leave with him, and bang, within an hour she was back. And then the tension that we would build up—you could see it, feel it."

"Until I saw him back in the house, it was just awful," Irene says.

"We were waiting—waiting for her to come and get him, and then waiting till he came home," Bernie says.

"When she did come," Irene adds, she came very erratically. This went on for a year and a half. She has not seen him in three years."

"When he was having contact with her, what did he call her?" I ask.

"By her name," Irene replies.

"But how did he know her?" I ask.

"As sister," Irene replies shortly. Then, "Well, he does talk about her ... he does *remember* her ... he *absolutely* does ... *absolutely*. He does remember her." Irene rambles as she picks at the tablecloth in front of her.

"How do those conversations go?" I ask.

"He loves animals and she has a couple of cats. Just a couple of weeks ago, he came out with, 'Susie has Buttons.' It's a cat named Buttons. I bristle. I can't help myself ... I, I just ... I ignore it. I don't continue the conversation at all."

"And you bristle because ... ," I prompt.

"Because I don't want her involved at all in our lives. I appreciate the fact that for whatever reason she doesn't come, I am thankful. I don't want any contact with her. It's very difficult for me to admit that. But that's the way I feel. I don't want to have anything to do with her ever again. I want her completely out of our lives." Her voice is very tight when she tells me these things, but she remains composed.

"I don't know how that's going to be later on. Right now he doesn't ask any questions. He knows he's adopted."

> When adoptive parents or other primary caregivers such as grandparents intentionally keep information about the birth family from children, generally those children view the "hidden" information as a secret and, in turn, assume the secret is something to feel ashamed about.
>
> Regardless of the intensity or severity of the information, at some point during their childhood, children need to be told. It is not only helpful, but also necessary for children to have a clear picture of their past, specifically their biological past, and the events that led up to their separation from birth parents.

"How did you approach that?" I ask.

"We had never really said anything one way or the other. He was going to a Jewish day school. He was about four. And they learned among other things that God produces miracles. And there is a story of Abraham and Sara. Sara was in her old age when she had a child. And this is how we refer to it. We tell him how loved he is and that God made a miracle—that I wanted a little boy so badly and 'You're my miracle!' And he just let it go. That was enough for him at the time.

"He never seemed to ask about being born ... and it just went on because he's not lacking love or attention or anything from any of us. In fact, sometimes I think we're a little excessive." She laughs. "We're the parent *and* the grandparent. We're the spoiling grandparent." She laughs again.

"And then about a couple of years ago, he had some buddies. And the parents were the kind of people that felt their children should know everything, everything about everything! And these children were extremely bright children. However, as bright as you are, when you are eight years old, there is only so much you can absorb and understand. And these parents would tell them everything about how a child is born, how a child is conceived—I mean things that are completely unnecessary. And he came running in one day screaming hysterically. We got really frightened and said 'What happened?' It just so happened that my oldest daughter was here that day too. And he came into the house and we all ran to him and he started to cry and scream until he could get it out of him. 'So and so told me that you're not my mommy. That I'm adopted. And my mommy didn't want me!' And I said, 'Just a minute ... calm down.' And I said to myself, "Uh-oh, here it is.""

When Aaron comes home frantic because neighbors have told him he is adopted and that his "mommy didn't want him," he demonstrates profoundly how desperately he needs to hear the truth and how much he needs to hear it from his family. All children need to know that they have birth parents. They are ready to hear and understand this information as early as four or five.

"All the wheels started turning ... what do you do? ... all the books, what do they say? So I said to him, 'Now Aaron, you know that Mommy did not *have* you.' And he started banging me in the stomach. "Was I in here? Was I in here?' And I kept saying 'No.' I said, 'In a woman's life she's only given enough years to have a child. Her body is made that she can only carry a child for so many years. You weren't carried in my tummy, but you were carried here in my heart. Now, who was the first one to hold you?' And my daughter quick ran to get the picture albums to show him. 'You know that you're adopted, and that means that I did not have you in my tummy but that does not mean that you are not our child.' And that was fine, and that was it. He never asked who his real mother was. He never asked why she didn't want him."

"You say that he knows he's adopted. How does he know he's adopted? When did he first know he was adopted?" I ask.

"I think that was the first time that it really sank in," Irene replies.

"Although we had been talking about it and brought books home from the children's library at school," Bernie chimes in. "There were some terrific books. And we talked about it and read them with him." He pauses and then adds, "He was a *little* boy!"

"He was a little boy!" Irene repeats in unison. "I don't know how much he absorbed."

"Around the time of the adoption?" I ask.

"Yes. And I don't think it made a difference," says Irene

"He loves the program 'Punky Brewster,'" Bernie interrupts, "and she's adopted—"

"By an older man," Irene finishes.

Irene and Bernie are one of those couples who talk simultaneously so you're forced to either choose one over the other or flip eye contact between them as if watching a fast-moving tennis match. When they are not doing that, they finish each other's sentences. Neither one seems to mind.

"He talks about that a little bit and I think he empathizes with her and sympathizes with her," Bernie adds.

"So whatever you initially told him around the time he was adopted, when he was around three years old, he somehow absorbed enough of that?" I ask. "And you didn't talk about it again?"

"No," Irene replies, and Bernie shakes his head no.

"And he never brought it up?" I ask.

"No, and he's never questioned." Irene says. "We give him so much love and attention that right now he doesn't require anything else."

> Many adoptive families believe that love and love alone is all children need. They believe that love will make everything all right and heal all wounds. However, children need the truth too. All children thrive when they are loved; all adopted children thrive when they have love and the truth about their past. They need their information. They need to know why their birth parents abandoned them or why they are unable to take care of them; they need to know why they are living with their grandparents. They need to know about their past. They need to know they didn't do anything to cause their birth parents to fail at parenting. They need to know the truth.

"The more he's with us, the more we're Dad and Mom," Bernie says. "We are constantly here as his dad and mom and that's the way he talks about us."

"What do you plan to do when the question comes up?" I ask.

"I don't know," Irene replies. "I think it would be much easier, as far as I'm concerned, if it were a completely strange person or an agency that we got him from. I think it would be easy to tell a child in that instance. How do you tell a child that his mother is ... you know ... my daughter? I don't know how I will deal with it. I hope that it will never happen. Maybe that's wrong also. Depriving him of ... I don't *know* what. But right now, I want him exclusively in our family. Maybe it's also wrong to try to shelter him so much. But life is tough and he'll have other problems to deal with, and I just hope that it'll never come for him that he has to deal with it."

Irene sighs heavily and looks away. "What will happen, I really don't know. And then I say that maybe we should tell him because I don't want it to ever happen when we're gone. Then the girls are going to have to tell him and that'll be difficult also. It's not fair to put this burden on them, and it *is* a burden."

"Do you worry that she will come back into his life?" I ask.

"Yes, constantly." There is a long pause before Irene continues. "I don't know what she could do. ..."

"I didn't mean that she would try to take him from you, I mean just show up at the door." I explain.

"Yes she could, she could. I know she wants to come back into the family. I know she does want to come back. Just the fact that she calls every now and then. She has the right to call and to speak to the child. She calls consistently knowing that it's like a stone in my heart," she says placing her fist under her bosom, her voice tightening. "She calls knowing he isn't home from school yet."

Bernie joins in, "She calls asking for menus, and recipes," he says waving his hands in the air over his head as if brushing away flies.

Irene says, "She called up out of the blue to ask for the most bizarre things that you just wouldn't believe. The last time I spoke with her she called—she was pregnant again—and she called because she wanted the Hebrew names. In the Jewish religion, you name the children after deceased people." The Winetraubs are Orthodox. "So I told them to her.

"From what I understand, she had the baby," Irene continues. "And I don't know anything about it. My husband spoke to her the last time. I don't know what that conversation was, I don't want to know.

"If she came back at all, she would only come back on her terms, I feel. It would be the same nonsense all over again. Promising him to come, promising him she'll buy him this or she'll do this, or take him there, and then disappointing him. You can't do that to a child. You just can't do it."

"But now he has a half brother or sister," I mention.

"I guess," Irene replies curtly.

"We don't know anything about them," Bernard breaks in quietly.

> It is very common for birth parents of adopted children to have subsequent children; thus, many adoptees have biological siblings. Hiding this fact from a child may make him distrustful of his grandparents. The reality is, children eventually find out about having siblings. If the existence of biological brothers and sisters has been purposefully hidden from them, they may wonder what else was hidden from them. This may place a wedge in their relationship with their grandparents.

"You read about these extended families and say 'Oh my goodness!' Irene says. "I think they're horror stories. This one is married to this one, and that one is married to that one. My husband was a school teacher for so many years, and the kids didn't know which end was up."

"The last ten years in school I never saw such needy children in my whole life," Bernie adds. "And it was getting worse and worse. I don't know what the reason was ... If I knew, boy—"

"You could write a book and make a fortune!" I kid him.

"A fortune! A fortune!" He laughs.

"So you feel like you want to avoid that kind of mess?" I say.

"Right," Irene answers. "It *is* a mess! The children have a hard enough time just coping with what they're going to do tomorrow. You have to provide stability."

"This is the way it has to be," Irene says finally.

When I leave, Irene walks me to the door. She asks me if she can be of any help. If I need anything, please call, she says. She's always willing to help.

The Randalls

Another couple, the Randalls, have also adopted their granddaughter. But while the Winetraubs fear contact from the birth parent, the Randalls long for it. While the Winetraubs actively conceal the true familial relationships, one might describe the Randalls as sidestepping the issue. They both pray for more time and inwardly hope the time never comes when they will have to face facts with their grandchildren. Both couples, as do most other grandparents, deal with issues like resentment and loss, sibling rivalry, and the "name game."

Betsy Randall and I are members of the Grandparent Support Group Network in Massachusetts, which is an offshoot of the Massachusetts Executive Office of Elder Affairs. She is energetic and talkative, a tireless worker. She has told me that in her little town, she knows of several other grandparent caregivers in Sara's kindergarten class alone.

She promises me lunch if I drive the two-and-a-half hours out to meet with her and bring donuts.

It's only the first of December, but it's flat, dead cold, and Christmas is already in full swing at the Randall house. Plastic evergreens and red holly berries wind around the lamppost, while Santa looks out each first floor window.

Millpond is small-town by anybody's standards. Only about 2,000 people live in this former mill town deep in western Massachusetts. There are homes that seem etched into the densely wooded landscape and farmhouses that appear to have landed onto fields lining the scenic route that meanders through this neck of the woods.

Then there are the houses—village colonials we called them when I worked in real estate—that remain clustered around the town's sparse center and old mill factories; sharply peaked roofs top the narrow-shouldered old girls circled by porches that droop in spots like uneven petticoats. The Randall's gray clapboard home sits neat and at attention, virtually in the back yard of what was once a thriving paper mill and now houses Mother's Mincemeat.

Six-year-old Sara bounces out of the kitchen door like an eager puppy, excited to have a visitor. I'm glad she's still home, I like to meet the grand-children when I can.

She is getting ready for afternoon kindergarten, putting on her winter jacket and thick, homemade purple mittens attached by long strings that loop through her sleeves. She keeps up a running dialogue as she dresses— silly talk about her dog Boots and her favorite hat, which is in the shape of a cat's face, whiskers and all. She dearly loves the hat. It looks at least a year too small, and the white fur has taken on a yellowed cast.

Sara is not precocious or demanding, she is simply chatting as she would with any friend. She is truly friendly, in fact, and her openness is remarkable. Her plain little face tilts upward to look in mine as she sits on the floor and slides her legs into puffy, pink snowpants. When she speaks to me she doesn't fidget, but looks directly into my eyes.

"My name is Sara. What's your name?"

I don't think it's just a thing to say, I think she really wants to know. She stops struggling with her pants while I answer.

"Deborah," I reply, and Betsy simultaneously answers, "That's Mrs. Dudman, Sara," as she fixes lunch for us and her husband, unexpectedly home on his lunch hour.

Dan Randall looks exactly like a drill sergeant; perhaps it's because of all those years he spent in the Marine Corps. He is stocky, barrel-chested, and has a wiffle, or is it called a flat-top? His old warrior stance belies the quiet attention he shows to both Betsy and Sara.

The grownups sit at the kitchen table for soup and salad. The Randalls have raised four children here, and I try to picture four boisterous teenagers, three of them boys, sitting around this table and thundering through the tiny house. We exchange small talk while Sara concentrates on dressing. Serious business getting into snow pants; there are straps, buckles, snaps *and* zippers to tend to and a lot of slippery fabric. Sara, smallish for her age, has chin-length, dark-blond hair and glasses. Her eyes swim overly large and earnest behind pale, tortoise-shell, child-sized frames. Her bangs flop over the tops. She looks a lot like Betsy.

Sara is finally into her entire outdoor ensemble—snowsuit, boots, cat hat, and mittens-on-a-string. She walks stiff-legged over to me, her bulky nylon pants swishing noisily with each step. She brings her face close to mine, as she looks up at me with a serious expression, to ask me a little question—I don't remember what. I only remember the utterly unself-conscious trust in her eyes. It touches me, and I think of it sometimes still.

I answer her question and she maneuvers around the chairs to sit next to her "Dad." She asks him politely if she may have a cucumber slice from his salad. He picks one out, then another, and we both watch in fascination as she deftly, delicately sprinkles the tiniest bit of salt and the teensiest bit of pepper on each green sliver before popping it into her mouth whole. The school bus comes at last and she springs from the chair, runs over to me, and gives me a hug—spontaneous, huge and loving—tucking her head into my shoulder as if she really will miss me. I am touched again by her sweet intensity. I wish she didn't have to go.

After the others leave, Betsy and I settle onto the couch by the woodstove with donuts and mulled cider and I listen to another tale of irresponsible parents, a drug-abusing mother, and an infant with failure to thrive. Betsy has horror stories to tell about the Department of Social Services—incompetency, inconsistencies, and rules and regulations interpreted differently by whomever she spoke to last. In addition, there seemed to be little or no cooperation between states regarding the placement of children with out-of-state relatives—a complaint I've heard frequently. Yet another bureaucratic mire for grandparents to wade through.

Sara was two months old when their son Donnie arrived at their doorstep with her.

"It was Halloween," Betsy recalls, "We always joke that she came for trick-or-treat and she never left." She lets out a bubbly laugh and her eyes crinkle up. Betsy is short and, she would admit, somewhat overweight. She has curly, light brown hair—short in the front and long in the back, and big glasses. She talks a mile a minute and takes in deep breaths of air or lets out long sighs in between. Betsy has that soft, motherly look that fairly oozes of baking big batches of chocolate chip cookies for PTA meetings, knitting fuzzy wool mittens for church fairs and having several useful craft projects made from common household items going at once—sort of a down home Martha Stewart.

But Betsy thought she was done with the cookies and school thing, and like most grandparents thrust into parenting again, struggles with bouts of resentment. Indeed, as Irene Winetraub remarked to me hotly, "Anyone who says they don't feel resentment is lying." Fueling that resentment is the loss of friendships with peers who no longer have the extra baggage of small children to complicate dinner plans, visits, and vacations. Betsy tells me, "There were times that I wanted to say, 'Forget it, I'm not going to do this. I want to go on with my life—I want my life back!' "

When Donnie first brought Sara to them, the Randalls thought that their new situation was temporary. "We really believed—for years—that one or the other of them would get their life organized and get straightened out." She half laughs and half sighs.

"And I think that was one of the saddest things, the hardest things as a parent, was to finally realize that it really wasn't going to happen. And then in 90 days we got permanent custody. Neither parent cared enough to even find out what was going on. They never asked." She takes a big breath and continues, "A day never went by that I didn't look up the street to see if the mother was coming down the street. Not in fear—I didn't live in fear at that point. I really hoped that some way, somehow, she would find her way from Texas out here and want to be a mother to this child.

"You know, I imagined that—because I was a mother myself—I imagined that this girl would just beg, borrow, steal, hitchhike, whatever, to find a way to be with this child.

"By the time Sara was a year old, the mother was pregnant with another child by another boyfriend. She was still back in her old lifestyle. And with her and my son, it was one of these on again, off again, type of things."

"Donnie would call but not that often. He didn't really call to find out how the baby was. They *would* want pictures of the child. I was very, very good about it. I lived in a little dream world so to speak. I would send them letters and I would send pictures to both of them. I really wanted them to be part of her life.

"And then she would call, 'Well, how come Don got two pictures and I got only one?'

"So then I resorted to writing a note to each of them, each one saying the same thing and each of them getting the exactly same snapshot." Her voice rises to a high pitch, which it invariably does when she becomes agitated.

"When I found out she was pregnant, I thought, 'Oh God! She's going to come and want this baby. She's going to have maternal instincts." Her voice zings skyward. "Well it never happened, and that child was in and out of foster care and in and out of DSS.

"So another year later, she had another child by another boyfriend. Now understand, she and my son were, and still are, legally married. She traipsed around Texas, the whole nine yards, and the two kids are on again, off again, taken back and forth. In the meantime, we're raising Sara. Nobody seems to care what's happening to her.

"When she was two, my son came to see her. I was really excited that he was coming because I thought that he really wanted to become a part of her life. Well, he came here and the first thing, the absolute first thing he did when he walked in the house was open the refrigerator and take out a beer." There is a long pause as she looks at me wide eyed. She is smiling, but it's a smile that says, Can you believe it?

I can picture Betsy busying herself in the kitchen, hovering nearby, giving him sidelong glances and waiting for her son to ask for Sara. Waiting for the moment when he would scoop her up in his arms and give her a hug or tousle her hair affectionately. Surely any minute now, she would be thinking, he's going to want to see her, hold her.

I had seen a photograph of Sara at two. In it, her hair is platinum and falls around her face in happy disarray. She is dressed in yellow. Babyhood clings to her still and in the sunlight she appears incandescent. She is golden and delicious, sweet as a lemon drop. But her father never asks to see her.

"Before he went, he used the telephone, and he called his wife and he said, 'I'm in Massachusetts and I'm getting to see Sara and you're not. Ha, ha!' Those were his exact words.

"Well, Sara, who loves everybody, wanted nothing to do with him. He had no patience with her. He didn't do anything with her. He took no interest in her at all while he was here.

"I tried to get him to go to McDonalds, I tried to get him to go to Friendlys, I tried to get him to do things with her, things that a two-year-old wanted to do, to have him be part of her life. He wanted absolutely nothing to do with her. Nothing.

"Sara, to this day, does not have one material thing that either one of her parents have given her. Which is very sad because someday I can't even say to her, 'Your Mom or Dad gave you this.' "

The Randalls' three other children dote on Sara. One son, who is in the Marines, sent her a map so she can keep track of where he travels. The Randalls have it posted to the pantry door in the kitchen at child's eye level. He makes sure to send her a little something—postcards or a picture—from every place he goes.

Donnie came home again once more when Sara was four and didn't stay long enough to even look at her.

"I cleaned everything in sight while he was there! That's what I do when I get nervous, I either eat or clean. Most of the time I eat." She laughs.

He would not leave an address with them. "I know where you are," he told them. "You don't need to know where I am."

This is one of the things that hurts Betsy the most. Her son has walked away from everything he had been "born and brought up with all those years." They have a very large and close family. Her husband Dan is one of eight children. But Donnie hasn't stayed in touch with anyone or anything from his past.

"The family traditions, the holidays, the community traditions, not a holiday goes by that I don't wonder, 'I wonder if he thinks about us?' I look at Sara, and all the things that she can do, and I think, 'You've missed all this.' "

> While in many families grandparents continue to have a very positive rela-
> tionship with their grown children, sadly, in others, relationships are
> strained at best. For some, the lack of contact with their adult children is a
> loss akin to a death. Grandparents must accept and grieve the loss of the
> adult child and make peace with themselves in order to move forward.

Betsy tells me, "At one point during Donnie's visit, we were having an argument and he said to me, 'I don't know what you're crabbing about, I let you have her!' I think she's more of a possession to him. I could never make him understand that, at this point, she was a little person. When she was six months old or a year old, if they wanted to pick her up and take her, that would be one thing. But when she got to be two, three, and beyond, she was a little person. You don't uproot her from her life.

"Nothing would have made me any happier than for one or both of them to come here and be part of her life and really share in her life. I used to hesitate to buy clothes from one season to the next because I always imagined they were coming for her. I lived kind of in a dream world. I guess I was really hoping." Her cheeks are flushed and her eyes fill, but the tears don't spill over. She smiles through her tears as if to say aren't I foolish?

"And, to be very honest, it wasn't until a week before we went to court to adopt Sara. ... " She talks slowly now and chooses her words carefully, very uncharacteristically. "She had got bitten by a bee and spent all night in a hospital. I was driving home with her and she was in the car seat in the front, and I looked over at her and I literally burst into tears. And I said out loud, 'They really aren't coming for her.' And it wasn't until then that I realized *they really weren't coming for her!*

"And that was the hardest ... I looked at her and I thought, 'Look at what they're missing!' " Betsy takes a deep breath. Her face has pinked up again and the tears are filming her eyes behind her glasses. But she continues to smile through her tears as she talks. "I really have a lot of mixed feelings. I think that when you have a decent relationship with parent, you can at least talk to them about the child and share some of the things. But when they literally, *literally* don't want anything to do with her. ... " A tear finally starts to escape and she places a finger behind her glasses and lifts it from the edge of her eye. "It's very hard." She swallows back the lump in her throat and says dejectedly, "I don't know which is worse, to have the parent of these children that you're raising in and out of their lives and disappointing them or, one that never sees them at all.

"What's happened now with Sara in our situation is that all that hurt and all that heartache is ours and not hers for the time being. Because she doesn't know the disappointment. She doesn't know as yet what she's missed. She doesn't know that they haven't had anything to do with her."

> Many times it is assumed that because children ask very few questions about being adopted and/or about their birth parents, the children aren't thinking about it. However, I have seen in countless adoptive families that many children will not ask their parents any adoption questions because they sense their parents' discomfort or fear of the subject. Children may remain cautious because they are concerned that if they ask too many questions, their caregivers may become hurt or angry. They fear this anger could lead to rejection, a situation few adopted children are willing to risk.

"Tell me, what does she know?" I ask.

Betsy reflects, "What does she know? She knows she came from Texas. She knows she came on a big airplane. She knew that we were her Gram and Gramp.

"When she first started to talk, it was Mom, because that's what children say first. And we would say G-G-G Gram. And she would say G-G-G Mom!"

"And it would break my heart when she would say, 'I'm gonna keep you forever. Are you gonna keep me forever, Gram?'

"And I could never, ever say to her, 'Yes, I will keep you forever.' All I would ever say to her was, 'I'll always be here for you.' Because that's about the time that that baby Jessica thing was going on, and all I could envision was me promising I would keep her forever, and them coming and taking her and her screaming at me saying, 'But you *promised* you'd keep me forever!' So in my own mind, I just could not tell her I'd keep her forever."

"But then she got so that she would ask the question more and more and more. Even though we literally stopped talking about her situation whenever she was around or in the house or anywhere within earshot. So we knew that this was bothering her.

"Well when she was five, my husband said, 'We're gonna go for broke. You find an attorney, we're gonna go for broke and we're gonna go for adoption."

It was then that the Randalls ran up against a road-block of incompetence within their local DSS district. The local social workers could not figure out how to comply with the requirement of the "home study" because Sara had not been in their system. Normally, when a couple files with the probate court for adoption, the court requires a home study to be completed by a licensed social worker for the state or a private agency. The Randalls could not afford to hire a private agency, but DSS in their area would not do it; they just couldn't figure it out. It took months of wrangling with officials both high and low before Social Services was able to sort out this simple procedure.

"There were many, many times when I just wanted to put her in the car and put her on DSS's doorstep and say, 'Here you go. Now you figure out what to do. And when you finish, let me know.'" She tells me this in a shrill falsetto.

Betsy went on to say that some days she would feel so frustrated and tired and down that she would want to give up. But fortunately, her husband would be able to buoy her spirits. And when he was discouraged and wondered if it was worth the endless struggle, she was able to keep *him* going. "Luckily," she tells me, neither one was down at the same time.

"I'll be honest, there were a few times when I thought, Do I really want to do this? Do I really want this for the rest of my life? Maybe I should just try to find her parents and just say 'Hey, this is your job, now you do it!' But of course I didn't, because I love her."

I ask Betsy if Sara knows she has birth parents.

"Well, yes. ... " She hesitates. "My husband would show her pictures. I couldn't do it, I'll be honest. I could not do it! But she loved to look at family albums and pictures and my husband would get them out and they would look at them together. I couldn't even stay in the room."

"Because?" I prompt.

"Because I didn't really know what I felt," she expels in a big breath. "I—I wasn't comfortable with what I was feeling.

"My husband could show her these pictures and say, 'This is your dad.'

We had pictures in the album of her first couple of weeks of life in Texas— snapshots that her (maternal) grandmother had sent of Sara and her mother and her father. And my husband would show them to her and say, 'This is you when you were a baby and this is your mom and this is your dad."

"And did she ever question it beyond that?" I ask.

"No. Because I think she was young enough that it was only a name to her. It was like saying this is your brother, this is your uncle, this is your sister. It didn't really click in her mind. So she didn't really know.

"Then it got to be that she was almost five. And I had very strongly told my husband, and he went along with it—I'm not sure he agreed with me, but he honored my wishes—I told him that if by any chance the mother or father should ever arrive on our doorstep, that Sara was at an age where I don't want to confuse her, and I would not refer to them, or tell her at that point, that they were her mother or father.

"Because, I didn't really know how to explain ... I didn't know how I felt! And I couldn't deal with my emotions about it, and I didn't know how I could explain it to her, and I didn't want her to think of them as some kind of 'knight in shining armor,' these wonderful people that have come, and confuse her. And I said, until she's old enough to realize, I don't want her to know who they are."

> It is important for the adults to separate their fear and anxiety about sharing information from the child's right to know. I am not suggesting this is an easy balance or that one could expect to be always comfortable about discussing the past, but the child's need to know takes precedence over the adults' need to protect themselves from anxiety. Grandparents may need to speak with a counselor or family therapist to work through their own discomfort.

Betsy falters and takes several deep breaths. "If either one of them came into her life right now, I would not tell her, at this point, this is your mother or this is your father. She hasn't asked.

"Nobody's told her and it hasn't dawned on her yet. And I just ... I haven't. ... " She falters again and struggles to give voice to her feelings. "The opportunity has not come up to explain this to her," she finally says firmly and emphatically.

> Grandparents need to recognize that opportunities are always there, and they must not allow their insecurity and anxiety to prevent them from finding them or, if need be, creating them. Grandparents must take the oppor-

tunity to explain to their grandchildren the different people, situations, and experiences that have made up their grandchildren's lives. If they wait too long, they risk having someone other than themselves let the cat out of the bag. As previously mentioned, this can set up a potentially devastating breach of trust no matter how well intentioned.

"Have you fashioned an answer in your head for when it does come up?" I ask.

Her voice rises a notch. I think she is annoyed with me. She lets out a breath and says, "Well, yeah. Depending on what the situation is, I would probably tell her, Well, you were born in Texas, you had a mom and you had a dad when you were born, but when you were only two months old, a little, tiny baby, they just couldn't take care of you so you came here to live with us. And I guess that's about all I would tell her for now.

"I always said I would never, never bad-mouth them. I don't want them to sound like dirt bags. But yet I also refuse to make them sound like some kind of heroes, that because they loved her so much, they've sent her to live with us." She looks at me steadily and with conviction.

> Sometimes what is said is not as important as how it is said. I never recommend that adoptive parents tell their children that "Your birth parents loved you so much they gave you to us," because its implications can be confusing and even painful. For example, an adopted child may be confused as to how someone who "loves" them so much can give them away. Also, the adopted child may wonder, "If you love me, will you give me away too?" It is far more useful for grandparents to share with their grandchildren that "Your birth parents made a decision because they cared about what happened to you. Our love and commitment means you are staying with us. Our decision means you will always stay."

Betsy continues, "And I guess what I am thankful for is that each day that goes by that she doesn't ask any questions, she's that much older and a little bit more mature so that I can explain it to her. And she would have to be quite old, or quite mature, before I would explain it to her. I don't want to go into the whole story with her of what I explained to you today, of how she came to be here and all that. Sara doesn't need to know that.

"I'm sure I'll know how to handle it when the time comes. But to try to fabricate a story, try to figure it out ... ? I guess my only answer would be, 'They just couldn't take care of you.'

"We never hid the fact of where Sara has come from (in the community). It's no secret. Everybody in the area knows who she is, they know that she belongs to my son. So I mean it's no big, deep, dark secret. And I don't want it to be a secret from *her*. It's just something that because I feel that at this age they can be so ... "

Betsy begins to tell me a story about one of her support group members to illustrate the point she is trying to make.

"We have one woman in the support group whose child is four or five years old. And the mother is probably never going to be able to take care of this child. And the father left the mother of this child when he found out she was pregnant and has never been back. He just blew the area. And yet, they've told this child about this father, and so the child sits there and fantasizes that this father is going to come for her one day.

"So I mean Sara at this point is a very well-adjusted, loving child. And I guess I've been through enough with raising four kids of my own to realize that you'll know what to tell them and what not to tell them when the time comes.

"I'll tell her when she gets old enough, and I mean *old* enough, that I feel that she can really handle this and she really honestly wants to know. By that point, if you feel that she can handle it, then you can tell her the whole story as to what has happened and why she came and everything. But it's going to be a long time from now before she's ever ready for something like that.

"It's always very hard because they have never had anything to do with her, and because it was always very one-sided on our part. How long can you keep up the charade of 'This is your mom and this is your dad.' If we had told her earlier by now she'd be saying, 'Well, where are they?' "

"But your husband has done that," I point out.

"He doesn't do it anymore. He hasn't done it for a long time. I don't think she remembers.

"When the adoption was getting ready to go through—I'll be honest—I probably have a dozen photos of Sara and her mother or father up until she was about two months old. And I'll be honest, I took them out of the picture album and put them away. I put them with her adoption stuff and I put them away. I guess I'll know when the time is right to show them to her.

"I just don't want this little child fantasizing, thinking that they are going to come rushing down the street and make this wonderful happy family for her. And on the other hand, I don't want her to think, 'How come they don't want me?' "

All adopted children experience sadness and loss because they were not kept. My advice to adoptive parents is to not attempt to take away this sadness and loss, but instead create a family environment that allows it to occur and be worked through.

"So I just don't say anything for now. It may be right, it may be wrong. I don't know." Betsy's voice is rising again. "I guess there's really no right way and no wrong way. You just have to do what you feel, and you know the child well enough to know. That's the way you do it."

"She knows she's adopted," I confirm.

"Oh yes! She was almost six years old when we went to court and she was adopted. And when you ask her what does "adopted" mean, she says, 'It means I am going to live here forever and ever and I never have to leave you.' "

"Before the adoption went through she had an inkling that her place wasn't permanent?" I ask.

"Right. She had the feeling that she wasn't going to be able to stay here forever. She didn't know why, she only knew that there was some reason why she might not stay here forever."

"And now she doesn't feel that way?" I ask.

"No!"

"The solution to that feeling was the adoption? And she never questioned beyond that?" I ask.

"No. She used to say it all the time, it was an obsession with her, 'I'm going to keep you forever, are you going to keep me forever?' And now only very occasionally she'll say, 'I'm going to keep you forever, Mom, I love you so much.' And now I'll say, 'I'm going to keep you forever.' "

Children hunger for open, honest, accurate information, even if it isn't always joyful or easy to hear. It is far more painful not knowing the truth than it is to know why the pain exists. Most important, children need to hear the information from loving caregivers. The facts need to be presented lovingly and truthfully, not sugar-coated or with some information strategically removed.

By the age of five, children should be given an age-appropriate family history by their caregivers. Grandparents should then begin to discuss the grown child who is also their grandchild's birth parent. They should start by talking about the adult child's history and then ease into the fact that he or she is, in fact, the child's birth parent. Then, briefly, describe why the birth parent was unable to take care of the child and how the child came to be in the care of grandparents. This is a discussion that will need to be revisited all during childhood and into young adulthood.

When caregivers do not share important information with children and the information is discovered as a teen or adult, a huge break in trust occurs from which some families never fully recover.

In a healthy environment based on truth and trust, issues can be resolved and children can make peace with their past.

3
When Grandparents Don't Agree

"When those closest to us respond to events differently than we do, when they seem to see the same scene as a part of a different play, when they say things that we could not imagine saying in the same circumstances, the ground on which we stand seems to tremble and our footing is suddenly unsure."

—Deborah Tannen, Ph.D., *You Just Don't Understand*

Throughout my daughter's pregnancy, there were times when I mentally walked myself through the adoption scenario—giving our grandchild up for adoption. I would get to the end of the scenes playing like a loop of film over and over in my head, and find a brick wall. I knew these were scenes I would never actually be in, places I could never really go.

My husband, Richard, never considered it as an alternative for us even for one moment. He would not play out the imaginary adoption scenes with me. Whenever I would point out the difficulties ahead of us, he would merely listen quietly and say "We'll manage." I knew that was true, we would manage, we *could* manage. Financially we would struggle, but probably stay afloat. For many grandparents in similar circumstances faced with a daunting array of decisions, whether or not they will be able to manage is far from certain, even doubtful. Disagreements are common. Allowing a baby to be put up for adoption or standing by while a child is placed in foster care may be a viable alternative for some. For us and others like us, it simply is not.

Our personal feelings about whether or not we could cope with raising another child were not the only challenges we faced. Outside our family circle, what we encountered was shock and disapproval. Friends, acquaintances, doctors, therapists, became divided into two camps; those who didn't "get it," and those who did.

A very dear friend, during a conversation in which she listed all the ways adopting my granddaughter would be fraught with problems and just plain "odd," finally announced, "The child will grow up warped!" One person called me "selfish." Many people told us we were crazy. A therapist I was seeing at the time to help me sort things out remarked, "You're trying to sabotage your life." I stopped seeing him.

My physician, the man who delivered all my children, told me he understood completely and said "of course" he would do the very same thing. He said words like "family," "heritage," and "flesh and blood." He got it.

My husband and I had the luxury of having all our puzzle pieces fit as far as this decision goes. We were in agreement, saw things the same way. Nearly all our large and extended family saw things the same way. But what happens when husband and wife don't agree?

Decisions are not always black and white, the way not always crystal clear. Are the children in danger? Can we *do* this? Can we afford it? Is this temporary or permanent? Guardianship or adoption? How will we manage? Where shall we turn?

The Harrises

I met Laurie Harris through the Massachusetts Executive Office of Elder Affairs. She attended a couple of Grandparents' Network meetings before she had to drop out because of her busy work schedule as a nurse. She spoke with me one afternoon by phone, taking time out of a crammed full day to tell me about the conflict pricking at the fabric of her marriage like a thorn on silk.

Laurie and her husband Bob are grandparents in their midforties. Their daughter put her baby into foster care when she felt overwhelmed by motherhood. When Laurie discovered what had happened, she intervened, waged a short but intense battle with Social Services in another state, and finally took the baby home. Working on what she describes as "gut instinct," she did not discuss the issue with anyone, not even her husband Bob. "I did what I had to do," she told me.

Laurie and Bob have been married for 24 years and have raised five children, the youngest is 19 and in college. They had just begun to take vacations alone together, to go out on weekends to dinner or a movie, to enjoy themselves as a couple.

"We did without a lot when we had our own kids, sacrificed a lot," Laurie told me.

When the dust settled and temporary custody was awarded by the courts, three months extended to six months and it became clear that this was more than a short-term situation. Laurie filed for permanent custody. Bob said, "I don't want this. Put her up for adoption." Laurie's reply, "No one is going to keep her from me."

Laurie told me, "Most of the burden, the responsibility of her care is mine. He wants to love her as his grandchild, but he doesn't want her to be here. He says, 'I don't want this, I don't want to give my freedom up, raise another child.' My answer is, 'There's the door.' "

They still see this as a temporary situation, although more long-term than they would like. Their daughter is in the service and trying to pull her life together. Laurie believes that within a few years her daughter will be able to shoulder the responsibility and have her child returned to her. She hangs on to that hope. Laurie works hard at preserving the connections between mother and child. She shows her granddaughter pictures and letters and talks about how much her mother loves her. "When she slips and calls me Mommy, I correct her," Laurie tells me.

Laurie is trying to juggle her granddaughter's well-being and a marriage while holding on to the fragile tightrope of faith she has in her daughter She is doing everything she can to shore up the relationship with her husband without sacrificing her grandchild. At the moment, she seems to have all the balls suspended in midair.

Laurie and Bob sought counseling and are trying to work together to keep the marriage going. Laurie tells me, "We have to come to terms with how we are going to have a relationship for ourselves—what can we do to make things better for us?"

Laurie believes they will make it.

> Parenting can test the strength of any marriage. Parenting your grandchild, however, adds the burden of unexpected stressors to couples ready for an entirely different stage in life. Parenting attempted, at any stage, without mutual support and respect can break a marriage. Caregivers need to make their marriage a priority. They need to do this for themselves and they need to do it for their grandchildren. Children sense the tension in a marriage, and they may assume that the tension and stress are because of them.
>
> Bob may feel that he wasn't given a choice and thus may feel some resentment toward both his wife and his grandchild. Laurie and Bob need to be in this together. They need to spend a significant amount of time actively discussing the pros and cons of raising their grandchild. They need to respect and listen to each other's feelings and opinions. Clearly, they cannot be successful as caregivers if they approach parenting as adversaries instead of as partners. In fairness to each other and their grandchild, Bob and Laurie need to continue to address these concerns with the help of ongoing counseling.

Part 1 of the Parks Family Trilogy

The story of the Parks family is one of rescue and redemption, a life-or-death struggle. Ben and Elisabeth Parks' marriage hangs on by threads. But those threads are strong, like the warp and woof that remain when the nap wears away on a rug.

Ben and Elisabeth's story is a good example of what happens to marriages when couples don't agree on the issue of raising grandchildren. As their story unfolds, many other important issues surface as well—anger, denial, grief, and loss. First, Elisabeth and Ben tell their story together, then Ben alone, and finally Elisabeth alone, as I fully chronicle their journey. In a later chapter, which focuses on making room for birth parents in their children's lives, Marion, who is Ben and Elisabeth's daughter and the mother of the children in their care, also reveals her story.

For the Parks family, the road to gaining custody of their two grandchildren was murky, confusing, and perilous. Ben and Elisabeth viewed the picture laid out before them with very pronounced differences. It was if they were looking through the same kaleidoscope of fractured pieces and colors, and interpreting what they saw in different ways. They became frustrated and angry when the other could not see the patterns adding up to the same whole.

Their methods of coping, expressing their feelings, and their approach to the unfolding situation were at opposing ends of the spectrum. They struggled and fought, split and came together. But the fracture went deep. It has not yet healed. Perhaps someday it will.

Ben and Elisabeth

When I finally find it, the buff-colored contemporary waits on a narrow lane surrounded by 1930's and 40's capes and cottages. This area was once a vacation retreat complete with Big Band dance halls and an amusement park. Now, the curvy little roads that wind around this lake and a few others like it are flanked by modest but updated older homes as well as pricey newer contemporaries like this one, which take advantage of the spectacular views that the lake affords.

The house is just as pretty on the inside as it is outside. Enormous expanses of glass bring the idyllic setting into every room of the house. The house is an eclectic mixture of comfortable contemporary seating combined with formal antique furnishings handed down through the close-knit family. Homey treasures touch down everywhere—porcelain butterflies, pictures of the children and grandchildren, and handmade dried flower arrangements. There is a white bisque angel sitting on the wood stove. She has a mauve French ribbon, edged in gold, around her neck. She is blowing kisses.

Elisabeth tells me this was to be their retirement home—they are both in their late fifties—until their lives were turned upside down shortly after they moved here. Marion, their oldest daughter, had gotten pregnant at the age of 16. With the birth of their grandson, Craig, their story begins.

"Marion was home with us," Elisabeth tells me. "And he (Thomas Connor) was coming over bringing diapers, baby food, providing support—you know, this wonderful, charming guy."

"Did you think he was wonderful and charming at the time?" I ask.

"Well, I didn't, because he got her pregnant, and I didn't think that was wonderful and charming. I was pretty angry that she had gotten pregnant. But let's just say that we were trying to make the best of the situation not knowing. ... Who was I to judge? She was too young, but he was wanting to help. She made the decision to marry him when Craig was a year old. She was close to 18 by then, wasn't she?" Elisabeth turns to Ben for confirmation.

Ben has a rugged, deeply tanned, craggy face covered by a trimmed-short mustache and beard. His hair, slightly balding, is neat and evenly close-cropped. His voice is cavern deep and loud. The air vibrates when he speaks. He talks quickly, pushing his words out machine-gun fast with force, as if he's in a rush to get it out and over with.

"Yup." Ben barks.

"They were going to move right around here and they would be close by, so we just figured we would give them a lot of support. But what started happening was she was starting to drink. And the more I tried to get close to her, she was holding me away. But she was also deathly afraid of him. It had started very early on with him hitting her."

"You were not aware?" I ask.

They both answer at once.

Elisabeth, "I had no idea!"

"We were not aware" Ben mumbles.

"Absolutely none!" Elisabeth finishes.

"And her brothers didn't," she continues. "I have *big* boys. One is a police officer. But they had no idea at the beginning."

Their sons eventually became aware of the problems Thomas and Marion were having, but never told Elisabeth and Ben what they knew or suspected.

"They were all doing the drinking. But, at that time, that wasn't unusual for high school or college age kids to be having a beer. Right?" She asks, looking to me for affirmation. "But we were totally unaware of how much drinking might have been going on. And how much pain they were in. We did not see. I was beginning to see the dangers of too much partying—*that* I saw. And I was worried about it, concerned about it, tried to talk to them about it, but it was, 'Oh, Ma! Everybody drinks!'

"They were starting to party in a house over there," Elisabeth gestures to the other side of the lake. "Right where you parked your car as a matter of fact," she laughs. I had become lost on the way here, in the maze of streets that weave around the lake. I had called her on my car phone and she had to drive over to lead me to the house.

"That place has a lot of horrible memories for me. There was a bar-room there that they've taken down."

"Really?" I say in surprise. The place I had stopped was a lovely residential neighborhood of brand new homes overlooking the lake—swing sets, people dressed in sweat suits walking dogs, flower boxes overflowing with impatiens.

"This is a small town, but there are a lot barrooms in it. Not a lot of nice parks or things to do but. ... " Elisabeth begins.

"There are more barrooms and liquor licenses in this town than Las Vegas has, per ratio of people—how's that!" Ben interrupts, his deep voice reverberating through the dining room. "Twenty-seven liquor licenses—the town has only 4,000 people—there's only supposed to be one," he says. Ben seldom meets my eyes when he talks. He looks over my head, or across the room to some point beyond.

Elisabeth is sitting quietly with her hands gripping her tea cup. She has an elegant, almost patrician look about her, with a shock of short, thick, gray-white hair brushed back from her face. She wears no makeup, not even lipstick, which gives her a somewhat weary, washed-out appearance. She looks out from enormous brown eyes, through glasses with delicate, rose-colored frames which sit on her aquiline nose.

Her usually pale face is flushed and her eyes are filling. "I didn't realize how much emotion I had about this, that *house.*" Elisabeth pauses, tries to compose herself, then continues, but her voice is full of pain. She talks with difficulty as if she's choking on her words. "But that's where the children got hurt so bad, and she did. A lot of suffering went on there.

"I was always on her (Marion's) back about getting help—going down, checking on the kids, checking on her. I was going to Al-Anon to see what I could do to help, I talked to counselors, I did everything I could to try to help. I couldn't get her *in* (to counseling). And, I would approach him (Thomas) and his lovely family and say, 'Would you help me with it?' And he'd say, 'Ugh. Your daughter is disgusting, she drinks!' Like he was this wonderful guy. It's amazing how these guys can con everybody! In this town I am sure everybody thought he was the nice guy and she was the slut."

"Well, they did!" Ben interjects.

"And the school system ... by the time I got into the school system with my grandchildren ... I could just feel it!" Elisabeth bursts in.

"We had just moved into this house, our retirement house, about 10 years ago," Elisabeth continues, "We had a wonderful summer. This place is so beautiful. Our dream home, this peaceful place by the water. She (Marion) came to us, and I was so grateful, I was really so grateful. By that point, I was out of my mind with worry about the drinking and what was going on over there at that house."

"She hit bottom, but she came here," Ben adds. "She did it on her own."

"She brought the two children and said, 'Please help me,' " Elisabeth says.

"Not financial help, but help to get into the recovery unit," Ben explains.

"So she went into the hospital for rehabilitation for alcohol and drug abuse," Elisabeth explains. "She wasn't even in there a day or two before the counselors called to say, 'Please do not have Mr. Connor come with the children. Could you please bring the children, Mrs. Parks?' Now, right up to this point I was almost alienated from her because all I could see was the externals, like she was hurting these kids by the drinking and the neglecting. And I was really angry at her, but I was still trying to appeal to her, to tell her I would help her and support her."

> It is good that Elisabeth is able to admit that she is angry with her daughter. It is very common for grandparents to be angry with their children for their failure to parent adequately. Admitting the anger is a healthy first step toward mending strained relationships.

At this time Marion was in her midtwenties, Craig was seven, and Christine was two years old.

"Whenever they (the counselors) would try to talk about the marriage, she would get hysterical, hysterical. And they would back off. But evidently they got enough to know that it was okay for us to come (to visit), but it was not okay for him (Thomas) to come.

"So, the first day we were supposed to go—it was visiting day—we had to tell him to please not come until she was ready. But he said he was definitely going down to see his wife. He had roses.

"All I can remember is getting off the elevator with the children, walking into her room and saying 'Hi, you're looking good!' and she went cowering back in the corner screaming, and I didn't even know at *what,* until I turned around and saw *him* in the doorway. That was the first time I had any idea of what my daughter was going through. She *ran* down the corridor, didn't she, Ben?"

"Yup."

"And screamed hysterically. They (the staff) came up and ordered him out of the hospital. And even during the rest of the 30 days of counseling, not a lot came out. They said she had posttraumatic stress syndrome and also amnesia to severe abuse that caused her to either blank it out or she couldn't talk about it. That was the first hospitalization."

> Posttraumatic stress disorder (PTSD) is frequently seen in survivors of violent crime, physical or sexual abuse, battering, or any other physically and emotionally traumatic event. Symptoms frequently include powerful and vividly frightening nightmares, flashbacks, difficulty trusting others, withdrawing, mood swings, insomnia, and paranoia.

After her first hospitalization, Marion had begun to pull away from Thomas Connor. She wanted a divorce. During that period of time, the children were being coached by Thomas to put pressure on their mother to stay with him. Marion started drinking again. Also, although no one was aware of it at the time, Thomas was going to her while she was working as a waitress at the local country club and threatening that if she wouldn't go back to him, he would kill her parents and the children.

"She knew he was capable of it," Elisabeth tells me. "He also offered her booze and drugs to go back."

> Batterers use fear and pain as their tools of control. Children who witness the cruelty found within a violent relationship will need long-term, intensive treatment to help them understand what they saw and why they saw it. The children may suffer from fragile self-images, and their caregivers will need to provide safe, consistent surroundings and boundaries for these children to heal.
>
> Children will benefit from caregivers who are united and mutually supportive of one another, otherwise they may feel vulnerable, or fear that this home isn't stable either.

Elisabeth continues, "After she went back to him it was a horrible time, nothing but beatings. She left him again and came here again, and went into the hospital again for drinking.

"It was during that second hospitalization that I noticed that Christine was being hurt. I was giving her a bath and I noticed that her vagina was all red. I knew that something was terribly wrong ... as a grandmother ... as a nurse. I just talked to her, as I washed her, about her private parts and how you never let people touch, and it just kind of went into this kind of conversation, because I was dumbfounded. She spit right out that day, 'My cousin always hurts me there, Nana.' This was his (Thomas') sister's son. He was 11, but very big for his age."

"My grandson, Craig, was seven, very small for his age—slim, tiny, a little bit of a thing, never ate. But Alan (the cousin) was a very big boy for his age, big-boned, heavy-set. I did not like that child. That's a terrible thing to say, and I don't usually say that type of thing about kids, but he had a terrible mouth. He once swore at Ben's mother. That was a real eye-opener! That concerned me about my grandchildren going to their house at that point. What kind of people were these? What's going on here? So we began to have a lot of concerns, but until that day in the bathtub, I had no idea of the violence. ... "

Ben interrupts, "It continued into the summer because they would go camping. What we didn't realize was that he would take the kids, and we weren't aware that what he was doing was going to New Hampshire, dropping them off at his sister's so that he could go do his thing, play golf or whatever. And she ended up baby-sitting for the weekend and they (Craig and Christine) would go through this torment.

"To make a long story miserable, that boy today has already been convicted of rape, armed robbery, assault and battery. He has broken out of jail twice. This all started with (what happened to) Christine."

"Christine started talking—" Elisabeth interrupts Ben.

Ben interrupts Elisabeth, "Worse things were going on with Craig but she didn't know at the time. He wouldn't come near me I couldn't talk to him. To this day he shies away from men. And he is not gay either. He's a normal boy, but he does not trust. ... "

Elisabeth interrupts, "Well ... he's a boy with a lot of problems."

Ben continues, "He does not trust men at all. Even myself, to this day. But, he went through hell with those guys!"

Elisabeth says, "With Christine's story, I immediately went to DYS (Department of Youth Services) in New Hampshire. I was working for Franklin Pierce Medical Center in New Hampshire at that time as an L.P.N., and when I first became aware of Christine's problem, I immediately took her to a pediatrician there to document it. But she was a new doctor, and at that time I don't think she was aware—she says so now—she was not aware of abuse. Even (later) when the therapists would call her and say, 'Christine's telling us she's being touched. You say she has vaginitis. Can you document that (sexual abuse)?' And she would say, 'Well she hasn't told *me*.' So this thing dragged on for a while.

"I tried to talk to the doctor about Christine's manifestation of the 14 danger signs, the red flag signs of sexual abuse—migraine headaches, stomach aches—that she was starting to exhibit around this time. We thought Craig had Tourette's Syndrome—he was doing this when he would come back weekends (she throws back her head and twitches her face). Angry. Couldn't concentrate in school. Then they would start to calm down a little during the week.

"I tried to approach my daughter on a visit and asked her if she had any idea (what was happening to Christine), and she went hysterical, screaming about migraines and, 'How dare you? Don't you talk to me! That's not true! What are you doing?' And then the counselors asked me to stay away, that I was upsetting her. They did not know the whole story.

"And it was kind of looking like I was this interfering, crazy mother. So what I decided then was I had to help the children and just let that piece go. I couldn't get any help from her to help the children. She was obviously much sicker than I realized.

"At that point I filed a 51A in the state of New Hampshire (at DYS). One of the counselors at the hospital also filed a 51A (naming Thomas Connor's nephew, Alan, as the perpetrator). Marion did accompany me even though she couldn't seem to get involved or handle any more than that. And then they brought the children in and asked the children. "And ...," she drops her voice to a whisper and leans across the table, past the basket of apples, past the squeeze bottle of honey, past the child-made napkin holder, toward me, " ... that information all disappeared. The woman social worker that did the intake left her job, nothing ever was followed through, it fell through the cracks, whatever—nothing ever happened.

"At this point they (Thomas Connor's family) started putting a lot of pressure and violence on the children. Unbelievable pressure. They started presenting with a lot of symptoms." By then Craig was eight and Christine was three.

"He (Craig) was totally falling apart. This was when my daughter totally separated from Thomas, during her second hospitalization. He was taking them to his apartment in Dorset, or to his mother's in Lakeville, or the sister's house in New Hampshire. The children were touched in all these houses."

"Oh boy!" Ben expels, shaking his head. This is so hard for them to dredge up.

"The man was insane!" says Elisabeth. "He's an insulin diabetic and he drank. He was this (seemingly) quiet guy."

"He was a weight lifter," Ben recalls.

"As we look back," Elisabeth says, "when he would come in with the children, the children never reacted with him like my father and us growing up, or Ben and the children—you know, affectionate. They would come in the room and stand like little toy soldiers."

"Like when they came into a room they would just stay against the wall and look at you," says Ben.

"And I was always thinking it was the drugs and alcohol (that Marion was abusing)," Elisabeth says. "They would be angry at *me*."

The fury the children are unleasing on Elisabeth is, of course, misplaced rage at their abusers. They feel comfortable enough with Elisabeth to vent their anger. They feel rage toward their abusers, and at the world for allowing this to happen. These bottled-up emotions can only be released where and when they feel safe. Although Elisabeth and Ben may have been confused by the children's behavior, it is a normal reaction to abnormal circumstances.

"That was very early on when my friend Mary Ann Alden started helping me." Elisabeth says. "I was helping her with her mother who had Alzheimer's. And what happened was a gift from God."

At this point Ben becomes irritable. His body language changes. He tries to interrupt Elisabeth several times and finally succeeds.

"Tell her about the boys," Ben begins.

"Let me do this piece," she says to Ben looking at him from the corner of her eye. "I was helping her with her mother. ... "

"Wait a minute," interrupts Ben.

Elisabeth whips her head around to him and he laughs a little nervously saying, "I'm not saying that you're wrong. But the most important thing that took place is that we went to social services over the abuse thing," he turns to look at me now, holding the floor, " ... and Thomas' best friend's wife is the receptionist!"

Elisabeth raises her voice now as she says, "I haven't even got that far yet!"

Elisabeth and Ben lock horns over the best way to tell the story. Elisabeth clearly has a sharper command of the facts but it seems that Ben wants more control over this interview. Elisabeth won't give it up. Ben is becoming agitated in his chair, impatient.

Elisabeth's raises her voice again saying, "But its a very important piece! Because Mary Ann is a very important factor in my rescuing the children. She was starting to tell me to prepare me that there was a lot more going on here, and, whatever was going on here with my daughter and her children was not because of me. The whole world was beginning to look in here and say I was this bad mother and that we did a terrible job. It was awful. I guess I was very low and depressed at that time because I felt that I was being "pooped" on by everyone!"

"Who do you feel was blaming you for your daughter's behavior?" I ask.

"Even my own family, my sister, my parents," Elisabeth says.

"To this day," Ben interrupts.

"They were just looking and saying, 'God what a troubled family!' Elisabeth says.

"Yeah, we're the black sheep of the whole group," Ben mutters. He is turned around in his chair with his back to Elisabeth, facing sideways, bent over at the waist, his arms resting on his knees, his hands clasped between his legs. From where she sits, all Elisabeth can see is the expanse of red plaid that stretches over the cold curve of his back, like a dull rebuke.

Elisabeth continues, "Well, they didn't understand what was going on. And it certainly looked like we did this lousy job. The externals *were* that. And I was feeling like I didn't think I could help anybody.

"My friend Mary Ann is the one that started giving me the support and made me strong, helped me get stronger. I wasn't strong at that time as I started seeing what was going on with my daughter and my grandchildren. It was mind blowing! And then when my grandchildren started telling me little stories, it was ... " Elisabeth drops her voice to a whisper again and leans forward. The whites of her eyes are showing all around her round brown eyes. She grips her tea cup and her lips tighten to white lines. "... mind-blowing!

"I don't know. I grew up in a family—my mother's Italian, my father's Irish—that was, shall I say, protected? Naive? I mean you knew things happened. But not to us. My parents weren't educated, my mother only went to the sixth grade. So college for their oldest daughter was not something they encouraged. You know, your boys went, but. ... "

Elisabeth blames herself for not realizing the extent of what was happening to her grandchildren and her daughter, Marion. Like many women of her generation, she feels uneducated and, perhaps, not very smart after a lifetime of deferring to the better-educated males both within her family and without. In the absence of any real support from Ben, she grew to rely on her friend Mary Ann, who has a master's in early child care and whom Elisabeth admires and respects.

Elisabeth continues, "She was a tremendous help to me by pointing out the mannerisms of the children that pointed to more than just alcohol and drugs, that I was not this lousy mother. She could see what I was feeling. 'You did the best you could. You're going to buck up! And we are going to do this thing together.' She made that promise.

"I was helping her with her father who was dying of cancer and her mother who had Alzheimer's. But I had all this going on, too. When they were both buried, she walked into this house and never left. She had a computer at home that she helped me put the chronology on. Terribly important! Told me all the time, 'Write down! Write down everything! Document! Call the doctor! Tell her how they came home, whether they want to hear it or not! Tell the lawyer this! Tell DSS this! Don't tell DSS that!' She was an unbelievable help to me."

At this point, Ben leaves without a word. The door slams shut behind him as he goes outdoors.

I try to lead Elisabeth back to the events in chronological order, and she tells me that after her daughter left Thomas for good, after her second hospitalization, he had sole custody of the children.

"Those children started going downhill, they couldn't even function in school. In the '85-'86 school year, I got my foot in the door by calling the school to say that I had concerns about how my grandson was doing in school. I explained to them about the drugs and alcohol and my daughter's hospitalization. I told them I thought they were not getting the support from their father that I felt they needed. So I started getting my foot in the door like that.

"In February of '86, my daughter finally went for the divorce. We helped her put the down payment on her lawyer to get the divorce started."

I ask her if there was any follow up with the 51A that had been filed initially in New Hampshire.

"No," she said. "We didn't have anything. They couldn't even find the papers. When we went into court, all we talked about was the divorce. She wanted to get away from him. We didn't know that much then either. Christine had just told us about her cousin touching her, so at that time that's all we knew about.

"So when we went into court—I say *we* because the children were going between us and Thomas Connor, so when we were mediating, it was sort of like a three-way divorce. So when she filed for the divorce, what of course happens is they (the court) want the best interests of the children. ... "

"Yup. That's what they say," I mutter.

"That's what they *say*! I say pfft!" She makes a dry spitting sound and laughs mirthlessly. "As far as the courts helping them, pfft!" We both laugh, but we don't really think it's funny.

"But what they (the courts) tried to work out was where were the children going to go—how many days here, how many days there, what school.

"Now as I was going to the school, I was more able to—not have control—but I was more able to represent my daughter, shall we say. So that's what I would do. I started taking that role on, calling the school and saying I was concerned. 'How can I help the children in any way?' So then they started telling me things. 'This little guy seems to be going through a lot.

He's falling asleep. He doesn't have lunch money. He's unkempt, dirty.' Oh, God! I would be so upset. So I would call the court person.

"Mary Ann would give me some good advice. She would say, 'Make sure you ask them how you can help them. Maybe you can ask if they can go to the Lakeville school system.' "

Ben has come back in and is moving about in the kitchen right next to where we are sitting.

"We were going to a family therapist who was helping the whole family," Elisabeth says. "Marion was out of the hospital. Ben and I didn't know if we were going to do this piece."

"She (the therapist) was working with you and Ben on whether or not you were going to do this '*piece*'? I ask.

"Well, um ... this was putting pressure on ... um ... everybody ... ," Elisabeth falters.

She is obviously uncomfortable. I try to help her to clarify. Ben is moving around busily, but silently, in the kitchen. Elisabeth is trying to be cautious.

"So, in other words ... ," I prompt.

"There were a whole bunch of pieces here that were kind of pulling apart, all the family was falling apart," Elisabeth blurts out finally. "The children would not talk to my husband and tell him the things they were telling me. He was having a hard time believing it. I was having a hard time with all of it. So in other words, we were going to counseling for *all* the pieces!"

> It really appears that Ben let Elisabeth down. She needed his support and guidance, but most of all, she needed him to believe. She needed him to be part of the "team," the team that put the children's best interest first.
>
> I recommend that Elisabeth share with Ben her disappointment that he had to struggle to believe the magnitude of the abuse. If this issue does not get resolved, Elisabeth's feelings of disappointment and hurt may continue to act as a wedge in their marital relationship. Relationships need not be perfect, but children will heal more thoroughly in an environment in which their caregivers are respectful of one another. If hurt feelings are left unattended, those feelings will continue to grow and so too will grow the distance in the marital relationship.

"The pieces of my daughter falling apart, and how can we help her ... ," Elisabeth falters again.

"And whether or not you should get involved in helping your grandchildren?" I ask. "Was that one of the pieces?"

"Right," Elisabeth answers.

"Taking on another burden?" I continue. I watch Ben in the kitchen, but he does not acknowledge this conversation, does not look our way.

"Yes! Because, you know, it looked like it was going to be a long fight," Elisabeth says.

> That they sought counseling is very useful, but it is fairly obvious that Elisabeth was more invested in the process than Ben allowed himself to be. Even though Ben does not appear open to any long-term counseling, he might benefit greatly from some individual short-term counseling to address his feelings of ambivalence and frustration.

"At that time, Marion was also going to counseling. They were telling her to stay away from *me*. She wasn't telling them everything that went on. She couldn't bear it, I guess, or her mind covered it up and she was denying it.

"It was very, very difficult. I was walking a terrible road. Because my daughter would be denying it. When Christine would tell me something horrendous, it would blow my mind. It would take me off my feet for a couple of days."

"Like what?" I ask gently. She has been, up to this point, tentative about giving details of the sexual abuse. She makes references to being "touched" and "hurt" words that are easier to say, but mask the true nature of the violation and suffering that occurs when children are sexually abused. Although I don't wish to make these revelations any more painful for her than they already are, I want the real version of events, not the polite one.

"Well, I am trying to think when she started telling us about her father touching her," Elisabeth begins. It was a long route. "It was the cousin, then an uncle that touched her over at 'Grammy's house.' He was starting to hurt her upstairs in the upstairs bedroom—"

Ben calls out, "There are nine brothers and sisters!"

"—and the grandmother went up and tried to interfere and he hit the grandmother," Elisabeth continues. "And all this whole time, this other grandmother never told what went on, because, obviously, this has been a family of generations of abuse and a weak lady that was hurt too, a battered woman I am sure. I compare her to Marion.

"My daughter was frightened. So frozen with fear and the threats—and they were so damned violent—that she couldn't. ... He knew what to do, I think, to keep her that little, weak girl that she was. And maybe I make excuses for her, I don't know. But I hear battered women, I have gone to seminars, I've taken a rape crisis counselor course—anything I could take that I could learn about what I was dealing with and who I needed to deal with and how to handle it as best I could."

"At that time your daughter didn't want to hear these things, Craig was denying it, so you were looking like the 'crazy lady?' " I ask.

"Yes. [They thought] I had this vivid imagination. Even when we started therapy, we had terrible experiences with therapists for the children, terrible experiences.

"In the summer of '86 is when I really got going with this thing. We went to court in June at the end of the school year because I had been calling the court person and telling her, "Look, I can't help these children! I can't take them to the doctor, I can't take them to the dentist. They need help! This father is doing nothing. I need a piece of paper saying I can help these children legally.

"So we went to court in June of '86. And every time we went it was sort of like a little neglect charge was being thrown in. He had been taking them to his sister's where we *knew* they were being hurt. I told the court this and the court ordered him not to take them there, because by that time we had a little proof. Teachers. A doctor. Counselors."

"I thought that was when we were going to the DSS," Ben calls from the kitchen where he stands, arms folded across his chest, listening now to what was being said.

"No, no, no, no ... they weren't even involved yet," Elisabeth cuts him off. "So at that point I got a piece of paper that we signed, Marion signed, and he (Thomas Connor) was supposed to sign giving me authority to be able to take them to the doctor, give them medicine, etcetera. During the course of the summer they were supposed to go on a ten-day camping trip. I told the court, 'They are supposed to go on this camping trip with his sister and we know her son hurts them all the time.' Craig would admit to being punched and hurt that way at this time. 'And they are supposed to be in a camper with them for 10 days for God's sake!' The court told him he couldn't go with his sister camping.

"You know what he said when he came out (of court)? He came right to the door and said, 'No one was going to tell him what to do with his kids! Get the kids and get them in the camper!'

"They left for 10 horrible days. They were sexually abused by all of them! Because Christine had opened her mouth." Elisabeth has welled up and can't continue. Ben has come back to the table and is sitting with us. He tries to say something a couple of times and then gives up. We are all trying to compose ourselves. It's several minutes before anyone can continue.

Ben finally says, "And a lot worse than that!"

"That was the beginning of the nightmare," Elisabeth says, her lips quivering and looking away from me. "When I started finding out how bad it was, I was hoping it wasn't as bad as it *looked*." She says this as a question, blinking as if to hold back the nagging guilt along with the tears.

"When they came back from that camping trip, they were in horrendous shape. They couldn't play ... they didn't care about anything ... they were in terrible shape." Elisabeth's voice is low, and full of pain. "Christine could barely sit down.

"I was very upset and I called the abuse hot line for some advice and they said, 'Take her to Saint Joseph's hospital.' They had a nurse there that dealt with abused children. And I said that I didn't know if she would let anybody examine her. She was hysterical. But I did, and God bless that nurse.

"She told me she had worked with abused children and she knew how I felt. She was wonderful. She let me go with her and had Christine sit on my lap when she examined her, first of all with the dolls. And when Christine told her with the dolls what had happened to her on that camping trip, I asked her if there was anybody else who could document it. Being a nurse myself, I knew that documentation was going to count. This was going to count finally! But, I wanted someone else too. And she suggested a social worker. I asked if it was a woman because she wouldn't let a male near her. And it was. And so twice that day they documented what had happened to her through the dolls and by Christine telling them.

"When the doctor came in to examine her, she started screaming. Didn't want to go anywhere near him. He was very cold. Christine wouldn't even talk to him. He examined her and just wrote down 'vaginitis' even though we told him what she told us. 'Well it could have happened on her bicycle,' he replied. He wasn't very helpful, shall we say. Covered his butt, covered his tracks.

"A 51A was filed. One by the social worker, one by the nurse that day and it was documented in the hospital records that day. And then I told our pediatrician about it and she, again, hesitated filing a 51A. She either didn't know much about abuse or didn't want to get involved, I could never quite figure that out.

"At that time we still thought it was only Alan that was hurting her."

"The story she was telling with the dolls was just about Alan?" I ask.

"Right. She was too fearful of him. ... " Elisabeth begins.

"Too fearful of her father?" I ask.

"Yes! Too fearful of *him* to say anymore. But, what she was doing, when she would draw pictures of the family at preschool—and I took those pictures to the therapists—the *whole page* was a picture of her father's face and in the corner over here ... " (Elisabeth hunches over to make herself small and bends over to a little corner of the tablecloth to show me what it was like.) "was a little picture of her mother, and even tinier than that was her brother Craig, and tinier than that—almost like a dot—was Christine. There was a picture of a house, and what was supposed to be window panes looked like jail bars. That's how she would draw her pictures. I was keeping track of all those things.

"I started doing a complete work-up on Craig. I hooked up with a pediatric neurologist. They were presenting with so many physical problems, medical problems. Mary Ann had suggested a complete work-up at Children's Hospital with a neurologist because it looked like he had Tourette's Syndrome."

"You did not suspect that Craig also was being sexually abused?" I ask.

"At that point, no, because we thought it was the cousin touching a little girl," Elisabeth replies. "I can honestly say no. I think Mary Ann did. She started saying things to me, getting me ready. 'It may be more than this.' But I had so much going on at that time."

"We were taking care of my mother," says Ben.

"Yeah, I'm a great caretaker," Elisabeth says dryly.

"But Mary Ann didn't really get involved until later," Ben says to Elisabeth.

"But we started at this point. Now we start with all the testing so I can bring all the test results to the Lakeville school system when the children start school there. I had him tested the year before, but in the face of all that (the results) the Dorset school system said he didn't have any problems— this kid who was failing every subject." Her voice rises sharply. "It was a matter of money, they didn't want to give him Special Ed. So with Mary Ann's knowledge of the school system, how it worked, she would tell me, 'You get your own work-up done. You get the neurological work-up, psychological work-up. And when you walk into the school system, they have to help you by law, they can't say no then.' And that's what was done."

Elisabeth told me later that no matter what she described to the schools, they would tell her they'd seen worse, children who were more depressed, more needy. Her grandchildren, even now, are sometimes described by teachers as being "insubordinate" and "not trying hard enough." When Elisabeth explains, once again, the children's history she is told that, "They look fine in the hallway, they are talking and chatting." Elisabeth's struggles to get the children the services they need and are entitled to are ongoing, and unfortunately, the unresponsiveness she has encountered in the schools the children attend is quite common elsewhere as well. Most school systems are overwhelmed and ill-prepared for the numbers of special needs students, particularly those who have been affected by the traumas—physical, emotional and mental—caused by using and abusing parents.

"A woman—God bless her—a pediatric neurologist from Northrop Children's hospital said to me, 'I think what you need is a Guardian Ad Litem. He (Craig) is not having seizures. There is no brain damage. This is all emotional.' So after that I went full speed ahead with therapy, calling DSS. ... "

"But what was their (DSS) response to the 51A you filed after that camping trip?" I ask.

"Pfff ... nothing," Elisabeth says.

"Nothing," Ben seconds.

"Nothing ... nothing. ... I was this 'crazy grandmother' putting ideas in people's heads, and even at Northrop Children's hospital ... ," Elisabeth lowers her voice to a whisper, "we found out much later. ..."

Ben bursts in with his booming voice—this is the story he has been wanting to tell, "The secretary there was Thomas Connor's best friend's wife. We all had to go to therapy there and this woman is his closest friend's wife! He was going too, by the way, at different times. Anyway, they all took his side. They didn't believe anything we said, and they believed him." Ben's voice is filled with disgust.

"They believed him when he was saying what?" I ask.

"That he never did anything really wrong," Elisabeth jumps back in. "And that I was the 'crazy grandmother' trying to take his kids away." Ben nods in agreement and says, "We never tried to take his kids away."

"Every time we went to court it was *never* over my wanting custody of the children. Never!" Elisabeth says. "It was over neglect and abuse of the children."

"Right," Ben says.

"His story was that I wanted custody of the children," Elisabeth says.

"And that it was their mother that was the unfit parent," Ben adds. "His whole defense was against her (Elisabeth), saying she was a grandmother talking from outer space, wanting to take over the grandchildren."

A report had been filed by a psychologist at Northrop Children's Hospital that characterized Elisabeth as an interfering grandmother and that hinted she was putting a lot of pressure on Craig which was causing many of his problems. Both the court and the school had this report on file although Elisabeth and Ben were not aware of its contents at the time.

"I *was* calling like a crazy woman after these weekends when they would come back. They were so traumatized. So hurt. Nightmares. Couldn't sleep. I was up all night, getting no sleep. I was getting nuts too. And I was calling up saying I want them to know the condition that the children are in. I want them to know! I want them seen like this! I want them seen on a Monday when they've come back on a Sunday night! I wish they could be seen Sunday night! Or Friday when they're getting ready! They ought to come out here Friday when they have to go with him and see what they are like—they are almost killing each other, and angry, and scared!" At times like this she becomes a ramrod of fury—trembling, fists balled up, thin lips like slashes drawn across her tense face, her brown eyes bulging circles, with the whites showing all around behind her glasses.

"So I was calling and making a pest of myself, and that's basically what they thought of me," she says more calmly. "But Mary Ann was wonderful. She would tell me not to be hysterical. 'Make sure when you call, just calmly give them the information. Only talk facts.' You know, because I would be so upset and I would ramble sometimes. She was coming and giving me all this support and telling me how to stay clear and focused, telling me to write down on a piece of paper what I wanted to say before I made the call. Because she knew me." Elisabeth laughs in reference to her tendency to ramble on. When she smiles, her face takes on an impish quality. Her round eyes narrow a bit as the laugh lines take over.

"But what was happening was my lawyer was patronizing me, DSS was patronizing me, event the therapists were. Christine was confirming what I was saying (to the therapists), but then they would take Craig in and he would say we were all lying."

At this point Ben leaves the house again. He does not come back this time. But I can see him through the big windows all afternoon long hauling lumber, digging stumps, repairing his boat. He never stops working.

Elisabeth confides in me whispering, "And my husband was not supportive, you can see the anger in me via my frustration. He would go away on business trips."

I ask if he was one of those who thought she was just a crazy lady.

"Yes! And he was almost befriending him (Thomas). I have a lot of rage—not anger—rage!"

"He was denying that there was a problem and taking Thomas Connor's side?" I ask.

"Right. So he would not have to believe it. Usually what he'll do when I am talking about it with anybody is change the subject—defer it onto something else. I get so angry!"

> In cases of sexual abuse, sometimes a family member will doubt the truth because if they accept the truth they must accept the anger and all the painful consequences that come with it. Ben does not appear to be very comfortable with painful emotions, and to acknowledge that his grandchildren have been sexually tortured may be far too emotionally overwhelming for him. It's as if he feels that, 'If I can't imagine it, then it doesn't exist.' This denial is preventing him from emotionally supporting his wife and grandchildren.

"We had a few problems before this, but what happened when I wasn't getting any support and he was pulling me apart ... " (She drops her voice to a nearly breathless whisper.) "... I could not walk away from those children. So that's what happened at that time ... I couldn't walk away ... and he was asking me to. I said, 'No. And if you are asking me to, it's telling me something about who you are as a person.'

"I am not saying my decision was right, but I knew I was the only one who could save the children. They would have been on the streets, using drugs, thrown from one foster home to another because they were almost like two little animals at the time.

"We are working things out because it's easier for the both of us financially, staying friends, salvaging what pieces we could. There was so much damage, and I keep hoping that someday we could get back to what we had but I'm afraid ... so far it hasn't happened."

"Do you think that he is now glad that you kept the children?" I ask.

"I don't know if he is glad. I think accepting it might be closer to what we have here. He wouldn't leave me even back when I couldn't deal with him. But even at the end, when I would show him something as concrete as that ... " (She lifts up a newspaper clipping bound in plastic reporting on one of the criminal trials for child rape.) "... he would ... " She imitates a dismissive gesture with her hand, a disgusted wave.

"So it took a long time to die. I think that's what it is. Something died in here" (She points to her heart.) "... as far as he and I go, and I feel very sad about that. It's very, very painful. That's another painful piece."

To save their grandchildren, the Parks need to save themselves. Elisabeth is making it very clear that she feels much pain and sadness over the current state of her relationship with her husband. She needs Ben to be her partner. Without his partnership, I am not sure how much more pain their relationship can bear. I would like to see Ben and Elisabeth actively pursue and participate in couples counseling. If Ben will not go, Elisabeth would benefit from therapeutic support to help her either accept Ben as he is or possibly make some very painful—but necessary—changes.

The Parks' story is lengthy and complex, a roller coaster ride of sharp twists and turns. It contains many highly charged issues: sexual abuse, drug abuse, domestic violence, denial, and damaged children as well as an ineffective social service system and protracted court battles. All of these elements took their toll on the Parks' marriage.

For now, we will put aside the Parks' struggle to free the children from devastating abuse (to be concluded in chapter 4, *Healing the Wounds*) and focus on their marriage.

Ben's point of view is the final puzzle piece of a picture that shows the disastrous effects on a marriage under stress when grandparents don't agree.

Ben

It's a cool, early fall day when I travel back out to talk with Ben. Sunlight has taken on a hard, yellow slant. The hydrangea next to the Parks' front stairs are turning now from creamy white to a deep raspberry pink, and miniature green and gold leaf tornadoes swirl at my feet as I step onto the front walk. I have been sick for days with a relentless intestinal flu, but I have also felt driven to keep this appointment. I was concerned that I left here last time with a bundle of negative feelings and questions left unanswered for Ben. So, armed with Maalox, crackers, and ginger ale for the long car ride, I had set off.

When I first met Ben, I had a sense of deja vu. He was so familiar, very much like many men I grew up with—a doer, a builder, a hard worker, uncomfortable with feelings, and possessed with a low tolerance for and about women.

After that first meeting, I called on a psychologist friend of mine, Dr. Kimberly Gatof, and anguished over it. "What's with these guys?" I asked. "Why did Ben have such a hard time believing Elisabeth? Why did he treat her efforts with disdain? Why can't some men value and validate their wives without feeling threatened by them?"

She told me that each time we enter into a dialogue with someone, we carry with us a lifetime of collected experiences and biases. As we drag this heavy baggage into conversations, it weighs on us, influencing how we hear and understand what is being said. I knew I had a few leftover issues from my childhood, even from my own marriage that I was hauling around, and I was afraid it was affecting my objectivity regarding Ben.

I do not dislike Ben; quite the contrary. But I have pigeonholed him, I know, and I know I need to free him from that box I've put him in—for both of our sakes. My friend tells me I must meet with him once more, just him and me.

I make this second trip to Lakeville to meet with Ben alone.

I drive through the town past the American Legion Hall and the "Meat Shoot Saturday Night" sign, past the other small lakes that dot the landscape and are ringed by new home developments, past the little strip malls scattered like matchsticks along the winding roads—uninviting boxes, indistinguishable from one another, strung together like cars on a train. There are stubby dry cleaners, seedy package stores, and the pizza parlors, glowing dead blue with fluorescent lighting that serve as hangouts for the local kids. I stop at the high school and look around—newly built brick buildings, somewhat fortress-like, but crisp and clean, with apple red trim. I don't know what I'm doing here, what I expect to find. Clues? An answer to how this happened to this family—how this happens to any family? I drive on with the question trailing me.

As I sit with him at their table once more, Ben points out a great blue heron perched on a piece of jagged drift wood at the shoreline. We admire the handsome bird for awhile and then I begin, gingerly, by asking Ben about their home—their dream come true. I know that they had planned for it to be their retirement home—this beautiful sanctuary by the water. Fishing. Boating. Gardening. I try to get him to talk about that period of time just after they finally moved here, when Marion got pregnant.

Ben talks about his mother who lived on this site for many years in an old house that he replaced with this one. He talks about the differences between prefab homes and construction, between Acorn Homes and Deck. And he talks a lot about his children, his pride in them. "We've been very lucky; we've got a good bunch of kids," he tells me. He does not talk about disappointment or lost dreams.

I chat with him about real estate and building, hoping to make him comfortable enough to open up. "I was a real estate broker for twelve years," I tell him, and talk about the houses I've renovated and the ones I've built. I ramble on a little about being a grandparent and how I feel about raising my granddaughter.

Finally, I try to stop beating around the bush. "Well, I guess what I'm driving at is that—and I guess it's true for all grandparents who are in this situation—you get to that age when you think that you are going to start to enjoy yourself, and you get pushed back to square one." I say and watch him as he responds.

"Of course, at that time, when we built the house, all of this hadn't come about," says Ben.

"Pretty soon after that," I lead.

"A year after that," he says.

I wait a few beats. "So ... you sort of feel like you're back in it again ... and it's hard." I am prodding, dangerously close to putting words in his mouth.

"It was harder then than it is now, even though I am out of work right now. I don't know what the future's going to bring within the next year when our finances run out. We had had a *savings*. You know, I always had a good job. I always had a good paying job, so financially it was never ... even with the gang—you know we had six children—we got by pretty well.

"I am angry at the lawyer stuff. They did absolutely nothing and we went through our total life savings. But anyway. ... " He pauses a while. "But see, this thing just built up—I'm sure Elisabeth explained it to you—it just built up and built up. From the nephew abusing them to the point where ... I had never ... I couldn't even believe that it was the father."

"Did you have a hard time believing?" I begin to ask.

"I *did*, because the boy, to this day, has never ... in fact he told me that his father never touched him," Ben says. "But, he doesn't tell Elisabeth that. He tells *her* a different story."

"I guess that's typical of boys that have been abused." I am dangerous again. Who do I think I am, Anna Freud?

"We knew that Christine was being abused by the nephew. *That* we knew for a fact. That came out at the time with the examinations she had. It looked like the father was taking her up to the nephew, because they're a close-knit family too. There's chaos in that family, they are a violent family. I've known the whole family long before Elisabeth has. I grew up with the father."

I find myself saying "Mmmm. Oh! Uh huh." continuously. I am sitting to his right at the dining room table, he is at the head. I turn my body fully toward him, nodding my head, leaning forward, urging him on. I'm trying too hard.

"But anyway, one thing led to another and Craig told us about the father abusing him," Ben says. "Plus knocking Christine and Marion around. We didn't even know about that." Ben says.

"So when it was all happening ... it probably took years to unravel ... but there was probably a long period of time when it was really hard to believe," I say.

"It was one thing after another. The whole of the seven years, all that was discussed was the abuse thing and the kids." His voice is down to a quiet, gravely mumble. "It got to be old hat after a while. I don't discuss it because I get so sick of it. I never discuss it with people at work. I never did, you know."

"Well that's understandable," I say.

"It's something, I guess, that will never go away," Ben says. He sounds wistful. "We have everything going here. We have them at home. The kids are healthy. But emotionally they're damaged, the boy more so than Christine. And he shows it. He's very quiet. He's a good kid. It's a shame. He loves sports.

"We were lucky that we had this home to raise the kids in, too. Really! We had a lot of things going for us." Ben pauses again.

"So it put a lot of stress on the marriage—that's true for a lot of grand-parents," I say, fishing, fishing.

Ben responds by telling me, "It put a lot of stress on all the kids."

I change the subject. "Do you think the Connor family got any fallout from the court trial or anything?" I ask.

Ben responds enthusiastically, "No! That's a good question! All of their kids were big time athletes in the school. Girls too. I am talking, *excelled*. They led everything. If it was a boy, he lead in basketball, football, touch-downs. Each kid. And the girls excelled in soccer and girl's basketball. They were always the captains. Nine kids, every one of them excelled.

"Most of the boys have been in all kinds of jams. They always got out of it because of the prestigious name. The town backed them and all of that. Our kids took a back seat. Like Joanie (their youngest daughter) had to suffer through high school being rejected by a lot by teachers who liked *them*."

"No kidding!" I say, truly amazed.

"Oh, she went through a lot of that. Now these two (the grandchildren) are going through a little bit of it."

"Even though he was found guilty?" I butt in.

"Yup."

"Why do you think that is?" I ask.

"Well, they were very active, like I said, in the sports end of it. ... " Ben drifts off.

"Were they likable?" I'm really trying to understand this myself.

"Oh yeah. They're very personable people. It's like anything else, Deb, if you sat in a room with them you'd say hey, no way does he have these types of problems. And they probably all don't. I know for a fact that two of them do. But you can't blame the others either. You know what I mean?"

"You knew their father?" I ask.

"Oh yeah, I grew up with their father. He was a great athlete, too, when he was younger. I played ball with him."

"So, there was never any real fallout for that family, and in fact there is still some loyalty left around," I confirm.

"Yeah, there's a lot of that. But we got a lot of support from people, people who knew what was going on even before we did."

"Who knew?" I ask.

"Oh, the police, the peer groups all knew what was going on. When it all came out, then they'd all start coming over saying, 'It's too bad you never knew.' That kind of stuff. But, you can't take that to court. It doesn't mean a hill of beans when they start investigating things.

"It's a stigma. We all see them (the Connors). You have that feeling when you're in a store and you see them or one of their neighbors, you try to go in the other direction," Ben confides.

"That must be uncomfortable," I say.

"It is. I mean this is a small town," he says.

"So does that bother you to the extent that you wish you lived somewhere else?" I ask.

"No. ... " Ben pauses again, then starts and stops a few times before he continues with, "I wasn't around here. When I was working, I did a lot of traveling with the job I had. I went overseas. I was on the road an awful lot. So I wasn't involved as much as Elisabeth was. I wasn't involved at *all* in fact, because I wasn't *here*. I was in and out all during that time. It wasn't until the last three years that I've been home. But up until that time, she was taking the burden, brunt of everything.

"And, there was nothing I could *do,* Deb," Ben says. It sounds like a plea, a bid for understanding.

"Craig never would discuss it with me. Never. No way. Only once I asked him when I thought he'd be comfortable with me and he went violent. So we never discussed it again. We can discuss sports. We get along fine as far as the sports go. We generally watch it together. And I enjoy watching him play. He's a very good athlete, *very* good. My kids were too. I played a lot of football and baseball when I was younger. So he's got the genes in him—from both sides really, you know."

"Now, as you look back, are you glad that you have them?" I ask.

"Oh yeah! I agreed. I've got no problem with that at all. We both, I think—well I shouldn't talk for Elisabeth because she's not here—but I thought that maybe Marion would've come to the point of taking them. But it never happened. But I don't hold that against her either."

"Well, most grandparents do that," I tell him. "They wait—they hope that their children will get their acts together."

"Which she did! But she just couldn't cope," Ben says.

"Elisabeth mentioned that you all went to counseling. And one of the things you discussed at that time was whether or not you would continue on that path ... to keep the children." I am not being direct enough, I know. I am finding this difficult. I can sense the discomfort in Ben. It rubs against the air between us like sand on glass; I wish I could brush it away.

"We went to so much counseling. with so many different people, you wouldn't believe it. She's into this counseling thing that just blows my mind. No one gets to the root of anything, as far as I'm concerned. And one of the things was ... uhhh. ... "

The seconds tick by; I really do not want to take him where he does not want to go—perhaps *cannot* go. But I want to give him the opportunity to tell it the way he sees it. Ben sidesteps.

"When it came time for education ... all I wanted was that this guy was going to pay for their education.

"I already had three girls in college. And Joanie is the last one going. It's a big expense. Anyway, that never came up (in court) and I was a little upset at that. Although Craig may not be college material because of his emotional problems. He's a very good artist, by the way, this boy. And Christine will go, I'm sure Christine will go. But, I don't know ... at our age then. ...

"He did that poster over there." He proudly points out a pencil sketch, a woodland scene with a fox, framed in silver and hung on the brick wall behind the wood stove. "He just did that in about ten minutes! He's very good with human figures. My daughter is too. He must take after her in that respect."

"You were trying to secure their education for them." I let him take me where he wants to go. "Was that one of the disappointments you had with the lawyers?"

"I still have a problem with it. Thirty two thousand dollars so far! And we've got nothing for it as far as I'm concerned."

"Does he (Thomas Connor) pay child support?" I ask.

"Twenty-five dollars a week per kid. I could care less about that." He harumphs. "That's not even food money for a week!

"I am more or less on the outside looking in," he reveals suddenly.

"So all this mess was sort of swirling around, and you felt like you were on the outside looking in," I repeat.

"Well, I was," Ben tells me. "I gave her no support because I was. ... The stories changed every day. I perhaps should have kept a diary of my own. I made a lot of mistakes too, as far as not recording things for my own benefit."

> It is good to see Ben acknowledge that he made mistakes too. Sometimes the only way to get on the path of forgiveness and healing is to acknowledge our own mistakes. Sexual abuse impacts every family member, even those not directly suffering the abuse. In many ways, Ben and Elisabeth are victims too. I can tell Ben does not like being a victim, yet he needs to admit he hurts too. The entire family needs to heal from the aftermath and scars of the sexual abuse that occurred. For Ben's healing to begin, he not only needs to acknowledge he has made some mistakes, but also needs to admit that his grandchildren were sexually abused by their father. Sometimes, half of the battle is admitting we have a battle. I don't want to see Ben lose the war.

"How do you think that would have helped you though?" I ask.

"It would have helped me because ... it would have helped me with the wording when I had discussions with the lawyer. Like I say, I wouldn't be here during the day and I didn't *go* to some of the meetings that she did have with the lawyer because I was working so. ...

"Elisabeth's got a whole file. She's got the file and she's got names, dates. I have to give her what's due to *her* and that's a hundred percent. She did it all, I did nothing. I was ... tagging along."

> We all need validation. We all need to know that the people we love appreciate what we do. Ben should tell his wife, frequently, that he recognizes she did do it all. He should let his wife know that he recognizes that this time, she was stronger. Partners can get a lot of mileage from validating what the other has done. I'm sure there have been many times that

Elisabeth felt unappreciated by Ben and perhaps even doubted herself. She needs to feel appreciated and recognized for her dedication toward her grandchildren. She needs this from Ben.

"Obviously you had mixed emotions at the time," I say. "It was a great big mess and you weren't hearing the same things she was hearing. So the question for you was, did you want to continue with all of this? The court battles? " I fumble, afraid to shoot the arrow too directly, and wound him.

"Oh yes! Because of the fact that I was hoping that the nephew was going to get dragged into this who was the biggest offender as far as I am concerned, which we know! The kids came right out with *him!*

"I thought it would've finally come to that. I figured this guy (Thomas) would *never take the heat,* that he was *covering.* ... " Ben begins this startling revelation, but I cut him off. I don't realize the significance of what he is starting to say. He mentions Alan and I am off on that tangent.

"He never went to trial though did he?" I ask. "Just the father did."

"Never."

"I wonder why not."

"Because he was a juvenile at the time, 16. This guy at 16 years old—I have two sons that are six footers—and this guy is bigger than them at 16. And here's this *baby* ... Christine was *two!*" He shakes his head still in disbelief.

"You must have a lot anger."

"Oh yeah! Toward both of them! After him (Thomas) going to trial and being found guilty, and I would have bet my *whole life*—I would have laid down my life—that there was no way. ... He is finally going to crack and say, *I* didn't do this, the nephew did. He didn't. He *took* it!

"Then I figured, well, he *is* guilty then. For him to sit there and take it, being found guilty, and then *plea bargain* and then come to Massachusetts and plea bargain! I said 'Oh boy!' That's when it really hit me!"

"Do you think there are some people who think that he was merely covering for his nephew?" I ask, stunned.

"I don't know, I really don't know, Deb.

"I'll tell you something that has something to do with him maybe making that decision. I coached him and all his brothers in softball when he first married my daughter. Then I found out their temperament. Their violent temperament and their decision making—they were *stupid*. They were really stupid! You had to tell them exactly what to do. These guys had all played high school sports, graduated from high school and had jobs ... and, they didn't have a brain! They were like Little Leaguers. They were all stupid. I couldn't believe it!

"So I can believe now, after looking at that. The bad decision making just in the sports thing, for him to make a decision of whether he was going to go to bat for his nephew, cover for him. ... " Ben trails off.

"So you think he might have made a stupid decision like covering for his nephew and taking the blame?" I try to keep my astonishment from showing.

"Probably. I don't know. One thing led to another at the trial in New Hampshire. And the repercussions we were getting from the police department about his nephew and his sister, who was in all kinds of trouble. We were getting this feedback and I said, Oh man, this family is more whacked up than I thought. We thought there were just stupid things, but there were serious things they were involved in. *Then* it wasn't hard for me to make a decision, okay this guy is a loser! He didn't seem like it. He seemed a little different from the others. But maybe I was just trying to make excuses in my own head about it."

"It was a long process for you to come to that point," I confirm.

"It was!" he states. "This was very confusing, this whole thing."

There is another long pause. The seconds stretch out into the silent room. I think Ben is done with talking. He is looking out the big glass slider, past the deck and over the water. I can actually see the choppy lake reflected in his glasses. He has been remarkably patient with me. I recall something he said, with his dry sense of humor, the day I met Craig. This trait also seems to apply to Ben. 'That boy only says nine words a year, and he said eight of them today.' I like Ben. I ask him one last question.

"Do you think that you and Elisabeth might get back to the point where you were before ... before all of this began?" I ask.

"I don't know. I really don't know. It doesn't look too good. Too much damage. We get along but ... we're just existing here. ... " Ben drifts off staring out the window with a faraway look in his eyes.

> One of the important questions here is, can Ben allow himself to grieve the loss of his grandchildren's innocence? Events have unalterably changed the nature of the Parks' relationship. That is not to say they cannot have a very mutually satisfying relationship together. They can. However, the sexual abuse has claimed Ben and Elisabeth as victims too. Because of this, they both must learn how to grieve the loss and pain that sexual abuse creates.
>
> I don't believe that there is "too much damage" although it's plain to see the extent of the damage caused by this ordeal. However, if Ben and

Elisabeth want their relationship to succeed, they must put a substantial amount of time and energy into it. To that end, Ben must allow himself the opportunity to heal, which can only begin by admitting the need for healing and moving forward from there.

For both families presented in this chapter, we see what happens when there is a substantial breakdown in communication or even no communication at all. For couples contemplating the important, life-altering decision of parenting their grandchildren, much heartfelt, thoughtful, mutually respectful discussion needs to take place with each other before, during and after the arrival of the grandchildren.

Even though grandparents may not have much time to discuss new living arrangements beforehand, they do need to take a great deal of time after the fact, to discuss openly with each other the potential for stress on their marriage and, together, make plans for dealing with it.

4

Healing the Wounds

"If you have faith as small as a mustard seed,
nothing will be impossible for you."
—Matthew 13:31, 17:20

After you have swallowed your bitterness and dismantled the secrets, after
you have rearranged the parameters of your life, taken stock, and assessed
the littered landscape of family relationships, where do you go from there?
It's time for healing.

Many grandparents move instinctively toward methods of healing in the
same manner that for eons grandmothers have provided chicken soup and
chamomile tea laced with honey to soothe the little hurts and fevers of their
loved ones. Some rely on their faith for inspiration and guidance, but that
alone is not always enough.

Support groups are often a good first step toward healing. Sharing experiences and information, breaking the isolation barrier, and connecting on a
personal level with those in similar circumstances can serve as a powerful
balm for families in conflict as well as offering much needed information on
navigating the "system." Each time grandparents are thrown into the melee,

they must reinvent the wheel. Where do I go? What do I do? Is there help for me? Very often the one place they can get the information they need is from their local support group and the people that have already been through it.

Some of the grassroots organizations that have sprung up throughout the country are connected to local Councils on Aging or with Departments of Elder Affairs, but most have formed through word of mouth among grandparents in crisis. Some have the benefit of professional facilitators, but most are run by grandparents just like you and me. Grandparents use their support groups to help them over rough spots or to garner information about legal rights, aid, and the like. Some just like knowing others are out there going through the same things and take enough comfort from that to keep going.

Additionally, groups such as Alcoholics Anonymous, Al-Anon, and Parents Anonymous can be useful resources. These groups are easily accessed in most communities and offer helpful tools for coming to grips with issues such as substance abuse, codependency, and family relationships.

Stress is the little black cloud that can be found following grandparents around, hovering overhead, raining droplets of resentment and guilt, self-doubt, and depression. Stress management seminars and literature on relaxation techniques can be helpful to those open to new ideas and remedies. Stress is the one universal element to parenting your grandchildren whether grandparents are young or old, financially secure or scraping by, in a custody battle or one big happy family. Stress is the natural by-product of caring for children all over again just when you thought it was time to think of yourself for a change. Learning how to overcome or manage the stress in your life, prioritize and put events into perspective, value yourself and your efforts, and work toward attainable goals, while letting go of things you cannot change—these are the lessons essential to healing.

Another component to healing is empowerment. Sometimes grandparents, specifically grandmothers, feel as if they are in a black hole of events over which they have no control and are powerless to alter. This feeling of powerlessness often leads to depression. Women are usually the keepers of the peace in families. To achieve that, they learn early on to sublimate their own needs and desires for the good of the family as a whole. They are unfamiliar with the power that is theirs, and do not know how to use it to effect positive change for themselves.

One of the grandmothers that attended my support group was caring for her teenage granddaughter. Her daughter, the child's birth mother, was an alcoholic. Although the grandmother was having some difficulty dealing with the angst of an emerging teenager obsessed with cars, boys, and parties, her life was on a pretty even keel. Then her daughter lost yet another job and apartment and asked if she could live, temporarily, at her home. It wasn't long before she was wreaking havoc on the household and the grandmother was slipping into a vortex of helplessness and depression. The daughter was utterly dependent on her, physically and financially, yet for some reason, this grandmother had assigned her all the power in that situation, and had abdicated her own in the process. I said to her, "But it's your home, your food, your car, your gas. You hold all the cards!" But she couldn't see it. She had lived a life giving her personal power away and didn't know how to reclaim it. She was the lost bird, trapped inside a room, growing weak but within reach of an open window and freedom if she could only see it was the way out.

Professional therapy and counseling are often necessary before real healing can begin. The complicated circumstances implicit in family dynamics often require outside help for sorting out feelings and managing circumstances that can seem overwhelming. Family therapists can offer help on the issues of family relationships, conflict resolution, and marital stress. For children, issues of abandonment, loss, and grief may be best addressed through the expertise of therapists specializing in adoption issues whether or not the child has been adopted. Like any other search for professional help, it is always best to go to specialists. Children who have suffered sexual abuse should be taken to therapists specializing in that area. Grandparents whose marriages are under stress should seek couples counseling, and those who are having difficulty dealing with troubled birth parents should look for a family relationship expert. It takes some time to "shop" for the right fit, but it is important not only to find the right category of therapy, but also to feel comfortable with the therapist. The special circumstances requiring grandparents to become parents, either temporarily or permanently, usually require some level of expert counseling.

Unfortunately, the older the caregiving grandparent, the less open they may be to seeking professional help as well. Those of the "old school" wouldn't hear of going to counseling or seeking it for their grandchildren. "Psychiatrists are for crazy people," they might say.

They may be unfamiliar with terms like ADD or hyperactivity. A grandchild affected by these conditions may appear to elders as merely naughty or willful. A negative triangle can result between an afflicted child, an overburdened teacher, and an uninformed grandparent. These situations and others like them could be ameliorated by education, awareness, and sensitivity on the part of professionals in the fields of education and health care.

Professionals—the teachers, school administrators and counselors, pediatricians, health care providers, and social workers—should work together to provide a safety net for these new intergenerational families. But they are generally unaware of or blind to the special circumstances involved when grandparents are primary caregivers. Grandparents may be out of touch and out of step with child-rearing guidelines, health care requirements, nutritional standards, and teaching practices of today. Positive attention must be focused on the intergenerational families that turn up at school and pediatricians offices, or that turn for help to social workers and clergy. Professionals must first be made aware of the differences in approach grandparents may bring with them to childrearing. Often they may be dealing with caregivers functioning within a fog of culture shock. Those suffering the worst effects may be raising adolescents across the great divide of decades worth of changes, in some cases half a century or more.

Grandparents need help as they maneuver through the obstacle course before them. Systems in place to help children and families are as yet ill-equipped to deal with their specialized needs and concerns. Grandparents exist in a kind of limbo with regard to social service agencies across the board. They do not fit easily into categories set aside for aid; trying to jury-rig a fit such as requiring grandparents to become foster parents—like the square peg in a round hole dilemma—just doesn't work. Even when grandparents are entitled to assistance by law, such as medical benefits, the ignorance rampant in bureaucracies results in denial of, or barriers to, their receiving what they deserve.

Grandparents will not get the help they need to heal and move forward until the people and places from which assistance is available realize grandparents' importance in the equation of holding families together and decide that it is in the best interest of society to value that importance.

Grandchildren cannot get the help they need until decisionmakers, politicians, and bureaucrats decide that it makes economic sense to strengthen and assist grandparents thereby lessening the overload on the foster care system, decreasing admissions to costly residential facilities, and perhaps even stanching the flow of rootless youth toward the dead end of prison.

Grandparents have a few things going for them that you cannot train into foster care providers or pay residential staff to do. Grandparents love their grandchildren. They offer children connections, roots, and belonging.

They think their grandchildren are the best things to come along since sliced bread—better. Ask them. No where else can a child get such things.

It is out of that love and devotion that grandparents look for and find ways to heal themselves and their grandchildren. Some don't know where to look or what questions to ask. Some falter and stumble and may lose their way because they are overburdened and underhelped, but they all try.

Reverend Yarde

Reverend Eduardo Yarde is what we all hope for in our clergy. Caring, sensitive, and open-minded, he struggles to deal with the extreme needs of families in extreme circumstances—families often ripped to the core by bitterness, shame, and grief. Families in need of healing. I visited with Reverend Yarde at his church one cold Sunday this past snowless winter to talk about his philosophy and his methods.

The Morning Star Baptist Church rises up as graceful and important as the Parthenon on a bleak city block. White columns, brick front, and crisp white trim declare the building's dignity, while sheets of crumpled newspaper and stained coffee cups blow into the shrubbery stretching along the sidewalk. Cars are double- and triple-parked out front all up and down this section of the parkway that runs through the center of the city of Mattapan.

Mattapan Square is a mixed bag. Flourishing establishments like Brother's Deli and Restaurant, Zodiac Domino Sports Club, and Lavinia's clothing store press up against hollow-eyed shells like TC's Variety, barely held together by graffitied, plywood planks. Other businesses are closed for the day; corrugated gray metal sheets or black grates are pulled over windows and down tight to the sidewalk, like a slap in the face. I rubberneck as I drive through, worried that I'll miss my turn. The city bustles, even on Sunday morning. Groups of boys stand outside places like Store 24, and men and women stroll with baby carriages or wait in clumps for busses.

I pass several churches—St. Angela's, Lilly of the Valley Baptist, and another Christian denomination I can't quite catch as I go by, housed in a low-slung brick building that looks as if it may have been a garage in a former life. They each seem to be full and busy.

It's too early to be spring, but the unfiltered sunlight, squinty bright, forgets it's only February and builds up strength as the morning moves along. After pushing open the heavy oak doors at Morning Star, it takes a few minutes for my eyes to adjust from the raw daylight to the dimmed, recessed lighting inside. I find myself at the back of a crowd of people yet to be seated. Ushers are helping families to the pews. There are lots of ushers; the men wear neat black suits and white gloves, the women wear white dresses that look like uniforms, white shoes, and white gloves. Some have three-cornered paper caps on, just like nurses. Behind me the big doors open with a whoosh of cold air mingled with the scent of perfume as a trio of stylishly dressed women enter, all heels, hats and color.

I can't find Rev. Yarde, and as more and more people brush past me on their way to their seats, I feel more and more uncomfortable. I tap a nearby usher on the arm to ask if he can direct me to him. The usher, a wiry, smallish man in his fifties with graying hair, turns quickly and when he sees me, recoils a bit—it's an almost imperceptible hop backwards. It shakes me and I suddenly feel like a terrible intruder here. He doesn't know Rev. Yarde, he tells me, and slides off. But other ushers come by and offer me a seat, and help, and I relax and begin to enjoy the service while I wait.

The place is packed. I find out that there is a Jewish group from the Anti-Defamation League here on sort of a cultural exchange. They come for a service one Sunday and in turn members of the black Baptist congregation visit them for Seder. The pastor tells his flock that they are "blessed" to have their Jewish friends here and adds in jest, "You are Baptists today!" Then he says, "Hit it!" to the organist and choir and they begin a joyful, belting hymn to the clapping and laughter of everyone seated under the soft glow of the curved, white ceiling. Fans hanging above rotate in time to the music and there is a warm feeling of fellowship moving in the air.

One of the ushers motions me to follow him and I lope along behind, disappointed, like a child taken from a grown-ups party and led to bed. Music and amens fade as we walk down the side corridor to the back where the offices are.

Rev. Yarde is a big man, bulky in Harris tweed, with a calm, open face. He is young for a pastor, I think, somewhere in his thirties. He is soft-spoken and smiles broadly and often as he talks.

"Growing up I had a very difficult childhood," he tells me. "There were people who reached out to me. And now that I am grown and look around, I realize that it made a difference. Because someone took the time out to care for me. So rather than be judgmental, I just reach out to the young people. I'll be driving by and see some of them on the street and start talking to them. And I get to know their families. Most of them are living with their grandparents. They are taking on that responsibility all by themselves, so then I offer to help in any capacity I can. I find most of the time that a word of encouragement or just being there helps."

We talk about the younger children and what he does to help them through their times of trouble.

"I thought of the mustard seed according to The Word. I thrive on the saying of Mrs. Rose Kennedy—I'll never forget that, it stays with me forever—she said that if the Lord was to take everything from her and just give her faith, that she could thrive. And then I applied that to my own life. And that little mustard seed seems so small and insignificant ... ," Rev. Yarde extends his arm and holds his thumb and forefinger together as if he held one of the tiny seeds in his thick fingers, "... but then you nurse it and it begins to grow." Each of the children is given a mustard seed pendant to wear as a symbol of hope and faith and a reminder that someone cares.

He speaks with a Panamanian accent—sort of a Panamanian/Boston drawl—and is sometimes difficult to understand. I lean my head forward and cock my ear toward him, hoping that on tape his words are more clear. But soon I become accustomed to the lilt and cadence of his speech and find it a pleasure to listen to.

"So the idea started from that and transcended to the parents and grandparents and even those who are incarcerated. We try to make a bond between them," he links his fingers together to illustrate, "and find a positive program to help because I feel the church needs to take a stand, because we have left everything up to the government to provide for us and the government is really overwhelmed. So I just go into their homes and try to see what their need may be or I see sometimes that they are so stressed out by everything that's going on. So what I do is try to get them together and sit down with them and start sharing with a word of encouragement and let them know what a wonderful job they're doing. Sometimes I might take their kids and take them to a movie or something and relieve them from that pressure a little. Other grandparents in the same situation have come together and we've formed a spiritual support group."

When he says "we" he refers to himself and a wonderful African-American woman named Vera Lenox. Vera is a social worker, now 58 years old and nearing retirement, who has been working for over 25 years with the inmates that come through the Nashua Street Jail in Boston. Several months ago Rev. Yarde, there to offer healing services, met Vera and forged a bond with her over their mutual concerns for the mothers and fathers of the inmates who were taking over the care of the children left behind.

Vera, too, has made it her personal mission. She takes the grandchildren to Sunday School, has weekly "rap sessions" with them, baby-sits, and hosts a Sunday afternoon spiritual service for grandparents in her home with Rev. Yarde presiding. She personally works with the approximately 13 families and over 20 grandchildren with whom she has connected through her work at the jail.

"We have several grandchildren that we are working with, myself and Mrs. Lenox. One grandmother has seven grandchildren. With another grandmother, one of the grandchildren began acting up in school, so we suggested to her that he needs to see his dad (who is incarcerated). Because he was very close and then that was taken away. So she started doing that.

"They depend on us for so much, so much support and uplifting because sometimes the burden gets *heavy*." He draws this last word out and bends forward as if that weight was pressing down on him. "I always try to give them a shoulder to lean on, just give me a call and I'll try to be there. And what is very important is there has to be a consistency also. You know I can't be there today and then tomorrow find excuses."

"What are the problems you hear of most often?" I ask.

"The problem begins financially. For the grandmother that has six or seven, its really hard on her. And having to deal with the grandchildren *and* with the children's parent. The problem has divided both at times. It's very difficult especially when their own child is demanding from them and they don't know where to turn to."

"Do any of them have anywhere else to turn besides the Church?" I ask.

"Many of them are not aware of places to turn to, and that's where we come in as sort of a consultant to them. We try to inquire, find out what are the places, what type of need there is. We try to make sure that it's a legitimate need. We try to find out what we can help with and we connect them with other grandmothers that are in the same situation and then they can communicate. And by listening to them and coming together and sharing, it really helps them a lot. But we find for most of the times, we are the only support they have so far. At times it's difficult, very difficult because we are not funded. Even though I am at Morning Star, most of this I do on my own.

"Most of the grandparents and parents that I work with, their children are in a drug program or incarcerated. And some of them are not ready to open up publicly. So rather than bring them into church against their will, if they don't feel comfortable coming here, I usually meet with them after service. Or we go to Mrs. Lenox's home. Or if there is a grandmother who is really going through a great deal, or they're depressed, or we haven't seen them for the past few days, we go to that particular person's home and just give them a word of encouragement. So that they know that we are still there and they're being thought of. And that alone is a lot to them. To know that someone has taken the time out to care. At times when we listen to their testimony they say, 'We didn't know someone else cared for us. We thought we were just in this ourselves.'

"And we say, 'We're here for you.' "

I find it remarkable that in the short time that he has been reaching out to grandparents he has been able to put his finger on exactly what their most pressing issues are: finances, support, isolation, and respite. I tell him about a grandmother in a neighboring city who, in her seventies, is caring for five grandchildren from seven months to eight years old, two of which are HIV positive. She has only her church for support, and although she gains comfort from talking with her pastor, the only other thing they seem to able do for her is to bring over food baskets now and then.

"It's so easy to give someone a basket of food and say, 'Well, here,' you know. This is why I try to make a difference. There is more. Because food you can get anywhere, but the thing is that they need someone there for them.

"Sometimes I have people give me tickets to different events. Vera will baby-sit with their grandkids so their grandparents can get a chance to go out. This past summer I took 33 kids to Water Country. Well, at the time I was single," he explains with a smile.

"I feel that the Lord has blessed me. So much goes back to my childhood. Because I almost became a dropout from school. But someone took the time to care. A complete stranger, I didn't know her, she was a pastor of the church here. Many times when I thought of walking away from the church, I always thought of her kindness and that's what kept me there. So I try to apply that.

"It's difficult to complete all the things that I would like to in outreach. A lot of people cannot see your dream, unless they live it themselves. Other people really cannot fulfill your dreams. So I try to do things on my own. And then I found Vera and now we work together as a team."

We talk about how difficult it is sometimes to get the right kinds of help to the grandmothers. "That's where the pastor or minister needs to discern when to seek professional help. Sometimes I see where it's no longer a spiritual need, but a professional is needed, so I refer them. I will follow up and speak to a doctor and give him some feedback."

There have been times that a school official has tried to talk a grandparent into obtaining counseling for her grandchild, but she seeks out Reverend Yarde instead. "Sometimes its a matter of convincing them to finding a new avenue and to feel comfortable with the idea. I tell them, 'Just try.'

"I'm a servant. I can do nothing else but serve," he says with a wide smile, spreading his arms outward and upward theatrically. "To whom much is given, much is required. And so much has been given to me and I try to return some of that."

We talk about how important the role of the clergy is and lament the fact that there is nothing in place for grandparents at the moment.

"We started a spiritual group on our own and we get no kind of financial support so what we decided to do is plan a musical at the Strand Theater (to raise funds). With the welfare reform, this is where the churches are going to play a crucial part. That's one sector that's been neglected. My philosophy is that these grandparents have already raised their kids, they are under no obligation to raise more kids. And to me they are doing us, society, a favor. They are doing the State a favor. They should be rewarded for that. If we can't see that, we surely have lost sight of everything. The State really looks the other way, 'Oh, that's grandparents.' " He gestures a dismissive wave with both hands. "They don't even consider giving them some sort of support, nothing. And it's *hard*.

"These kids are the leaders of tomorrow and if we don't help them now. ... I don't think building more prisons is the solution. There is a most serious problem and it's happening right in the home. No one will deal with it. This is why I am committed to this."

Vera Lenox and Reverend Yarde share a dream. To create a day-care center for intergenerational families where grandparents and birth parents alike could come together for the children. They would offer parenting classes and support groups where family members could re-bond. Rev. Yarde says he and Vera need help from other people, "who share the same concerns. The more help I have, the more people I can reach."

Elisabeth Parks, Rev. Yarde, and Vera Lenox all lean heavily on their strong faith, but wisely, they each reach out in other directions as well. However, while Rev. Yarde's story is uplifting, the Parks' story is discomfiting. While Rev. Yarde ministers to those in the midst of furious turmoil, he has the luxury of stepping back, of floating above it like a guardian angel. The Parks live it. A look into their story is a ride through a storm—jarring, unsettling, disconcerting.

Concluding this chapter is part two of the Parks' family trilogy. In it, Elisabeth's strong determination to both rescue her grandchildren and help them to heal, is highlighted. She not only saves the children from their abusers but also from the destructive infection of bitterness and hatred.

Elisabeth is driven, at times obsessive. She is not a saint, nor is Ben a sinner; they are flesh and blood people with failings and excesses, trying to cope with a waking nightmare. Elisabeth uses any and every method possible, from spiritual tapes to karate lessons for the children, to try to keep their lives, so ridden with torment, safe and sane. But her outrage informs everything she does, often giving it a breathless, ragged edge; we can only look on and flinch, at times, in response.

She enrolls in rape crisis courses, visits shelters for battered women, utilizes "Tough Love" tenets and advocates for her daughter at every opportunity. Elisabeth's foremost achievement is working toward forgiveness. She first finds it in her heart and then works to nurture it in her grandchildren. It is her greatest gift to them.

Forgiving liberates the spirit and is the key to healing. Yet it is the thing that many grandparents find most difficult to do. Some seem to savor their anger, jealously guarding their resentment for the offending birth parents with a self-righteous piety. They hang on to it for dear life, as if letting go would stop their momentum, their will to go on. The rancor that drags at them becomes a barrier to finding peace for themselves and their grandchildren. Bitterness is a heavy burden to haul; it requires energy better spent elsewhere. Letting go of anger, learning to forgive, working at forgiving, replaces that dead weight with a lightened heart and enables us more easily to move forward.

In the midst of the tooth and nail battles, the emotions rubbed raw, the fiery will to protect, Elisabeth provides her grandchildren with islands of calm, places of peace and healing. Elisabeth is in this chapter not because she is a fighter, but because in the heat of battle she kneels down to kiss away a hurt, stoops to patch a broken heart.

While she is fortunate to have strong allies in her friend Mary Ann, as well as those in her religious community, the "system" fails her at every turn. In many ways she is on her own.

There were 2.9 million cases of child abuse reported in 1992.[1] Abuse of grandchildren is one of the most frequent precursors to a grandparent's move to gain custody and is the reason the Parks' story is particularly important. Unfortunately, their struggle within the court system is all too common.

In 1990, I participated in the Massachusetts League of Women Voters' study on child abuse. Local Leagues in each city and town came to consensus over the issues involved. Here I will share an excerpt of my written presentation given at our League meeting at that time, which was based on the research done by me and other local participants in the study as well as the information supplied by the League of Women Voters at the State level.

"The League questionnaire went out to hundreds of professionals at DSS, the police, schools, hospitals, DAs, and judges. Each group had many recommendations and their concerns reflected an overall consensus on the issues that need to be addressed—education, funding, prevention, changes in attitude and judicial reform.

"Severe abuse cases funnel, ultimately, through the court system and it is the way the judiciary deals with those involved that has the greatest impact on victim's lives. Of all the groups questioned, the judges were, by far, the poorest respondents. 'Some judges declined to participate, stating that they were too busy ... or that they did not possess the factual information requested.'[2] Of the few judges who did participate, opinions were widely divided on virtually every issue.

"Some judges in the League sample still believe that children's credibility is questionable, that women are either shielding husbands or bringing vindictive, trumped up charges against innocent men, and that the current system is 'adequate.' "

I ended my presentation with a quote by Justice Francis T. Murphy. In a speech at a Fordham Law School conference on child abuse, he said, "Children have neither power nor property. Voices other than their own must speak for them. If those voices are silent, then children who have been abused may lean their heads against windowpanes and taste the bitter emptiness of violated childhoods.

"Badger every legislator from every county in this state, let no editor or reporter sleep, until the remedy you want is granted. For you are the only voices of the violated child. If you do not speak, there is silence."

Elisabeth Parks was not silent. And while she secured her grandchildren's freedom by relentlessly speaking out, regrettably, she also paid a mighty price for it. Rev. Yarde provided the calm in this chapter, and now we will enter the storm. Through it all, there is much to be learned about healing from Elisabeth Parks, much we can take into our own hearts and, in turn, share with others in need.

Part 2 of the Parks Family Trilogy
Elisabeth

Just beyond the living room windows, boats scud across the blue diamond water, their colors reflected on the uneven surface like iridescent scales on a snake. The view is broken only by Ben walking back and forth as he keeps busy outside. Elisabeth continues telling their story without him.

"DSS was involved and they were going very gingerly. No matter what happened on weekends, they would come out and say, 'Well, you know, there are two families involved here and we want to help them. We help fix families.'

"They don't help protect children, they 'fix families.' They don't fix families that can't stop themselves and are out of control. There's no *way* that they can," Elisabeth says this angrily, straining forward, pushing her hands against the table.

"By 1987, the therapists were beginning to believe the children. There was too much there to deny anymore. There were more 51As being filed. Christine went into a play therapy group in the fall and they did a segment on their bodies. It was an eight-week segment, and by the end of the eight weeks, many of the children that had been sexually abused were able to say it or draw it.

"Christine, for the first time, told that her father had touched her—her *father*! They told me what she had said ... but they didn't believe her."

"They didn't?" I am puzzled, shocked.

"No. They said that they thought she said that because the other children did. Now remember, I did not know the secretary that was in that office was a friend of the Connors. One of the therapists there later confessed that she had been influenced by this woman. They were still coming from that 'crazy grandmother' place.

"In December of '86, this counseling agency had decided that I was an unfit person. Based on the—I call him 'patsy psychologist' for Mr. Connor that was at this office. Based on the therapists all saying that I was coming there very upset all the time. And that they felt I was emotionally upsetting the children, putting ideas in their heads.

"My lawyer at this point was believing them, the court was beginning to believe them. And they (the counselors) were saying they wanted to take the children away from me and put them in a foster home. And they had decided they were going to do that, and they had the right to. I almost went nuts! And I would have lost those children at that point if it wasn't for Mary Ann Alden.

"She said, 'Like hell!' She told me to call my family counselor and have my lawyer tell the therapists at Northrop that she (the family counselor) had to be in on any meeting where they would be deciding the fate of these children. She advised me to call my lawyer and see what my rights were regarding that meeting. I thought that if they had that meeting, the children would be gone. Gone for Christmas! Mary Ann could not believe it. She was going crazy too.

"By this point, my Community of God's Light was very much invested in these children," Elisabeth tells me, and then asks if we could take a break.

We sip sweetened, milky tea as Elisabeth begins to talk, hesitantly, about a religious community she is very involved with. She makes an off-hand, guarded remark and gives me a sidelong glance to gauge my reaction. I ask her a few gentle questions, fairly sure of where she's heading. "Is this a Catholic group?" I ask.

"Oh no, we never ask what religion anyone might be—we don't care," she answers.

"Is this group all women?" I ask.

"Not necessarily," she answers lightly, as she spins around the kitchen, rummaging in drawers for spoons and bowls, preparing a snack for us.

"Let me put it this way, is the backbone of this group women?" I ask pointedly, holding her gaze.

She laughs, almost girlishly. She checks my tape recorder to make sure it's off, then laughs again in embarrassment. "Yes," she says and we share a smile of unspoken acknowledgment.

I can see how important this is to her. Through all the private things she has shared with me, she has never been concerned about recording it on tape. Until now. I am curious about why she is so secretive about it. I think it's because it's not mainstream. It's slightly fringe and she fears being tainted as strange after her past experiences. I am intrigued by this group—this "women's group"—and I press her for more information.

Although she says it is not a Catholic group, there is a priest that guides their Sunday morning service. He "allows" the women to read the liturgy. And therein lies the rub—or one of them; this is not done. They have been investigated by the powers that be within the church hierarchy. This is one of the things that drives her secrecy.

But as she talks on, I realize that this "community" is much more than Catholic women wanting to read the liturgy at Sunday Mass. This grassroots group is made up of thinking, spiritual women coming together to share their deep sense of spirituality, and empowering each other. Women unbound by the fetters of formal church doctrine, they test their wings. Here is another support group, but with a deeply spiritual base.

She tells me they have learned the Universal Dances of Peace, and I instantly think of the Salem "witches"—and persecution.

I have been reading a book by Alice Walker, *In Search of our Mother's Gardens*. Walker uses a phrase in her book that comes back to me as I listen to Elisabeth talk about her group: "Womanish ... i.e., like a woman. Usually referring to outrageous, courageous or *willful* behavior. Wanting to know more and in greater depth than is considered 'good' for one."

That must feel like a threat to many people. Perhaps it is why Elisabeth is hesitant, secretive. But I feel this is too important, this version of a support group. I encourage her to talk freely, and on tape, about it. So she does, and from now on, mentions the group frequently. However, I realize that whenever she has spoken of her friend Mary Ann Alden, there is a wider community of support that connects Elisabeth to Mary Ann—and beyond.

"By this point, my Community of God's Light was very much invested in these children," Elisabeth says laughing lightly, as if released, and speaking directly into the tape recorder for effect. When she is serious, her mouth is small, her lips thin and pale. But when she smiles, she smiles big. Her eyes twinkle with Irish mischief, and she laughs merrily, girlishly. Her face softens and colors.

"These, like I said, were professional people, many of them. Intelligent people. And it was a real eye-opener for all of these professionals to where the 'system' was and what was happening in the 'system.' They were all upset too."

Elisabeth speaks again of the meeting that was held to determine her suitability as a caretaker for the grandchildren. "I asked a pediatrician I was working for if he would please be able to be a participant in this meeting. I told him that I would insist upon it, so that we would have representation in there as well as they did. And that came as a surprise to them (the therapists at Northrop). I don't think they ever had anybody strong enough that would come with all the 'guns' to a meeting like that.

"At that meeting, representing me was a letter that Mary Ann wrote about who we were as people, and all the things I was doing and learning to become the best possible parent. Between that and the pediatrician, they decided they wouldn't take the children from me.

"A Guardian Ad Litem was assigned. I hardly ever saw her. We were granted temporary custody from the courts."

The Parks were granted temporary custody because they were the only ones doing the child care. They were taking the children to their doctors and the therapists. Thomas Connor was doing nothing. Thomas also refused to sign the papers relinquishing custody. He was "thumbing his nose at the court," as Elisabeth put it. So the court took matters in its own hands and signed over custody to the Parks. However, Mr. Connor was granted weekend visitation.

Elisabeth rambles on a bit, telling a story about the children's pediatrician who was so helpful at that meeting.

"Several weeks before that I was so angry at him because no one was really helping. I was real angry, and I had said to him, 'Why do you take an oath to help children, all of you? What is it? Are you afraid to lose a day's pay to go to court? Why is it that everybody walks around this thing and doesn't do anything concrete that will stand up in court to help these children?' I was furious! This was after I had heard that they were just going around saying they 'weren't sure' what was really going on with the children. That's all they were doing, these pediatricians.

"So I spieled off! And that really knocked this doctor into reality. I told him that the saying that 'all children had the right to liberty and the pursuit of happiness' was a bunch of bunk. And when all you doctors say you take an oath to help children, it's a crock!" She leans forward, her knuckles white where she is holding her spoon, and she is wild-eyed with fury. I am reminded that they thought she was a "crazy lady." How else could anyone behave but "crazy" in this situation? This frantic fury, this trembling, eye-popping rage—isn't *that* normal here?

"I was just so full of anger at that point. And Mary Ann would feel the same way—and these other strong women. Because I was meeting with them and my church, and because of their love for me and my children, some of those women started having memory returns."

"We started what we called a 'parachute group.' It was a group to talk about the book *What Color is Your Parachute?* It was a book that taught you how to look at your life experiences, how to write resumes, and how to change the direction in your life and all that. It was a course at some of the colleges at the time. It gave us an excuse to get together and we loved it. Saturday mornings early we would get together for coffee and we started out discussing the book, but the topic always got around to Christine and Craig. It was almost impossible *not* to talk about it. And the women were so supportive.

"So a lot of these women will be my friends until I die because of the connection. Way back it was a spiritual connection and a church connection, and then it became a connection with people who had 'adult child' things that they were talking about ... so that each level that we went into seemed to become a deeper and more trusting level and circle of friends."

Beyond the living room, framed by windows off to the side, is a square flower garden surrounded by knee-high, white pickets. Friends from her "community" came one day with shovels, flats, and fertilizer and planted it as a birthday surprise for Elisabeth. In the center of the garden, surrounded by tall pink and white phlox, blue delphinium, and sturdy, magenta dahlias, rests a small stone cherub; sweet alyssum tickles at her toes. She is bent forward with her elbows on her knees, her chin resting on her hands. She looks lost in thought and her wings are pointing to the sky.

"So all during this, when my days were very dark, I would get help from them. I always have been a woman of strong faith. Even when my bottom fell out sometimes. There were times I thought that's all I had.

"When my daughter was starting to drink, and I didn't know what was wrong, I remember falling on my knees one day and asking Our Lady, the Mother of God, who saw her Son hang on the cross, and saw her Child suffer, would she please help me, I couldn't take anymore. That was the Sunday before my daughter came to me. When I was feeling like a total failure as a mother, I laid it in another mother's hands.

"She has enriched me so much, because of that power. And I do believe every time I thought the worst was coming ... and it did, it did," Elisabeth laughs ruefully. "There was always a window that opened when a door shut. And these women would say to me 'Hang in there. It will change, and we're going to see that it does!'

"Mary Ann was wonderful in helping me to get the children relaxed, to get their minds off what was going on at the time. If they were going in for questioning with a detective or DSS or whatever, she would always be there, first of all, and she would always remind me to bring things for the kids. She would say, 'Come and sit with me and play dot-to-dot' to get their attention so they wouldn't be like this," Elisabeth bunches her shoulders up and stiffens her arms by her sides, "waiting to go in to be asked and having to talk about the most horrendous things that they said they couldn't do; because of what she would do to help me get them there, they did."

Elisabeth used to call ahead and say, "If you make these children wait an hour for that meeting, you won't get a damn thing out of them!" Or, " If you say you're going to question them at four o'clock, question them at four o'clock, we'll be there at five of. If those children have to sit there, they fall apart."

Elisabeth is getting a little ahead of herself I realize, and I push her back chronologically.

"We got the Special Ed things going at school that year, they got into therapy that year, they decided they wouldn't take the children from me—that was December of '86.

"At that time, he was still getting the children every weekend. It was just before Marion went into the hospital for the third time. She was living here and she had started drinking again. As she started getting worse, I told her I couldn't put up with that. She either had to get help or leave. So she left my house for a while, and her brother Mitchell took her in, thank God. She was not in good shape at all, but I couldn't handle her coming in all hours of the night and upsetting the children."

> It is important for parents not to buy into their children's addiction or addictive behaviors. Elisabeth was right to draw the line and tell her daughter to get help or leave. This is not easy, but by giving such an ultimatum, parents demonstrate that they are not buying into the alcoholic's need to be taken care of. It is easy to get sucked into a child's "neediness." However, the best thing you can do for an alcoholic is to turn your back, not on them, but on their addiction.
>
> It is common for parents to try to rescue their alcoholic child, but they need to be reminded that only the alcoholic can save himself or herself. Very often these rescue attempts keep the addict from hitting bottom. The substance abuser needs to hit bottom before he or she can begin the climb to healing.

"Then she went into the hospital for the third time. Saint Joseph's didn't want to take her and I called them up and begged them. I explained to them what was going on with the children, what we were finding out, and that she needed help and she wasn't coming out with it and I couldn't help her. They took her in because I knew one of the nurses there, thank God.

"I had gone up and had a meeting with a counselor up there and told her I had read this article in *Time* magazine about goals and schooling and how many people made it and how many didn't make it. And there was huge numbers of people that didn't make it but the ones that did had schooling." Marion had not completed her junior year in high school.

Elisabeth also talked with them about putting her in a halfway house "completely away from these people that she was around that were getting to her ... to get her completely away from here."

The disease of alcoholism is a powerful, tragic, gripping illness that afflicts over ten million adults in this country. Millions more are being raised by alcoholics with disastrous, lifelong effects.

Most children feel, at some level, responsible for their parents and their substance abuse. Grandparents need to be aware of this fact and give reassurance to their grandchildren that they are not the cause or in any way responsible for their parents' addictions. Grandparents also need to recognize that many children will not openly admit they feel responsible, frequently, because of guilt or shame. However, grandparents will want to approach their grandchildren with the option to discuss their feelings regularly, even if their grandchild gives the impression that all is well. Research proves that for all children with actively abusing parents, all is not well, but with guidance, a sympathetic ear, and a supportive shoulder, things can get better.

"We had a little session, Marion and I. She told me to stay out of her business, etcetera, but then admitted to me that she did want to come back to Harding so she could go right back to what she was doing. She thanked me afterwards for fighting in her behalf. She said, 'Ma, you know me. I was giving you a crock!' I said, 'I know you were, that's why I was up there doing that.'

"She went up to the Fairfield area to a halfway house. There is a Franklin Hospital up there that has marvelous programs for women. She went back to school. In the halfway house she got her GED. She went to Fairfield Community College that has programs for women. She is a wonderful artist, she draws beautiful pictures, as my grandson does.

"Mary Ann used to say to me that, 'This little girl was a victim of this perpetrator as well as the children. He picked on a weak, naive girl that he could use.'"

> Critical for all involved with the alcoholic is the understanding that alcoholism is very much a family disease. No immediate family member is immune to the devastation that alcoholism delivers to not only the alcoholic, but to, anyone who loves him or her.
>
> It is common for parents who have watched their child drown in the disease of addiction to question what role they had in their adult child's "need" to drink and to feel, in some part, responsible. Of course, no one causes someone to drink or abuse drugs. Grandparents may need help processing their feelings about their child's addiction and help in understanding the anger and ambivalence toward their child.

In 1987, the children were beginning to recant in therapy because their father was sitting in on the sessions with them.

"When the children had to go with him to therapy, they would get headaches, sick. ... I was trying to tell them that *they* were invading the children's privacy and safety factors by expecting those children to say anything if, in fact, this perpetration was true. Would I be able to tell anybody anything if my perpetrator was sitting beside me? Where were these therapists coming from? They hurt the children so much during that period of time. They would send him deliberately home with them alone. They wouldn't believe Chrissie when she said it was her father that was hurting them.

"After Marion went to Fairfield, I then became the person to try and reestablish a relationship between her and her son, who was almost completely destroyed by his father telling him that his mother was no good, didn't love him, didn't care about him ... all those other pieces.

"And every night we would be saying our prayers going to bed, that God would help all of us. And as I started explaining to the children that their mother was a victim like them, they completely lost all their anger for her. The therapists were saying that she neglected them, and she did this, and she did that, and she was this terrible mother." Elisabeth's voice softens, and catches. "She never hurt them. She never hit them. She wasn't there for them because she wasn't there for herself." Her voice breaks as she struggles to continue. "And as they started understanding this, at least it was a piece of healing and repair. No matter what a mother does to a child ... they need to know, if nothing else—even though she can't be there for them—they need to know she loves them ... to survive," she finishes softly. "And that's the piece I wanted to keep going."

> Grandparents should be aware that their grandchildren's sense of self is shaped and developed by their birth parents. By modeling forgiveness, Elisabeth demonstrates to her grandchildren that they can forgive their mother too. For their own emotional well-being and psychological health, at some point children need to forgive their neglectful parents, not only for what they did, but for what they didn't do or were incapable of doing.

"I would be so tired and so angry at her sometimes, I wanted to just kill her. But as I became more and more aware that she was a victim, it was okay. I just wanted her to get well. So we would pray every night for what we could be thankful for.

" 'What do you mean there is a God! How can there be a God?' my grandson would say, even though he wasn't telling me then (about the abuse). That's how he was trying to tell me what was going on ... how bad it was ... and there was no way there was a God that would allow what was happening to him and his sister."

Elisabeth glances down at her folder of notes, the typed chronology, and reads, " 'Why are you so strong, Nana?' she (Christine) says at breakfast one day. On the fifteenth of February, 1987, they returned after a two day visit (with their father), whining, crying at the drop of a hat. Not hungry for supper, didn't eat all day, takes a few hours to calm down. Christine wants a baby bottle and to be held close, sits in my lap for TV, circles under her eyes, takes some time to fall asleep.'

"They were going to karate then. I was trying to get them to feel stronger, that they would learn some power and have something that they could feel that they could hold on to, or learn something that would help them when they didn't feel safe." Elisabeth's voice is dragging heavily over her words as if the weight of them is too great to bear. "Because I was doing everything in my power to try and free them and it wasn't happening."

Christine flies in from outdoors. Her cheeks are flushed from bike riding, full tilt, with her friends, her sandy hair flying back from her face. "Where's the obstacle course?" she demands to know. "Grandpa couldn't put it together," Elisabeth explains apologetically. Christine is huffing and puffing with all the melodrama a 12-year-old can muster. She swings her arms around her as she marches out haughtily. When she finally leaves, we have to laugh at this mini drama. However, Elisabeth feels a need to explain to me why this obstacle course wasn't erected. "I am caring for aging parents too. And we had a birthday party last night. Sometimes you just can't get it all done!"

The "sandwich generation" is a term that describes people who are coping both with their own children and aging parents. Much has been written about that trend. But a new term is needed for grandparents such as Elisabeth wrestling with the added layer of grandchildren on their plate— perhaps the "club sandwich generation," or the "submarine sandwich generation"—large, with everything on it, including hots.

Elisabeth takes a deep breath and continues on. "Valentines Day that year was a horrendous, horrible weekend. Christine's birthday was a pure hell. Nothing but abuse went on in that apartment (where her father lived) by other members of the family. They were then putting the heat on the kids so bad because we were immersed in the system by then between DSS and the counseling, and people were beginning to suspect and put pressure on Mr. Connor. Counselors were beginning to believe Christine a little bit.

They couldn't deny what they were seeing in terms of the physical and emotional (symptoms) in the children even though they still couldn't even talk ... they were so afraid by then of talking. Christine was being brutally hurt.

"What happened is that around this time that things were accelerating, there was more abuse. They were coming home in terrible shape. I was taking them to the doctor almost every week after the weekends.

"Christine was taken up to the sister's house and abused by four members of the family taking turns on her because she was the one that was talking!" Elisabeth is tensing up again, her whole body stiffening, straining forward as she talks, eyes enormous. " 'This is what we do to little people with big mouths,'" she quotes.

She slumps back in her chair, her shoulders rounded, and continues in a monotone staring into her lap. "So during the period of '87 ... her birthday was hell ... Valentine's Day was hell ... Easter was the last weekend that he raped her.

"At Easter!" she exclaims jerking upward, her voice cracking. "Good Friday! Two weeks before Easter she couldn't *sit* for two weeks!" Elisabeth is crying now. "He was a basket case ... little Craig ... he was humming. ... " She rocks back and forth in her chair to show me, pulling on her ear and saying, 'Hmmm ... hmmm ... hmmm ... hmmm ... ,' pulling his ears so bad, he wanted to rip them off his head! He was twitching like he had Tourette's syndrome ... migraine headaches every other day ... stomachaches." Elisabeth is out of breath from the effort of speaking these things.

Elisabeth goes quiet for awhile and then diverges again. I believe she needs this breathing room. She talks about her daughter's boyfriend. She attributes much of Marion's continued recovery to him. They met in rehab in Fairfield and have been together ever since in support and friendship. "They do wonderful things together, all healthy things. He loves to fish, he hunts. I believe the reason my daughter is alive today is James. He was doing what we couldn't do while we were trying to hold these kids together, dealing with two states. After the year in Fairfield, they both moved to Maine, and I'm so grateful. He's big, he's strong, he is a very gentle guy. I believe she would have been hurt (if it weren't for James). He (Thomas) stalked her, he stalked us while we were up there, he stalked the children."

A few moments go by again before Elisabeth is able to get back on track. "Everything came to a head in April of '87 when they were finally stopped."

"The SAIN team is a team of all the agencies in Massachusetts that are connected with an abuse case. (The SAIN team is made up of a police officer, a therapist, a DSS social worker and supervisor, District Attorney's office representative, a victim witness advocate, a medical consultant, and a Team coordinator.) They come together in a room with a glass in it. They bring the child in the other room—this is supposed to make it easier for the child as far as questioning goes. The children have to know the other people are in there, unfortunately, which makes it doubly hard on the children. They actually show the children all those people sitting in the other room behind the glass. There are so many pressures on those kids it was awful! But the reality is that all those agencies get it at one time, the child goes through it once supposedly. But that was the time that they were able to stop the weekend visits. Thank God for that team—the SAIN team."

In May of that year Christine had to be examined by a physician for the upcoming court trial. "It was going to be a very hard examination for Christine. We did not know if Christine would be able to endure it. She was totally traumatized by that time. I had brought her to the pediatrician. The pediatrician even called in the gynecologist. She (the pediatrician) saw that she had really been hurt bad. She had bruises on her legs, her vagina had been stretched unbelievably.

"The gynecologist couldn't even get near her. Of course, he was a male. But they all attested to her traumatized state. Christine was so traumatized, he was hoping he could hypnotize her to examine her to see if there was any gynecology damage. He even invited us to his home with his children hoping that he could maybe hypnotize her so that he could take some pictures of her. But that didn't work out.

"So then I called the Abuse Hotline to ask who in God's name, what doctors were experienced in abuse that could help children in this area, and they told me Doctor Susan White. Susan had worked with many abused children. She started the Rape Crisis Center in Harding in the seventies when no woman was even looked at with any credibility in the hospital system. She has worked with abused children, she goes to court with them, she fights for them. She was known as a ... *my hero*, that's what she's known as!" Elisabeth laughs.

"We showed Chrissie a picture of Susan in a working situation. Mary Ann had a tape of her giving a talk about Alzheimer's. And we said, 'This is the wonderful doctor that works with children that you're going to go see. Chrissie, she wants to help you if you let her. Maybe she can help you. Maybe she can help free you. We don't know. And we don't want you to say anything that's not true. We only want you to tell the truth.

"Mary Ann would always tell me, 'Don't put any words in her mouth.

Be careful what you say.' And we were very careful. All I would ever tell both children is, 'All we want you to do is tell the truth. I don't know what you're going to tell them. I can't tell them anything; I don't know, I wasn't there.' So that was wonderful because those pieces helped at the trial.

"By repeating them over and over again, I was able to spit that out too when the lawyer was giving me a bad time about being this grandmother who wanted to take the children." Her voice gets loud and shrill. "I said, 'Ha! At 58? My retirement? This is what I *want*? Two disturbed children? Like Hell!" Her voice levels off. "But keep them safe? Yes! I *do* want them for that reason.

"Susan was wonderful with her. She used the teddy bears and was able to examine Chrissie. She explained how she helps people that have been hurt to get in a safe place, but she has to look and be sure. She said ... " Elisabeth's voice slows and softens as if she's talking to a child, " '... But Christine I hate to tell you this, but it's only a picture of your bottom that will make a judge even look. We have to shock the judge in order to get any attention. I've been working at this a long time and my heart's been totally broken at the children that are turned back. So I've learned that that's how much evidence you need.'

"The State of New Hampshire said they wished they had a Dr. White up there when they had this case. They would have given their eye teeth for a Dr. White.

"Dr. White took pictures of her bottom, her bruises and her vagina that was so stretched and hurt! Then left us to call the District Attorney screaming and hollering—I heard her from down the hall! 'What the hell is going on here! How long is this going to go on! Do you realize how long these children have been raped?' She raised total Holy Cain with the district attorney's office and so they said okay they would set up the SAIN thing right away.

"And still ... still Craig wouldn't talk. Christine did. Christine told Dr. White what happened ... that her father hurt her. It was the first time it was really totally documented. She was in a place where a female Doctor was saying, 'I can help you. We've got to go to court and stop this. We can maybe stop this if you will allow me to help you.' And that's how we got supervised visits.

"They still had to *go* ... and they would get sick every time we had to go there they would start saying, 'We can't go! I've got a stomachache! I don't want to go to the visit!' But it was a formality. The court still makes you go. My grandson still wasn't talking, so they still didn't have enough."

"Have enough for what?" I ask, confused.

"Enough to hold up in court for a court case of abuse. Because Craig denied, in front of that SAIN team, that his father hurt them. He said that she (Christine) was lying. So it was just this little girl's word against the father's, and they said it would never hold up. And it was too horrendous a case to risk losing. They felt he would kill them—kill them—if he had them much longer. And if they failed, and he got visitation ... Christine, they said, was very close to being murdered, she had been hurt so badly. And Craig was beginning to be raped as a punishment because he couldn't get his mother to go back, he couldn't get people off his (Thomas Connor's) back. So he was beginning to do a wicked number on Craig. He had always hurt him, 'pulled on his "pee-pee," ' he said, but now ... He was on the verge on insanity, my grandson.

"I think Hitler was a nice guy in comparison, after some of the things they told me. I couldn't even bear ... I cried myself to sleep ... when they started talking ... sometimes. But, I couldn't cry in front of them because ... The first time they told me ... something so horrendous ... the tears started coming to my eyes and coming down my cheeks and my granddaughter said, 'Oh Nana! It's okay.' And, she comforted me!" Elisabeth's eyes spill over. " 'It's okay, Nana we're going to be okay Nana.' She literally comforted *me,* and Craig clammed right up so after that, I learned that I couldn't show my emotions. When they told me something, I had to try to pretend that this was something I heard all the time." She laughs a little through her tears at the absurdity of it.

"Then my grandson started a little bit. I said to him, 'Craig, I know it's *there.* And I can't push you to talk.' He would start getting hysterical like my daughter would. So I would say to him ... " Elisabeth drops her voice down, slow and soothing, "'When you can, you will. When you want to be safe, you will. We know that it's true even though you say that it's not. This is not unusual for a child that's been threatened.' So, I would spoon feed him that, and then I'd lay off. I'd just say, 'It's okay, Craig. I'm not going to put pressure on you.'

"What I would do is play these spiritual tapes for him at night. 'When I was lost and all alone, you were there to put your arms around me.' And what they began to see was that maybe there was a God now.

"I had put up a poster in their room of a butterfly, and it said, 'Setting You Free.' I truly regret that they did not give my grandson medication to keep him calm during that time. But what I did have was my spiritual tapes, tapes that my friends would send me saying, 'Listen to this, listen to the words on this tape,' words like, 'When it was black and dark, I cried with you. I was there in the darkness with you, but I am going to send the light,' songs with words that they clung to. At first they would be angry. 'I don't want to listen to that! Where is He? He's not here!'

"I would say that I understood that, and it's okay to be angry. That He got angry. He threw things in the temple when they were horrible to Him. But He says in the Bible, 'If you hurt a hair on a child's head, I will be stinking mad! I'll take care of those kinds of parents!' And, they listened.

"These tapes are what I think kept the children going. And got me through it. That's how we got to sleep at night. They couldn't close their eyes. They'd scream in the dark. I had to sleep in the room with them until they got to sleep and their bedroom had to be next to mine, there had to be a light on. They would wake up with nightmares. It was awful! At that point there was no social life whatsoever. And the interesting piece was, I didn't even care!

"It was homework or I would lay in bed reading them stories. Anything to get their minds on something that a child's mind *should* be on. I worked overtime at that. I always had a friend in for Christine and a friend in for Craig. They were so fragile and they were so apart at the seams. They would fight with each other, bickering. But I constantly worked at keeping them calm, keeping the house quiet, not letting them hang around with kids that were hyper. I worked *overtime* at keeping them calm during that period of time.

"My grandson was a fabulous baseball player. What he was doing was getting the rage out with the baseball. He could pitch a ball so fast when he was in Little League that every coach in town wanted him. He would say things like he could picture his father's face on the pitcher's mitt. Wham!" Elisabeth's mischievous, Irish laugh peals out. "That ball would come slamming in and he would get cheers from everybody! But, they wouldn't know. ..."

Elisabeth continues, "Craig would have headaches, he would be white as a sheet. They would be nervous wrecks even though they didn't have to go with him (their father) after, they were still showing all the signs of the stress of the situation. She saw that, the DSS worker. I kept asking when can they stop ... would they please stop doing this to them. And she literally said, 'When Craig decides to talk. I'm sorry there's nothing we can do.'

"In around November of that year, Craig started saying some things to me, but then he wouldn't repeat it. He'd say to me, 'You really know what's going on, Nana, I know you do.' Or, 'I wish I could.' But then he would back off again. If I would tell the therapists and she would ask him, he would deny.

"At the Christmas visit they were supposed to have, this man (Thomas) came laden with gifts. We happened to look out the window and saw him. The DSS worker asked Craig and Chrissie if they wanted to see him, because it was Christmas, and I guess she had a tender heart that time. And he said 'No! You mean I don't have to?' He was sick, he was white, and I think he had to throw up. 'Please, please don't make me see him!' She really felt bad. So she said, 'Okay. I think I can tell the judge that.' So she took us down the back way. Craig was ahead of me, saw his father coming in, and went screaming back up the stairs. 'Oh my God, oh my God, there he is, there he is! Don't let him see me, don't let him see me!' There was just no denying what was going on. He didn't want the gifts. He didn't want any part of the man. So we went around the other part of the building and we ran, literally, to our car to leave. And I saw her still looking out the window at their behavior, running for the car like two little animals.

"We had to go see the DSS worker in January. On the way down, Craig asked me, 'Could a judge make me go with my father if we go back to court, Nana?' I said, 'I'm afraid I don't know that. You never know. You're denying it, so his lawyer can say Nana's lying. We can only try to keep you safe the best way we know how. But judges are crazy. I can't promise that that won't happen.' I *didn't* say I'd run from the country before I'd let that happen—I'd go underground. I didn't say that because at this point it sounded to me like he was doing a lot of heavy thinking—and he was.

"We had given him enough safety time now. He had six months of being here and with only supervised visits. He wasn't being raped. He found a safe place. He saw we were fighting for him. He saw the people around me that were plugging for him—strong people, caring people. People that didn't want anything to happen to these children or children like them.

"In church on Sunday, he would hear things from these wonderful people that were surrounding us from the Community of God's Light. Saying things like is there anything they can do to help. Playing certain songs that they knew the children liked. They always really put themselves out. And these children knew it. When they were in that liturgy, they knew the liturgy was literally for them. By the things that Father would say gently, not calling attention to them, not embarrassing them, but by praying for justice or by praying for other abused children in the world, these kids got the message, strong and clear, that all those people were behind them.

"It took six months of not being with him, and that January he said to me that time in the car, 'Nana, I know you know he *did* touch me. Who do I have to tell? Do I have to tell Jane (his therapist)? Will that make me safe?'

"So then they had another SAIN meeting. After that, we got the visitation completely stopped.

"Even during this period of time, when you expected something to *happen* ... like you'd tell the district attorney's office—nothing happened. They questioned him (Craig) ... nothing happened. Nothing was every happening! When we went to court, we stopped visitation—that's all we got!"

"Did you ask for more?" I ask.

"Right. We asked for permanent custody. That was like nothing. Nothing ever went anywhere in Massachusetts. Couldn't figure it out, couldn't figure it out," she mutters.

"Now that Craig was talking, Jane (the therapist) wants to make a video of Craig and his sister and hear some of what has happened to them, which she did. What had finally empowered Craig ... He was still having a lot of trouble talking. He was getting wicked migraine headaches. He was getting really sick when she would push him to try to get him to talk. So what happened was, what finally turned the tide was a couple of things. One was the death of Mary Ann's mother. He happened to be there.

"Mary Ann's mother had been coming here all the time even though she had Alzheimer's. Mary Ann would bring her here because she needed to be helping me. Her mother was still able to walk and sit but didn't know where she was.

"Now this was a woman who would be sitting there staring ... she couldn't see me or Mary Ann ... this is Alzheimer's disease, advanced stages ... but yet, when Christine or Craig would come into the room ... Christine would bounce into the room and tell her friends, 'Oh Josephine is here. Come and meet Josephine and watch what she can do. Here Josephine, put the peg into the pegboard.' And Josephine would put the peg into the pegboard We couldn't get her to do anything! But, this was a woman that always loved children, and in the deep throes of this brain demoralizing, degenerating disease, this woman, somehow, there became some awareness that there was a child in the room. When there was a child in the room, she would turn her head and look at that child and sometimes she smiled.

"The day that she died, I couldn't get anybody to baby-sit Craig. I said to Craig, 'I have to bring you with me. It's not something to be frightened of. I'm going to bring you movies to watch upstairs and we'll be in the downstairs apartment. You do not have to be down there, but Mary Ann's mother is dying and is going to die today. I need to be with Mary Ann.' I was afraid it was going to traumatize him and I didn't want that.

"But Mary Ann's whole attitude was so incredibly intelligent and compassionate—loving, *loving*—that the whole dying process was not a frightening thing. The day that she died, he literally came downstairs *as* she was dying. Right before she died, she opened her eyes. The hospice nurse was looking into her eyes with the flashlight and saying to Mary Ann there is no recognition, she is unconscious, and she was giving a whole medical spiel, da-da, da-da, da-da. Mary Ann and I were looking at each other and I turned my head. I saw this little boy come into the room and stand at the bottom of the bed. And all of a sudden her eyes went down to the foot of the bed and stayed ... and she was looking at Craig. And Mary Ann said, 'My God! She knows Craig's here!' She was looking right at this boy."

Both our eyes have filled with tears. I place my elbows on the table and bring my fists up to my cheeks to try and control the urge to cry. Elisabeth catches her breath, weeping as she continues, "Mary Ann said, 'Craig, this very day my mother is going to bring you in her heart to heaven, and God is going to know who you are.' And then she died. And he wasn't frightened, he didn't run." She sobs once and gulps a big breath, "He *stayed* there. He just held her hand ... and we hugged each other.

"But you know, that next day he told the therapist that he was going to have help with is problems. That was one of the turning points that gave him strength to start talking.

"Out of the blue came two calls one day. It was a DSS worker. She told me who she was and said, 'I can't believe all the 51As we have up here. We are horrified!' Out of the blue, out of the blue. 'We just came across this case,' she said, 'are you still dealing with Mr. Connor?' I said, 'Oh my God, *are* we!' She said, 'Oh dear! Well, I have a detective here that wants to know if he can help you, Robert O'Hara.'

"At that time, I was taking care—again the caretaker—of my father's oldest brother who was dying of cancer. My parents went to Florida, left me with him. Besides all of this, I almost died. So I was overseeing my uncle, who was Irish, and knowing the strong faith that I had came from my father's side of the family. My uncles all did rosary beads even though they were all big tough guys, and coaches of football teams, but they said their rosary too. And they were men that respected women. And my uncle was a godsend here. He drew cartoons for those children. It became a gift to have him, believe it or not, even though I was dealing with doctors for him, dealing with agencies, home health care, trying to fix his house up. I was doing all that and I get a call from this detective and I started crying." She begins to laugh out loud, her round eyes crinkling, twinkling. "That's my Irish side. That's my Grandmother in Heaven. Hooray!" She raises her fist in salute. "I said, 'You better get down here PDQ!' " and she laughs again.

"He said, 'I want to meet you at the therapist's.' I told him where we were, so far, in Massachusetts and he couldn't believe that it had taken that long. He felt really bad and asked if he could come down and meet Craig that day. He said, 'I would really like to gather some more evidence and get this bugger if we can.' They were looking for Alan at that time; all the complaints up there were about Alan. Then he found out that the father was involved. He said, 'What?' And the more he heard the more interested he got.

"So he came down to the therapist's that day, and met Craig in the office. We were waiting to go in. And he sat there talking to Craig, and he kind of let his coat fall open—it was marvelous the way he did it—and he had a gun in his holster. He said, 'Craig, I am here to help you if you want me to. I would like to help you. I hear that you had a really hard time and so far things aren't where you'd like to see them. Would you let me help you?'

"Craig was looking at the gun like this." Elisabeth widens her eyes and raises her eyebrows and shouts, " 'Yeah! Yeah! You sure can!' " imitating Craig.

"He said, 'I've called and asked your therapist if I can go in with you today and she said okay if that's okay with you. And Craig said okay. They made a tape that day and he came out with a few more things that day. Things like Thomas Connor had come to my daughter with cocaine when she had come home from the hospital with Christine as a newborn baby, and told her, 'Sniff.' My daughter said, 'No,' and tried to push it away, but he pulled her head back and hit her until she did, then digitally raped the baby."

Elisabeth pauses again. She is looking down at the table, her mouth turned down and her shoulders sagging. She takes a moment before continuing, slowly.

"So when that wonderful detective came in, things started turning around."

"Then he asked the loaded question, 'Did the father ever touch Christine at his sister's house?' I said, 'I don't know.' " It comes out like a desperate wail.

"He said, 'When you go home, when you get a chance, ask that question. Because I don't want to bother with this Alan case. It's too terribly important to rescue them from their father. That's too big. Alan's way down on the list now.'

"He told me, too, that it's terribly important under New Hampshire law that you have dates. And Mary Ann said to me ... " Elisabeth, imitating her friend, waves her hand in the air, " 'Oh pffff. We'll get dates! For God sakes, those kids always came back on birthdays and holidays.' I'm going, 'Oh my God! How are we ever going to get a date when it was going on all the time?" Elisabeth wails again in a high pitch. "Mary Ann said, 'Don't worry about it! It will be a holiday. It will be a birthday. We're going to nail him. You watch and see. You just ask Craig if he can remember a birthday.'

She leans in toward me, bending her shoulders down low over the table, her eyes boring into mine, and says, "Alan's birthday was on March the 17th." She continues on in a whisper, hissing out the words as if they burned her lips as they left her mouth. "Christmasss ... Christmasss ... ," a long pause and she breathes out slowly, "If you can abuse a child on Christmas ... Oh ... God. ..."

"Those were the two dates that got him a guilty verdict in 1989," Elisabeth says finally, limp, drained.

"When Mary Ann and I brought the chronology up there (to New Hampshire), for some reason they still felt that they didn't have enough evidence. And I said, 'Do you know what? You guys believe us and believe the children. I didn't have that luxury and that feeling before that I have with you. I know that God's using you to get these kids free. Please, please, I beg you, go with whatever little evidence you have. My whole gut, my whole being is saying this is it!'"

"I don't understand," I say. "If they have both children telling the story and you have a chronology, what other evidence do they need? They have doctor's pictures. ... "

"No, no they don't. That was Massachusetts. The medical records up in New Hampshire were weak in comparison to Susan White's."

"And they couldn't use any information garnered in Massachusetts?" I ask.

"Nothing from Massachusetts," she answers.

"How strange," I murmur to myself.

"They decided to go with what they had, which was Craig's say-so of what happened at that house. Four family members ... not only the father, but the father set up the others too. They would rape them as a punishment up at his sister's house in New Hampshire."

"His brothers?" I ask.

"Brothers. Sister. Her son. The father." She spits each word out.

"So he was convicted?" I want to be sure.

"He got put immediately in jail that day. That was the best psychological thing that happened to Craig in this whole period of time. He went in there shaking, twitching. They said the jury felt so bad for him they knew it was over the minute he walked in because he was doing this." Elisabeth shakes and twitches all over. "There was no one in the room besides Craig and his father. I couldn't go in. Thank God this Jay Sanders (the victim advocate) became his confidante and made this trial feel *empowering*. Just like Robert O'Hara did."

> Children who are sexual abuse survivors battle so many conflicting emotions. They feel responsible in some way for the abuse, but helpless to stop it. They believe themselves to be no good at all. For Craig, the day his father was convicted may have been the first time he felt validated and safe.
>
> Because many grandchildren in the care of grandparents may have been abused, grandparents need to be very aware of all the issues that arise for children who are survivors of abuse. Some psychological and emotional effects for children who have been physically or sexually abused are: difficulty trusting adults; insomnia, restlessness at night, nightmares or night terrors; acting out abuse on dolls, animals or even other children; a preoccupation with body parts and body functions; a preoccupation with their appearance; eating disorders; problems with self-image, self-esteem, self-worth; and shame.
>
> For grandparents, awareness that these are normal reactions to abnormal circumstances will help them understand the child's behavior. Obviously, it is critical that grandchildren receive the appropriate treatment and counseling. It is also important for grandparents to receive counseling or support to address their feelings of rage and shock. Sorting out all their feelings will make them stronger, more helpful caregivers.

Christine fell apart on the stand and couldn't be a witness, even though she had been the one talking all along. Craig had been too traumatized, but now he was able to speak up. "He got very empowered by the detective, Robert O'Hara. And the wonderful victim advocate, Jay Sanders, he was the saint in all this. "Thomas Connor spent 40 days in jail," Elisabeth said.

Connor appealed. A fund-raiser was held in Harding for him "this innocent man." The judge threw out nearly every piece of evidence except for Craig's testimony. The judgment was overturned on a technicality; Craig had used the word "bum" instead of "anal opening" when describing the abuse.

When Marion had to appear in court for her divorce, Craig told her, "Mama, you'll be very nervous and scared when you walk in, but once you start talking and telling them what happened, you'll feel much better."

The case in Massachusetts had been pending, with continuance after continuance from 1986 to 1991. The Parks family eventually accepted a plea bargain; they finally called it quits. Elisabeth explained that the children had already been through so much she couldn't justify continuing on for an uncertain outcome. It was time to move on, pick up the pieces, and try to heal the wounds. Thomas Connor never spent another day in jail. He pays minimal child support, and is able to go on with his life undisturbed.

There are some people in this idyllic, lakeside community that still believe he is innocent and that Elisabeth Parks is just another crazy woman.

Forgiveness is a two-way street. Grandparents need to forgive their child, and they need to forgive themselves as well; they need to acknowledge and apologize for what they are unable to do—stop their child's destructive behavior.

Therapy, support groups, and a compassionate ear are all vital tools that can allow grandparents the opportunity to find their path to healing. All of us have times when we need a non-judgmental, unbiased, non-family member who we can trust and who will help us help ourselves, someone who is on our side. That is what therapy is all about.

Many people fear therapy or feel that by seeing a therapist they are admitting weakness. This is definitely not the case. Admitting you need help and taking the initiative to finding that help demonstrates strength. We all have to recognize we have pain and disappointment that needs healing. For grandchildren to begin their journey into healing, grandparents need to begin the healing journey first.

5

Integrating the Birth Parents

"Dear Lord ...
patch this work. Quilt us
together, feather-stitching piece
by piece our tag-ends of living,
our individual scraps of love."
     —Jane Wilson Joyce, "Crazy Quilt"

"Once upon a time, Tyra had a baby growing in her tummy (because that's where babies grow before they're born, in their birth mommy's tummy). And Tyra said to me, 'You know, I really love this baby, but even though I can do some things really well, like write stories and sing songs, I just don't know how to take care of a baby.' So, I said to Tyra, 'Guess what! I really love this baby too, and I *do* know how to take care of a baby, so when this baby is born she can be mine!' And Tyra said, 'That's a good idea!' "

Sabra beams when I tell her this story. She calls it "my baby story." We tell it at bedtime when we snuggle together, and when I get to the end I say, "And who was that baby?" and Sabra says happily, "Me!"

She was three years old when I put together the facts of her birth in what I hoped would be an age-appropriate and positive way. But it wasn't the first step we had made to try to integrate her birth parents in a meaningful way into her life. After Sabra was born, we made a concerted effort to welcome her birth father as well into the family. When she was christened at three months of age, I asked Randy to be godfather. This gave him a role, a position at a time when he felt like odd man out. From infancy on, he and his family have been a positive and loving part of her life. We encouraged and supported open-ended visitation. In fact, I always say that I consider that the situation we have is a very, *very* "open adoption." It is not always easy to accommodate the needs of all the individuals in a large and super-extended family, but I think the end results make the effort well worthwhile. We feel that a child cannot have too much love in her life, and anything we can do to strengthen loving family ties can only be of benefit to Sabra. And we have been fortunate in having a wonderful group of people to work with who all have the best interests of Sabra at heart.

Although physically including all the players in Sabra's life seemed like the natural and right thing to do, confronting the obligation to explain the facts to her hadn't surfaced yet. Sabra was only three. Both my older daughters had been living at home with us. Tyra was attending the Boston Conservatory of Music, and Tasha was taking some time to work before entering college. One icy January, they both left home—Tyra, Chicago-bound to try her hand at playwriting and singing professionally, Tasha for Westfield State College in the western part of the State. Sabra took it hard. And it threw me for a loop. She began to have "accidents" night and day. Every day when I picked her up from nursery school, I was handed a plastic bag full of sodden pants, socks, panties, and sometimes even shoes, and a child with a badly mismatched outfit.

To make matters worse, Sabra wouldn't speak to either of them on the phone. I encouraged both Tyra and Tasha to send her little notes and trinkets by mail. But trying to maintain bonds long distance is a frustrating job. Although I think the effort is important, I often worry that the results are feeble at best.

I knew something more was needed. I began to have talks with her at night, when the house was quiet and there were no distractions, just the two of us cuddling together. Talks about her birth mother and her "sister" Tasha. Talks about when they would be coming home for visits and reassurances that *I* would stay. One night I started, "Once upon a time. ... " Sabra became so still and intent, her green eyes grew larger and larger; I knew I was on to something.

A narrative such as the one I finally fashioned can be a valuable tool for beginning the road to healing, for breaking down complex facts into digestible components and, ultimately, for initiating the process of fully integrating birth parents into the lives of grandchildren.

We hadn't, as yet, focused attention on explaining facts to Sabra because she was so young and because everyone was *here* for her. It was easy to take that for granted, and we were not prepared for a such a powerfully negative reaction when her family situation altered. Her birth mother, even though her role was as more of a sister, was very much a part of her life. When both she and Tasha left simultaneously, I was astonished and horrified at how deeply Sabra felt the loss. It made poignantly clear to me that she had abandonment issues, and no matter how well we think we have at least tried to handle things, she will always have those issues, and we will always have to help her deal with them.

I have been aware from the beginning of the need to nurture all the relationships at hand. We had always identified both Tyra and Randy as "birth parents" long before the term would have any real meaning for her because I felt that it would serve to make the transition to other details smoother. I believe its important to begin in small ways such as these, laying the foundation for the gradual inclusion of more and weightier information.

We were, however, drifting along at that time, blissfully unfocused on the way in which we would actually begin to explain the complexities of Sabra's interfamily connections to her. Events, as frequently happens, forced us to come to grips with her need to know. She required information to deal with issues relating to loss and abandonment, and issues relating to her place in the family.

One of the ways in which grandparents can show a grandchild in a tangible way how important her place is in the family is to keep a journal that would include her baby story, a family tree, events and milestones large and small such as the first time she walked or talked. Talk about how wanted she is and how happy you are to have her with you. A book I would recommend for reading to children from two to 12 is *On the Day You Were Born*, by Debra Frasier. It is a book about each child's importance in his own family as well as the family of humanity and nature. The last page reads, "Welcome to the green Earth" the people sang ... And as they held you close they whispered into your open, curving ear, "We are so glad you've come!"

The story I created for Sabra obviously was a story designed for a very young child. It is a story I will add to and expand frequently as she grows older. I am still trying to figure out how to include her birth father, Randy, in her "baby story" without having it turn into a biology lesson.

One of the mistakes I made as we struggled to make our interfamily adoption work, was trying to force a relationship between Tyra and Sabra. I was impatient, controlling. There is a wobbly line between encouraging and controlling, and I often fall down on the wrong side of it. I have learned to release, to let what comes naturally come and not press for more or for something different. They love each other, and they have worked out a relationship between them that defies labels. That's all right. It is enough that they are both content in their hearts when together.

Within the parameters of establishing and/or maintaining a bond between birth parent and child are definite lines that must be drawn. Roles which may have, of necessity, shifted or been replaced altogether must be clearly defined and firmly reinforced. When grandparents accept the parent role in grandchildren's lives, it is important to maintain that role with consistency particularly in the presence of a birth parent who has, for whatever reason, relinquished that role. Grandparents must learn to say 'No' to the birth parent and say it with confidence and authority. Adult children have to learn to accept the new boundaries, whether temporary or permanent. It is a step they must take before they can connect with their children in a positive and constructive way. If they cannot, it may leave grandchildren open to torn loyalties and confusion.

One of the most difficult circumstances for grandparents is when adult children continue to behave in ways that are disruptive and destructive for the grandchildren. Occasionally, under extreme circumstances, grandparents must let the grown child go to fully protect their grandchild. It is one of the most painful choices grandparents are sometimes forced to make. It comes down to this: Solomon-like, one must weigh the needs of the grandchild against the needs of the adult child. On one hand you have a youngster who is vulnerable, impressionable, and helpless without you, and on the other hand you have an adult child, frequently needy as well, but for whom you have already done your best and who is old enough to make decisions and choices, who has had his or her chance at life. The decision is wrenching but clear, the child must have *his or her* chance now. Luckily, I never had to make that desperate choice; others do.

Under those conditions, it is critical for grandparents to have a palatable explanation for their grandchildren—one that faces facts squarely but gently and leaves room for hope for better days to come. Integrating the birth parent is always an essential part of rearing healthy grandchildren under any circumstances and perhaps especially under those most dire ones. And if the only means for doing that at your disposal are effective narratives, then make certain that the facts you present neither glorify nor vilify birth parents, but present the facts in a way that makes your grandchildren comfortable with their heritage.

Hopefully, most of us will never have to face choosing between grandchild and adult child. Most of us need only to find ways to either maintain or reenergize the bond between birth parent and child. Sometimes, doing that means dealing with or putting aside our own anger and disappointments. Frequently, to achieve that, counseling may be the best course of action, but however one goes about coping with bad feelings toward birth parents, it is another essential step toward integrating birth parents and raising whole grandchildren. *For the sake of the child.* Let that be your mantra if it is the only way you can get through it. *For the sake of the child.*

Ann

Ann Leonardi, petite and trim as a girl at 53, lives with her two grandsons, Douglas, six, and Brad, five, in a sprawling multilevel home in an oceanside community at the northern corner of the state. She sits primly, the tips of her very short, dark hair barely brushing the navy blue frames that set off her baby-doll eyes. She is wearing a crisply ironed white shirt that makes the freckles running up her arms and under the rolled up cuffs stand out like cinnamon sprinkles. She tells me her story in a matter-of-fact, nearly businesslike way.

Her grandsons came to live with her and her husband a couple of years ago. Their son, Nick, discovered them at the home of his estranged wife being looked after by three strange men—"druggies"—and delivered the children to his parents. Ann and her husband, Joseph, acquired temporary legal custody of the boys.

Both parents went into rehab. "I thought that she was getting her act together," Ann recalls. "I thought that my son was getting his act together, but as it turned out, she left her rehab and started living with another man." Ann's son came to her home to live. "It worked out okay for about three months. He was really good about paying attention to the kids, and then I could see him backsliding. He wanted to get custody of his children back. He wanted to live here, have custody of his children, have me do all the work, and be able to call the shots. And I said that's just not going to happen. So we went to court and we had a custody battle over it. I got custody of the kids, and I asked him to move out because he was drinking, he was not working, he was not showing up when he said he would show up to be with the kids, and then he started gambling."

Meanwhile, Ann explains, the children's birth mother "had gotten into a pattern of calling me and saying, 'Can I come see the kids tomorrow?' and I would say, 'Yes, come at two o'clock.' Well, fortunately, I never told the kids Mom was coming at two o'clock, because Mom wouldn't show up. I never told them until she rang the doorbell, I just handled it like a big surprise. I didn't want them to be disappointed when she didn't come." She would call, make excuses and then make subsequent appointments that she would not keep. "It was bad enough when she did come and she left. I mean, she would come and spend and hour and be like ..." Ann snatches furtive, nervous glances at her watch to illustrate, " 'Lets hurry up and do this, Mommie's got to go quick.' And she'd leave them crying. Well you know how hard it is for kids to separate from their mother." Soon their birth mom stopped coming altogether.

At the same time, the Leonardi's marriage began to disintegrate. Joseph didn't want to raise children again. "He loves them," she shrugs, "but didn't want them here. He didn't want them in a foster home, but didn't want them here. He didn't know what he wanted. We always had some problems." That was the wedge that finally drove them apart.

Ann's family situation, as well as her grandsons', had unraveled, and it was up to Ann to begin to try to knit them all back together as best as she could. Ann's son never severed contact with the boys, remains bonded to them, and visits them regularly and consistently. While his destructive behavior is a source of pain to Ann, she must put her feelings aside to allow her son and grandsons the freedom to remain connected. She has developed a "hands off" approach to their relationship and his parenting style. That "hands off" approach can be a difficult one to manage and requires constant maintenance. Weighing when to make suggestions while trying not to control the course of events is tricky at best. But Ann realizes that she needs to do what she can to allow their relationship to flower without her constant vigilance. While working at all that, she also works at pointing out to her grandsons which behaviors are acceptable and which are not, an important aspect of raising a grandchild with troubled birth parents. She never denigrates Nick, but rather explains inappropriate behaviors.

Ann tells me that the boys' relationship with their father "improved since he moved out," but that he "had some not so great things to say about me—that I was this or that because I threw him out. And the boys brought it up to me, 'Mimi, Daddy says you're blankety-blank because you threw him out.' And I have to correct them, 'Daddy needed to go live by himself so he could learn to be responsible for himself, so that maybe someday he can be a very good parent.' Once they asked Ann, "Mimi, when we get to be Daddy's age, are you going to throw us out?' She told them, "No honey, you can live with Mimi as long as you want, as long as you follow the rules.' I just let them know that there are expectations."

> Most grandparents can expect that, at some point, their grandchildren will test them to some degree. This testing I call "the necessary test," necessary in that these children will feel that they must find out if they will be asked to leave or be removed from their grandparents' care. They will force the caregiver to prove that the child will be kept no matter what. Most times, this testing shows itself through verbal challenges and annoying and manipulative behaviors. Children expect that if they are "good," well behaved and polite, they will be loved and kept. However, they need to know that if they are moody, naughty, or willful, that you will still want them around and love them. Children know that it is easy to love someone who is perfect, but they need to know that you will love and accept them, imperfections and all. Being aware of this and expecting the "necessary test" will help you to understand and move through the trying times.

Ann continues, "Even when they've said Daddy's said this or that, it's always, 'Well, that wasn't very nice of Daddy.' Or, 'Daddy shouldn't have said that.' I can think what I want, but they need to be taught that there is another way to deal with situations, they don't need to hear the verbal abuse."

This is a very difficult situation, to say the least. But Ann is committed to encouraging and supporting the boys' relationship with their father. Their connections with their birth mother, however, are fractured, and Ann has not attempted to put those pieces together. Her face tightens up each time the subject of her daughter-in-law comes up.

"My basic explanation is that 'Mommie's real sick. And Mommie has to stay with the doctors and nurses so she can get better, until she's able to take care of you.' "

Ann believes their birth mother will either end up in jail or dead from drugs. She has heard that the birth mother is "looking to give away" the two children she has had since losing custody of Douglas and Brad.

"I know that she is their birth mother, and I know that when they are grown they are going to want to see her, but not now. I have always said that, 'Your Mommy does love you, but she just can't take care of you right now, she's just not well enough.' "

> Regardless of when or why the separation occurs, children will feel the loss of the birth parent very intensely and very deeply. And, at some very basic level, children will feel like they were not good enough, not good enough to be parented or good enough to be kept. Grandparents will need to provide an environment that allows for and encourages the children to discuss their feelings of disappointment and loss. To do this, grandparents will need to model for their grandchildren that it is good to talk about feelings, and the way to do that is for the grandparents to talk about their sadness and hurts. Grandparents should provide opportunities for quiet time where this sharing can occur. All children look for cues and leads from caregivers as to how and when to express feelings. They need guidance and support to learn how to share their feelings, particularly around abandonment issues.

Ann tells me that although the birth mother "never really bonded" with her younger son Brad, Douglas was very tied to her. She thinks the reason Douglas has trouble going to sleep at night is because he misses his mother. "I was looking through some pictures the other day, and I found some of him. I could see the sadness in his eyes."

Ann is also in the position of maintaining a relationship with her ex-husband, their grandfather. "He has never called me on the phone and said, 'Can I see the boys?' I have to take the boys to him. And I do that simply because the boys need to know this is their grandfather and they need to have a relationship with him."

I point out to her that she makes the effort to take the boys to their grandfather, but does not make that same effort to take the boys to their birth mother.

"No, I don't," Ann replies slowly, thoughtfully, "simply because her lifestyle has not changed at all. And now she has two babies. In fact, I don't even know where she's living. But it would only break their hearts to see her with other children."

Ann may be right, but it sounds as if Douglas' heart is already wounded. She needs to make more of an effort to include his birth mom in his life in some meaningful way. I ask if he has a picture of his mother and suggest that she place a framed picture at his bedside and say a few soft and kind things about her at night before the boys go to sleep, words to have sweet dreams by.

Group support for children who have experienced abandonment or separation is an excellent resource. They will encounter, probably for the first time, that they are not alone, that other children have experienced similar losses too. This can be a very healing revelation for children at any age.

Ann has a lot to deal with—her son, her grandsons, her ex-husband—she has few emotional reserves for dealing with the added burden of maintaining a positive link with a birth mother that she dislikes. She must dig deep to tap into the forgiveness that will enable her to help her grandsons heal fully.

Part 3 of the Parks Family Trilogy

Marion Parks Connor

In the Parks' case, Ben and Elisabeth's daughter, Marion Parks Connor, often rankles at the pressure her mother Elisabeth applies. Elisabeth Parks hasn't gotten the hang of "hands off," and it may be that in her case, more vigilance is required, it's hard to say. They still constantly bump up against one another—Elisabeth trying to get Marion to be more of a "mother," and Marion trying to find her own speed.

Marion's story, like Ben and Elisabeth's, contains many explosive elements. Marion was a battered woman and substance abuser, which made her an unwitting accomplice to her children's abuse. She cannot forgive herself for that, and the turmoil that she lives with because of it sometimes threatens to consume her. But Marion loves her children and is constantly trying to overcome the guilt and pain that gets in the way of her relationship with them.

While obviously a relationship with their father was out of the question, Marion's children needed to be reintroduced to her once she became clean and sober. The bonds needed to be reestablished and cultivated. Elisabeth had already laid the groundwork for their rebonding by talking to the children about their mother as a victim, her substance abuse as a sickness, and explaining her behavior to them in ways they could understand and forgive.

Marion's story is the conclusion of the Parks family trilogy. It gives us new perspectives—that of the rebellious daughter, the birth parent, the battered woman, the drug addict. "How could this happen?" Marion asks of me during the interview. Perhaps accompanying Marion down the dark path she took will give us some answers to that question.

Marion is a striking young woman, tall and slim with startlingly blue eyes and an enormous, infectious smile. She answers the door of her oceanside condo on this damp fall morning dressed in a turtleneck jersey tucked into shorts, white socks and sneakers. Her legs are long, tanned, and muscular—runner's legs. Her dark hair is drawn up into a ponytail. She has that slight slouch that some tall women develop in adolescence, trying to look shorter.

Marion and her son Craig look remarkably alike—the piercing, blue eyes, dark hair, and height. But while Marion's face is tanned dark and strongly angular, Craig's is fair and fine boned. I ask her to talk a little about her adolescence, the time when she first met the man that would become her abuser and, ultimately, their children's tormentor. I am searching once again for clues, a blueprint for disaster we can study and learn to avoid, a flow chart of flaws.

Marion folds herself into an easy chair near the palladian windows in her living room. There is a golden woodsy stretch beyond. I remark about the lovely setting and she tells me she likes it here, she likes the quiet. Marion is only a little wary, a little hesitant and nervous as she begins to talk about how it all began.

"I was in high school when I met Thomas Connor. Wow, I haven't thought of all this for so long. It's not very pleasant memories for me for one thing. And a lot of it I've blocked out." She swings her open hands up, slicing the air at the sides of her head. "A lot of it."

"Actually, I met him at a party that my brothers were having. My parents used to go camping on the weekend, and I used to go with them all the time, and my brothers would always stay home. I remember begging my mother and father, 'Please let me stay home,' because I knew they were having a party."

Marion was 14 years old. One brother was a senior in high school, one a junior.

"I remember my mother letting me stay home, telling my brothers that they were responsible for me. Of course, they didn't really care what I did. They kept an eye on me, but they were having a *party*. And that's where I met Thomas Connor.

"I just can remember thinking, 'This person is actually paying attention to me!' And his family was very popular. All the boys in that family played football, they were all wicked good athletes. I just couldn't understand how come they were paying attention to me, because I really had very low self-esteem. So that's how I met him.

"At that party I drank. My brothers didn't know that I was drinking. I felt like one of the big kids, you know. I just liked him the minute I met him. He was very funny, he was paying attention to me, and once he paid attention to me all his brothers paid attention to me. And it was like this big deal! And I thought that I was crazy about him. Now I realize I was just a kid with a crush.

"So I continued to see him behind my mother's back. I thought that he had just graduated and he was, maybe, a year older than my oldest brother. I didn't have a clue how old he was. He told me he was 17, and I believed him. Because when you're 14, somebody 17 is like all grown up. I didn't have a clue that he was 22 years old.

"So I snuck around for a long time. I would go to hockey games and I would see him there. For a good six months I would always see him places. I didn't really date him or anything like that, I was just crazy about him ... or so I thought.

"Then when I was 15 years old I got pregnant. I ended up sleeping with him.

"I went to a football game ... begged my mother to let me go. His family was going, and by this point, I knew all the sisters in school. Once they knew that he liked me, they became friends with me. His sisters were older than me, but I played sports with them. All of a sudden they just started paying attention to me and being nice to me and telling me that Thomas liked me, and I got to be really close with them.

"The football team was playing down at Martha's Vineyard, and the whole school was going. Everybody was going and they were going to stay overnight in a hotel. I begged my mother, 'Please let me go!'

"I just remember, that every single time I was with Thomas, he would always buy me booze. Then I didn't think anything of it. But today I look at it like ... I never knew him without drinking, ever! I never sat and had a conversation with the guy without him buying me beer, or smoking dope.

"When I went away to that football game, he came, and all his brothers came, everybody came. I think that's when I got pregnant. I do not remember it. It was a complete blackout most of the time I was there, because it was all drinking the whole time I was there. Of course, I hid it from Mrs. Connor. She was supposed to be watching me. The only reason my mother let me go was because all the girls were going, the Connor girls. And Mrs. Connor was going, and she said she would be responsible for me. Well, of course, I snuck out! It wasn't her fault. I don't blame anybody.

"I don't remember exactly where we were, but everybody was drinking.

Nobody was old enough to drink. And that's all I remember except that I have a brief flashback of getting out of bed in a hotel room—out of Thomas' bed—and there was a whole bunch of people sleeping around us. And sneaking back to my room, and praying that Mrs. Connor wouldn't know that I was sneaking in. She didn't, she was sleeping. I don't ever remember having sex with him.

"This is how I found out I was pregnant. I was on the basketball team in high school. I kept getting really sick around Thanksgiving. I kept thinking that I was having appendicitis pains. So here I was playing basketball, my coach kept telling me that it was just aches and pains that I had to work out of my system and she made me stay an hour after practice and run, run, run and do a thousand sit-ups and a hundred pushups just to get the pains out.

"My period was really irregular. I think I only got it like once or twice and never got it again. So it was no big deal when I didn't get my period. When I didn't have my period for three months, it was no big deal to me. I never in my wildest dreams thought I was pregnant. I don't even remember having sex for starters.

"I was at my mother's house. Everybody was there. It was a Sunday. I just remember keeling over at the dinner table with pain so bad. My father thought it was an appendicitis attack and took me to the hospital. There they did all kinds of exams on me—a pelvic exam, which I had never had before. I'll just never forget I was lying on the bed in the room waiting, waiting it seemed like hours. And a nurse came in and said, 'Are you still here?' and I said, 'I'm just waiting to go home. Can I get dressed?' And she said, 'Well, you're pregnant, and the doctor's telling your father now,' and she just closed the curtain and walked out.

"I'll just never forget how devastated and scared to death I was. I was just so scared to death! My father came in and I started crying. And he was crying and just hugged me and said that he would help me through whatever was going to happen, not to worry about it. He was hugging me, I'll never forget it. That's the closest I've ever been to my father. I always loved him to death and strived for his attention, but, he was very standoffish like he couldn't really show affection. I knew he loved me, but he had a really hard time with saying I love you. Today it's easier for him—he tells me today—but then he had a hard time with that. Maybe that's why I looked for older people, especially boys. I don't know.

"I remember going home that day, begging my father, 'You can't tell mom right now.' He had already told her. And I was scared to death, I didn't know what to expect. I got home and her sisters and everybody was there. When they're all together they're very Italian; they were all crying and yet they were all excited.

"My mother was trying to get a hold of Thomas and his family, because, we had to tell them obviously. He had been gone all day with all his friends. I'll never forget to where. He was at the brewery in Manchester, New Hampshire. It figures!

"He came with his sister, and they came into the living room and sat down, and both of them said, 'Well, you've got to get an abortion.' And I was like, 'Okay.' And I'll never forget, to this day, agreeing with them and having no idea what an abortion was. Not a clue.

"And that night I went to bed and I was really scared, and my mother came and got in bed with me. She was really good. Every night she would always come in and talk to us before we went to sleep. I really just loved that part of my life.

"She came in and she got in bed with me and she was hugging me and telling me that she loved me and that we were going to get through this, not to be scared. And I remember saying, 'I have to get an abortion,' and not even knowing what it was, that was the really crazy part. 'I'm gonna get an abortion, Mom.' And she said, 'No. You're not going to get an abortion, Marion. There'll be no abortions in this house. We can talk about, maybe later on, giving this baby up for adoption, or some kind of other options. But no abortions in this house, absolutely not, not under my roof.' And, I was like, 'Fine.'

"Anyway, Thomas stuck by me through this whole pregnancy. He bought me clothes, bought me baby stuff. Really put on a show. He said, 'Well, we might as well get married.' Then when we talked about it with our parents, my parents said, 'Oh no! You're too young. You have to finish school.' And Mr. and Mrs. Connor agreed with that even though Thomas had a really good job. For the next year, I lived at home. My mother said, 'In the next eight months, if Thomas proves to us that he's going to be good to you and a good provider, then maybe we'll agree to letting you get married.' Craig was about nine months old when I finally did get married.

"To me marriage was just the wedding, it was going to be a big party. I had no clue what I was getting myself into, and I thought I was in love with him. I really wasn't when I think about it now, it was just the whole glamorization of having my own house, and friends could come over, and I am going to get away from my mother. Because now, once I had the baby, me and my mother started clashing. A lot of it had to do with I was into drinking. I was really resentful that I had a baby. I didn't know that then, I realize it now. I was very headstrong, I knew everything; my mother knew nothing. She was telling me that I had to finish school. I didn't want to go to school. So it was a constant butting of the heads." Marion slaps her fist into her palm over and over again.

"My sister Joanie was a baby, and my mother got really sick with bursitis in both arms, and my mother told me I had to stay home from school and take care of Craig. This one day I really wanted to go to school because—this was really how selfish I was at the time—I had gone to the beach with my girlfriends and got really tanned, and that was such a big thing. It was all about how I looked on the outside. I guess when you're a teenager, that's what you go through.

"My mother had a hard time with that, the way I dressed. She was constantly picking at the way I dressed, constantly about the way I looked. Never, ever said a thing to my brothers, but it was always me and Charlene (her younger sister), about the way we dressed. I don't think she could deal with a daughter in high school and just with the teenage changing, of the things that I wore, the tight jeans. She used to say to me, 'You already got pregnant, why do you have to dress like that?' It was a constant butting of the heads every step of the way." Marion strikes her palm again with her fist."

> The struggle for teenagers between trying to separate and become a responsible young adult and the desperate vulnerable need to still be parented is one that usually turns into a battle with the family. The tried and true methods of conflict resolution are the best tools for dealing with this stage of development. First, pick your battles well. Learn how to distinguish which battles are worth fighting over and which are worth letting go of. Make respect an issue worth fighting over, respect for you, and respect for themselves. Make them responsible at home and make them keep their commitments to themselves and others. Give them consequences for their transgressions.
>
> Have realistic expectations, and hopefully your teen will rise to meet them. Keep expectations low and your teen will probably fail to achieve them. Make your teen accountable and set consistent, firm, fair limits and, with luck, you will all successfully get through the teen experience.

"When I think back today, there were things she was absolutely right about. Because I find myself saying the same things to my kids when I have them here. It's crazy. But I couldn't wait to get out, away from there, be all grown up and have my own place. We did a lot of fighting in those days." Marion displays a sheepish smile. "We've come a long way since then," she adds.

"Anyway, it started when they finally let me get married. And within two weeks," she says squinting, her eyes trying to remember, "this man who was such a sweetheart turned into a nightmare. My life turned into a nightmare in two weeks. All of a sudden he said, 'You can't leave this house. I don't want you going over your mother's house all the time.' He just completely turned, starting putting my family down."

"The first time he hit me, I can't even remember really. The first year I was married, I just remember going home and sitting on the back step of the house the first time I had a black eye and telling my mother I fell down. My mother sat down on the steps and said, 'Did *he* do this to you?' And I was petrified. Petrified to tell her. Like she was going to hurt him in some way." Marion laughs in disbelief.

"Within this year he emotionally put me down so much that I felt like I needed him and I needed to protect him. I got into this syndrome that it was my fault that he hit me. As much as it was inside of me that I was afraid of him, I was quite the people pleaser. I look back today, I was such a people pleaser, I didn't want anybody to think bad of me. I didn't want to do anything to hurt him, because what was his family going to think if my family was mean to him. I loved Mrs. Connor ... I loved her. She was very much like me. Obviously, she was being beaten; I never knew that till years later. I don't know what it was about her that I really loved. I still do to this day. And I feel really bad that I can't have a relationship with her. But I can't." Marion's voice softens. "I'm sure she doesn't want to have it with me."

Marion hunches over, her face draws down, and she is working hard at not crying. Her whole body is bent over as if recoiling. She seems to shrink until she is curled into a small question mark. She manages to say, "I still have a hard time talking about this." Her arms are wrapped around her waist, and she rocks forward.

"I don't want you talk about anything that you don't want to talk about," I tell her. I mean it. I am not here to cause her more pain. In fact, I am amazed she is willing to talk with me at all, to dredge all this up. Whatever she wants to say to me, I consider a gift.

"I don't actually remember a lot. I remember a lot of stuff. I don't remember a lot of Thomas Connor stuff.

"I remember my friend, Cynthia. I'm very close with her. She came over to my house all the time. And it's really weird because I didn't talk to her for many years—like a good six years. And I just went to a class reunion and rekindled our friendship. We talked a lot. She was really angry and it really blew my mind. She said, 'Thomas was very *abusive* to you verbally, but I had no clue he was hitting you! Why didn't you tell me?' She was really angry. She said, 'Another thing I don't understand is why did you stay in it. The first time he ever laid a hand on you, why did you stay there, Mare? I don't understand that!'

"I have another girlfriend that's living the same nightmare now out in Las Vegas. And she's like, 'Look at Dawn. She's doing the same thing And she's staying in it! It's beyond me.' She was furious." Marion relates it all in an angry, disgusted tone. She is either imitating her friend or feeling angry and disgusted herself, I can't tell which.

"I said, 'I don't know, you're just a different person, Cyn. I don't know. There was a lot of guilt, and he always made me feel like it was my fault.' I said, 'For one thing, I was in the midst of my alcoholism. I had a lot of other problems. I felt really guilty. I don't know ... I can't explain why I stayed in.'

Marion tries to explain it to me, "I just had a lot of fear. I had nowhere to go. Look at how old I was, I was 16 or 17. I didn't know how I could raise my kids alone. I knew I could go back to my mother's. Every time I *did* go back to my mother's, we ended up in a big fight. I just wanted ... freedom ... from everything. And yet I knew I couldn't truly have it."

Marion's boyfriend James comes in, and we are introduced. He seems uncomfortable with me there. Although pleasant, there is an edge of suspicion. He stands sideways several steps from me and does not come over to shake my hand. He leaves quickly after making a few arrangements with Marion.

Marion continues, "I was actually a little angry at Cynthia. I don't know how come I got mad at her for saying that to me. It was almost as if ... 'Didn't you know? Couldn't you *help* me?'"

"You were mad at her for not realizing the trouble you were in at the time," I confirm. "Were you mad at other people?" I ask. "Were you mad at your parents?"

"No. Never. Never ever! Because, my mother came down to my house. I remember she stood in the door and said 'Where is he!' She didn't like him at all. That actually made me kind of feel good. It's really weird. She didn't like him, and she wanted to protect me, and I knew that. You know, I held on to that. I almost expected that someday she's going to save me from him.

"She went downstairs and said something to him like, "How dare you. If I find out that you laid a hand on my daughter, I'll kill you!' My mother told me he said, 'Don't tell me that Ben doesn't slap you around once in a while when you need it!' And my mother almost flipped."

"I always used to get really nervous because my mother could see right through me. I think that's exactly why. ..." Marion seems to be talking to herself, getting some things out that she hasn't talked about for years and discovering a few things along the way. "She could see right through me and I was dirt. That's how I felt. I was dirt because I smoked pot and drank and my self-esteem was low. I really didn't like myself much back then. She always confronted me with stuff that I couldn't ... didn't like to talk about. I was very resentful because I always thought she was trying to run my life. Really she was trying to help me. But I didn't see it then. So I got really, really angry with her a lot. She was always right, and she never listened to me or anything that I had to say.

"She stood in the door and said, 'You and I have big problems, and he's right downstairs!' I didn't know what she was talking about. I was like, 'What?' She shook her head, and she had tears in her eyes and she just left. When Thomas came up I said, 'What did you say to her?' He said, "Nothin'! Your mother's a pain in the friggin ass. I don't want her here. I don't want her coming to this house.' He had a big fight with her—told her not to come to the house. That's why she used to come and stand outside the door.

"She used to come and check up on me all the time. She knew I was smoking pot and she was worried about the baby." Marion is lost in thought and memories. She sits hunched over with her head down as she talks. At times it appears that she is in conversation with herself alone. Thomas once locked Marion outside for hours on a screened balcony in the dead of winter, she tells me. She was barefoot and wearing nothing but a nightgown. "He told me, 'That would teach me. That would teach me.' Her head hangs, her voice is low, worn down. "I don't know what it was teaching me.

"I always had people in my house. I hated the way I lived. I lived in this little, tiny, tiny hole in the wall and I hated it. Always had people there. All his family, all his brothers were there, my friend Cynthia was there. I had no space whatsoever."

"What were his brothers doing there?"

"They would always come over to get away from their house. They were very close. I was very close to Andy. I don't even know if you want to know this stuff."

"That's up to you," I reply.

"His family was real sick. I was really close to Andy. Sometimes I think I married Thomas so I could stay close to Andy. He was in love with me. He used to tell me that all the time."

"How old was he?"

"Two years older than me. He protected me more than anybody did from Thomas. Andy practically lived with us the five years we were in that house. I ended up sleeping with him ... and it was just a way out. I couldn't stand Thomas, but there was no way out—I really didn't feel like there was any way out of that whole thing. How could I leave him? Where could I go? How could I hurt everybody? How could I embarrass myself?

"I really feel that if I didn't have Andy to love, I would have killed myself. I had tried to kill myself lots of times. Andy used to get really angry, 'How could you do this to me? How could you do this to Thomas and me?' I was just really hurting. And I think I would've if Andy wasn't in my life. I would have killed myself."

Marion's pain begins to consume her now. Her face, which had been animated, is crumpled, ravaged. She's doubled over. Tears stream and stream down her face as she talks.

"You really felt that there was no escape?" I ask her. She's unable to speak. She merely nods her head. "Even though you had a family there that you knew was concerned about you, you didn't see that as an avenue for escape?"

"The Connors had a lot of power over me. I don't know how come." She chokes out the words. She cries silently and wipes at her cheeks. "There's too much stuff!" she manages to say through her tears and pain—suffocating pain.

"Well, lets change the subject then," I offer. "You know I'm writing a book, and it's about grandparents raising their grandchildren." I speak to her softly. I believe this interview is too much for her to bear, and I don't want to leave her like this. I want to try and lift her out of this pain before I go if I can and leave her with some positive thoughts. "And the reason I wanted to interview you, Marion, is because most of the time when grandparents are bringing up grandchildren, it's because their children were involved in drugs and alcohol; it's a common thing. Drug and alcohol abuse touches many, many families, and this is sort of a by-product of that abuse. And the reason I wanted to interview you is that you've been through it and come through it and you've been in recovery. I wanted to talk to somebody that's okay now, that's recovered and come through that awful time into a better place. So if you were talking to people that might be in the same situation, what would you like to say to them?"

"That there is a way out. There is a light at the end of the tunnel, that's for sure."

Marion pauses and then, to my surprise, continues on. "I had to go through a lot of pain, but I wanted to get better. I think I wanted to get better for my kids. A lot of my pain has to do with ... not even Thomas Connor, but my kids. I wasted it. I can't beat myself up for it now, which I still do, and I wasted a lot of time. I don't even remember the first five years. Little Craig—I can't even remember him being in the picture." She says this with horror looking up at me, her blue eyes magnified through the tears.

"I feel grateful that ... I have a lot of pain today, but, I mean, I've recovered from alcoholism and drug abuse, and I'm not in an abusive relationship, which really blows my mind. I have a hard time with that one still. I keep waiting for something bad to happen, still to this day. It's really ridiculous. James compliments me all the time about what a beautiful person I am. He likes what's inside, you know. I keep waiting for the slams or the digs or something and they just don't come.

"I still have a hard relationship with my mother. We don't fight anything like we used to." Marion says this with a crooked smile and a laugh. "But I think it's because I've changed. My mother hasn't changed, but *I* have. When I first got sober, my counselors told me that I needed to move away from my mother. They said even to move away from my children. 'You have to do it to get better, Marion.'

"My mother is very controlling, very controlling. She wants to dictate my whole life and I can't live like that. I start to feel a closed-in feeling, and *that's* the feeling ... that's when I want to drink and drug to escape.

"It's like she can't understand what I'm saying to her. It's like we're still going to butt heads forever." She smiles that crooked smile again, and I realize there is affection leaking out. "We're different, but we're the same in a lot of ways. We get along much, much better today. I love my mother to death, and I am so grateful for my parents, that they could be there for my kids when I couldn't be.

"It's not crazy like it used to be way back when I was really sick. It was my disease. But I moved away. It was a very hard decision to make. My mother still, to this day, doesn't understand it, and I can't tell her 'It's cause of you, Ma.' I can't tell her that. She doesn't understand it—she thinks I'm horrible living this far away. She *doesn't* think I'm horrible—she's proud of me ... I know she is, I know she is."

"And your father too," I tell her. "I spoke with your father separately." I am so surprised she's still talking with me.

"You did?" she says.

"Ben talked mostly about you kids—his children—with a lot of pride. He talked about the sports. He knew I was coming to see you and he said, 'You'll really like Marion.' He talked about how beautiful you were. 'She looks like a model,' he said, and, 'You wouldn't believe it but Christine looks just like Marion did at that age.' He talked on like that."

Marion murmurs with surprise and is tickled pink when I tell her about comparisons with Christine.

"I didn't really ask him specific questions because I want people to talk about what they want to talk about," I tell her. "But whenever I tried to guide Ben to talking about those painful times, he mostly talked around it. He would shift the conversation, and it would mostly shift to his children. Positive things. He is very much a family man for his children, and very proud of them."

"I feel really bad for my father sometimes," Marion says. My mother has so much rage against Thomas Connor, and the fact that she couldn't stop it, and a lot of times she blames my father. 'He should have stepped in and done something! He didn't believe anything was going on!' He couldn't deal with it. Who could deal with hearing that Thomas Connor sexually abused my children? That was a really, really hard, hard time for everybody. It was hard for *me* to swallow. I didn't believe my mother for a long, long time. How could this happen?" She asks me with her hands outstretched palms up. "How could this happen!"

The pain is back, if it ever left. She is talking with difficulty again, struggling to get the words out. Tears fall down her cheeks onto her hands, her jersey, and drip down her neck.

"I blamed myself. I still have a hard time with Craig, my relationship with Craig, all the guilt I have. I'm much closer to Christine, but I love Craig to death! I know how much that kid loves me too. But we just can't talk about our feelings. We're both like my father, we beat around the bush and we talk about everything else." Her voice trails off to a whisper.

Marion tells me her mother is constantly encouraging her to talk to Craig about the past. But she says, "I can't! It's easy for her to say that, but its not easy for me to do."

> Marion needs to let herself off the hook. She needs to make peace with herself and the fact that she was rendered helpless to protect herself and her children. Years of emotional healing are required to mend the aftershocks of domestic violence. It may take years for her to feel that she can trust others again. It may take years for her to feel that she can trust herself to

make mature, responsible choices. It will be difficult for Marion to forgive herself unless she works through all the pain and conflicting emotions that have been part of her for so long. She needs to commit herself to the hard work of therapy to resolve her feelings of guilt and shame.

"Everyone has different approaches to things," I tell Marion, still trying to ease her pain. "And I think your mother finds it easy to talk about things. That's great for her, that's very healthy for her; she gets a lot out. And she has a lot of people to talk with. She told me about the community that she's a part of. It's hard to understand, I think, when other people have totally different approaches and can't deal with things in the same way—they just can't."

"My father can't," Marion concurs, "and my mother blames him wicked and that makes me so sad. It's over and done with! There's no going back to that time. None of us would want to go back to that time. Everything that happens to us happens to us for a reason." Marion uses her hands when she talks. She hits her knees with them sometimes for emphasis.

"Do you and Craig go to counseling together?" I ask.

"I did a long time ago. I'm almost afraid to—it's really crazy ... ," she trails off.

"It would be painful, that's for sure," I say.

"That's what I'm afraid of. I couldn't deal with it. It's bad enough that ... I feel like I have a hard time breathing when I start thinking about it." She clasps her hands to her chest.

"Maybe it would relieve you, give you some relief," I tell her. "Look at me, I think I'm a therapist!"

Marion laughs and I am happy to hear it. The pain that sits in this room with us is unbearable. I joke with her a little more, "That's what happens when you ride for three hours in a car with a therapist," and we laugh together.

"I went to counseling with him one time way back around the time he was being abused. They made me watch a tape of him. Ever since that time I could never go back.

"Sometimes I really, really wish I could be like my mother."

"In what way?" I ask.

"Well, she's so strong. She's the strongest person I know. Even though I know that it's been very painful for her. She blames herself for a lot of stuff. None of it is her fault. I do not blame my parents in the least for anything that's happened. My mother blames my father for a lot ... not protecting us and blah, blah, blah. She throws that back at him a lot. And that really makes me really angry when she does that. But on the other hand, she just stands up for all of us. She's been such a fighter for my kids most of all."

"So if you see your mother as really strong, how do you see your father? What would you say about him?" I ask.

"I see my father in a way that I'd rather be. My mother will tell the whole world everything that's going on, and I don't like that. She obsesses on things and she never lets them go. My father, on the other hand, wants to live in today more. I love that about him. I can go and see him and he's happy to see me, and we can talk about what's going on *now*. With my mother, she is constantly, constantly bringing up these poor kids and everything they've been through. Craig still has all this emotional shit going on because he was abused. And she talks about Thomas Connor like it was still today." Her lips tighten up over her teeth.

"I can't deal with that and *that* makes me angry! The part about her being strong and she's brought those kids so far through everything. My father, on the other hand, was always there for us, but in a quieter way. And actually I like that more ... its hard to explain. ...

"I can talk to my father about stuff. I can talk to him more than others can it seems. More in the past couple of years. Me and my Dad have become real close, and I know it's real painful for him to talk about the bad stuff."

"Does he? Does he bring it up?" I ask.

"Yeah ... ," she hesitates. "*I* have to him. I have *to* him. The day I had to go to my lawyers—when I got a new lawyer to get my divorce—it took forever. I had to rehash all this stuff again. More so what Thomas Connor did to me. I came home and fell apart." Marion is falling apart in the retelling.

"I get a lot of headaches because I can't deal with a lot of stuff. I know that I was beat up, but a lot of it I don't remember. All I know is when I get close to it, my whole body starts to hurt. When I had to go to court and my new lawyer wanted to know everything that happened to me, it was really weird because I talked a lot about it and it was really painful, but I couldn't remember a lot of stuff. I had a hard time breathing. But when we got to court, I had to go into the courtroom with Thomas Connor and say what he did to me. My whole body hurt! Every inch of my body started to ache.

"I got so upset. My father was the only one home. And I just lost it, I started crying. I could tell he just got really upset too. And he just hugged me. I know that he doesn't know how to say anything, but I know that he feels really bad. He said that he really wishes that it never happened and he could have done something.

"There was nothing he could have done! I told him that. But he's so positive to me, 'Marion it's all over with now! Now you can go on with your life and put it behind you. If your mother will *let* ya!' She laughs through her tears. "He's so funny, my father is wicked funny too. That's another thing I love about him is his sense of humor. I think he has a really good sense of humor, but it's to cover up a lot of pain. But thank God for that."

Marion begins to laugh again. "And it's so true because the minute I see my mother, we don't go through any time or any minute of the day without her bringing up the past crap. She's just never going to let it go. That's why I have a hard time going there. Because I can't get through one day without her bringing up something. She doesn't say it to make me feel bad. I can see where she is coming from. But God does it hurt when she says stuff like, 'These kids didn't lose one parent, they lost two.'"

"When she says that, what is she trying to get you to do?" I ask.

"Be there more. But I work, I'm trying to make a life for myself so I can have it for my kids if they ever need to come here. I want to be able to give them stuff, so I work my butt off. And I still have this 'my mother telling me what to do' thing. And like I'd go there as much as I possibly could if I knew I could go there without her calling me and telling me *when* I have to come there, *what* I should do with my kids every time I'm there. I don't spend enough time with them when I'm there, I'm 'not giving the right emotional attention to Craig.' It's like—*God*—I do what I can do! That's constant. And I can't deal with her doing that to me!"

"Do you tell her that?" I ask

"Oh, I've tried to lots and lots of times but, she won't listen. I am just 'selfish' when I say stuff like that. That's why I don't say that stuff to her anymore because it just brings up a big fight and she doesn't listen to me." She slaps her bare thigh with her hand. "I've done it too many years."

"Here's another thing you hear from therapists," I tell her kiddingly. 'You can't change other people, you can only change yourself.'"

She smiles her dazzling smile, "That's right! I can't change my mother and I never will, and she'll always be like this the rest of my life." She says this laughing and slaps her thigh again. "So that's the stuff that I try to avoid.

"My mother had my kids for a good two or three years when I left Thomas Connor and I moved in with my mother and father. But I was really into cocaine and drinking—just had no desire to stay home and take care of kids even though I loved my kids. The alcohol was so much more important. And the partying. And I felt sorry for myself that I'd missed out on a lot of stuff. It sounds really sick.

"In those years my mother had them there. Then, when I did get sober, the first year living in that halfway house was very hard. I had so much pain. Everything started coming out about Thomas Connor abusing my kids and that on top of trying to get sober. I really in my heart did not think that I could raise those two kids. I knew that my mother could. At one point, I didn't even think I wanted to." Marion breaks down again. "I just was scared to death. I still felt like a little kid myself. And I just couldn't do it."

"I've heard that the years that you drink and abuse are lost years in terms of growing," I tell her. "So you were still a little kid. You were still probably stuck at 14." I know I am crossing the line with Marion at every turn. I know I shouldn't offer up my opinions to her, but I feel the need to make her feel better somehow, to put a positive spin on things.

"I'm not very proud of myself," she tells me.

"Well, when you realize the way things are and where the best possibilities are for your kids, I think that's something to be proud of," I tell her. "You made the best arrangements for them that you could, and I think that's a good thing."

"It's good to know yourself," I continue. "I think its tragic when people don't know themselves ... try to do things they just can't do."

"Maybe today I could. I mean, I know I could today. I'd have a hard time adjusting to two teenage kids." She laughs. "The relationship I have with them is that I'm friends with them more than their mother," she says.

"That's what I've always said to my daughter," I confide, "that, you know, you're not going to be a 'mother' to Sabra, but that's okay. As long as you have a good relationship—whatever form that takes—that's all that's important."

"I feel that I have a good one with them. I love when they come here. I want to do everything for them, I want to give them everything. It's hard for me to go into the role of the mother. I say to them, 'Pick up your stuff,' and 'You have to go to bed at this time.' James watches them a lot. He had a really hard time."

"Is his style is more strict than yours?" I ask.

"I had a hard time dealing with that. Craig came over and he was pissed off about something, and he was stomping around the house and slammed the bedroom door. And James scared me to death and scared Craig. He opened the door and he was so mad he said, 'Nobody is going to talk to her like that, for starters. She is your mother. You have to have some respect. And for another thing, nobody is going to come into this house and slam doors!' And he was furious. And he shut the door very quietly and came out.

"I had so many mixed emotions, like 'How dare you yell at my kid, when it's bad enough I only see him once every couple of weeks! Let him be pissed off at what he's pissed off at because he never shows any emotion.' It was almost like I was relieved that he was actually getting angry at me for something for the first time in his life. I want the kid to tell me how he feels. And then on the other hand, I was so damned proud of him (James) for standing up for me and telling Craig he can't get away with that.

"Then, it was so weird, because Craig, within a half hour, calmed right down. I had never seen him calm down that fast. He used to always be angry and be angry forever. This was obviously because he had been sexually abused and he had a lot of anger in him. He was a very angry kid.

"What an emotional day that was, though. He calmed right down and came right out. And I knew right then and there that this kid was actually going to have respect for James. And James was going to have respect for him."

"So they worked it out in their own way?" I ask.

"But I went totally nuts. I was screaming at James after." James told her, "Marion, you can't spoil them."

"He's 17 years old now. He doesn't want to come to Maine. My mother says, 'You don't spend enough time with him when he's home.' I tell her, 'Ma, when I'm home, he's out the door. He's going to his friends house, he's going to play golf, he's going to play hockey. He's not 10 years old anymore, he's 17. He doesn't want to sit home with his mother and spend the whole afternoon with her. He just doesn't want to.' And that's all right with me. It's not all right with my mother though. She wants us to bond together and spend this time together. I don't know what she expects us to do in this time.

"And then after I think about it, I laugh because we are really close. And we do have a lot of shit to work through, and maybe someday we'll go to counseling and we will get over the hurt and the pain, but right now me and Craig get along great. He talks to me, tells me what he's doing, tells me that he loves me, tells me that he wishes I could be there more and that I could spend more time with him. And then when I get there, he's out the door. But so what? I'm not going to make the kid feel bad cause he wants to go do what he wants to do. I refuse to lay guilt trips on my kids. I try really hard not to." Marion laughs a bit. "I catch myself doing it. My mother is wicked good at it."

We break for tea and I dip into a bowl of candy corn as she lets Spike, their black lab, in for a visit. He goes nutty when Marion lets him in; his tail could knock over a small car. I feed him pieces of the chewy candy while Marion reveals that she was bulimic all during the court trials because she couldn't deal with it and was eventually hospitalized because of it. She felt guilty because she couldn't be there for her children, but she couldn't deal with being with them either. She tells me James is very protective of her but sometimes he goes overboard. He argues with Elisabeth occasionally, if he feels she's being too hard on Marion.

Marion tells me she really doesn't know how she finally made the break from Thomas Connor. She had been away from him for a year, but had begun to drink and drug again. He was able to talk her into going back with him.

"We got a new apartment. My mother was scared to death, she thought I was making a big mistake. But I was just *doing* it! We started fighting immediately. All I remember in that time, the last night I was there—I don't know why I remember this so clearly—he came and picked me up at work. He had been to a party. He was drunk as a skunk. He wanted to go back to another party, and I was totally exhausted and I wanted to go home. He started a big argument with me and became really violent.

"He drove to the party. I didn't even get out of the car. He grabbed me by the head and slammed me against the window. I just thought, 'Oh God, here we go again!' He made me get out of the car on the highway, tried to run me over. I don't know how come I can't remember all the other times, but this night I remember most of it. We got home, he pushed me down the stairs kicking me in the gut, kicking me in the face. His niece was baby-sitting—she was scared to death of him. I loved her. She's my Godchild, and I can't even see her.

"He was screaming at me, but nobody came out. I had a girlfriend that lived across the hall; she never came out. I always thought, 'How come nobody *ever* comes to help me?' I used to think that." Marion's voice sounds weary, drained. She sits round-shouldered in her chair, but she's composed and calm. "Except when we used to live in the other house and Andy was there. He used to beat Thomas up all the time."

Andy once told Marion that he was sexually abused as a child by his grandfather. He said she was the only person that he ever told and that he was fairly sure his other brothers had been abused as well. She feels that he told her to warn her.

"I don't believe, for a second, that Andy was one of them that sexually abused my children," she says straightening up in her chair, squaring her shoulders, her eyes narrowing.

"But I remember laying outside the door—I don't think I could get up—and Sharon, his niece, was underneath the door and she was whispering to me that as soon as Thomas went to sleep she would let me in. That was an awful night because my mother tells me later on that Thomas sexually abused Craig that night.

"I was scared to death to leave because Thomas always told me he would kill me if I left. Always! 'If you ever go with anybody else, I'll kill them, I'll kill you. You'll be nothing! You'll never make it on your own! You'll always go back and live with your Mother! I was really scared to leave and I really, really thought that I'd never be able to do it on my own. I couldn't do it. He told me that so many times, I really believed him."

But Marion did eventually find the courage to leave. She walked away and, literally, never looked back.

"I am really, really grateful for the way my life turned out, in one aspect, that my kids are safe. That's the only way I can close my eyes at night, knowing that my kids are with my parents. And they don't ever have to go with Thomas Connor."

> Ideally, birth parents and grandparents will be able to work together as a team; and in many families, that is the case. If they cannot work together, grandparents must recognize that the grandchildren will still feel a connection to their birth parents that needs to be satisfied.
>
> Honesty must always be maintained regarding birth parents. However, the amount of openness and contact between birth parents and children can vary from family to family depending on the situation. If there is concern about the birth parents' appropriateness with children, then a supervised visitation can be arranged. Supervised visitations can be arranged through a human services agency, mental health professional, or even the courts. Over time, if the supervised visits go well, unsupervised visits and contact can resume. Sometimes even supervised visitation does not go well and can be harmful to the child. If this is the case, all visitation should be suspended until the birth parent can demonstrate appropriate boundaries and behavior.
>
> It is so important to be aware that the needs of the children are constantly evolving and changing. Part of the caregiver's role is to change and adapt to those needs. Meeting the child's need to have positive connection, in some healthy form, to their birth parents is vital to their emotional well-being.

6
What's In a Name?

"The trees ask me,
And the sky,
And the sea asks me
Who am I?

The wind tells me
At nightfall,
And the rain tells me ...

Someone small
Someone small
But a piece
of
it
all."

—Felice Holman, "Who Am I?"

Nana, Grampa, Bubbe, Papa, Mom or Dad? What to choose, and who chooses? Allowing a grandchild his or her identity whole and unblemished is one of the reasons we give them truth and avoid secrecy. Their formative identity is also one of the reasons naming becomes imbued with such powerful significance. What your grandchild calls you, after all, defines your grandchild as well. It establishes a place, expectations, roles and indisputable belonging. It is no small thing.

One of the first questions I asked at the first Grandparents as Parents support group meeting I attended when Sabra was only a few months old was, "What should she call me?" I really didn't expect that anyone would be able to give me a definitive answer, but it was a place I felt comfortable wondering the nagging thought out loud. A few people kindly shared with me what they had worked out, but I left still wondering. Since that time many grandparents have asked me the same question and I have offered this profound insight, "It depends."

We grandparents come into this experience bewildered, with no frame of reference. But, looking back on that first meeting now, I think my uncertainty about what Sabra should call us was ridiculous. We were adopting Sabra, my son Dane was only four years old, they would obviously be brought up as siblings and there is no rational way for each child to have called us something different. My uncertainty, I think, was born out of a hesitancy to close that final door to Tyra. I think that other grandparents hold out for the same kinds of reasons—a thick and binding soup made up of loyalty and hope, love, and denial.

Grandparents wait for their adult children to get their acts together. They wait for them to go into rehab, to come out of rehab, to get an apartment, a job, to begin to show some sense of responsibility, some evidence that they can be parents. Sometimes the waiting works, sometimes it doesn't. When it doesn't, grandparents must begin to make a series of judgment calls. Although virtually all grandparents hope their sons and daughters will become the parents their grandchildren need and deserve. Failing that, other choices must be made. Those choices include "naming," and what grandparents or grandchildren choose depends on myriad variables such as: How old is the grandchild? How old was the child when he or she came to you? Was the child already accustomed to calling you an affectionate name such as Grammy and Grampy? Are the birth parents still a viable part of the child's life? Does the child know them as parents? How long do you expect the child to be with you? And finally, Who is the child's psychological parent?

I think it is essential to look to the grandchild for cues. If they were very young when they came to you, even if you started out as Nana and Grampa or Bubbe and Papa, a typical scenario may surface when the children reach school age: they begin to want someone to call Mommy and Daddy. They want to be like the other kids in this most basic way and may make the shift to calling grandparents "Mom" and "Dad" on their own. I have even seen examples—lots of them—of much older children making that shift as well. They make it because of the overriding longing to have that need fulfilled.

I never actually made a choice. Sabra called me Mama simply because it was a perfectly natural outgrowth of my "mothering" and her role as Dane's "baby sister." I think now that it was utterly thoughtless of me not to realize just how ludicrous, false, and ultimately damaging any other decision made by us would have been, but I can remember well the question ringing in my head at the time, "Am I a mother ... or a grandmother?" My answer now to myself is, "You mother, therefore you are a mother." And ultimately, my answer to other grandparents caring for grandchildren in what appears to be a long-term situation is that children need mommies and daddies and if there is no one else who can fill that role emotionally, physically, or psychologically, then the obligation—the privilege—falls to the caregiving grandparents providing they are in it for the long haul.

One would assume that having once experienced such confused thinking myself, I would be more tolerant of others' confusion. I am not. One of my pet peeves is a frequently asked question regarding biological connections versus family roles. For instance, "Won't it be confusing for Sabra because her brother is really her uncle?" Usually I answer a short and irritable "No." I don't believe that question is ever put to traditional adoptive parents. Would anyone dream of asking, "Won't it be confusing for your adopted child because his sibling is really not related to him in any way?" Of course not, because the unspoken "rules" of traditional adoption are inherently understood by society. Why this doesn't translate to a common sense understanding and acceptance of inter-family arrangements, I will never comprehend.

Here's another one that bothers the beans out of me, "Isn't it confusing to have so many people involved in Sabra's life?" "Excuse me? Haven't you ever heard of divorce?" I would like to shout into their knitted brows, their foggy, questioning faces. "What's the difference?" But instead I say, "The more the merrier," cheerfully, behind clenched teeth.

This is Sabra's life, she has known no other, she is not confused in any way. We have explained, and will continue to elaborate on, her family connections. We are her parents because we parent. She also has birth parents, just like any other adopted child. Sabra loves them too, but they do not parent; she calls them by their names. Fortunately for Sabra—for everyone—those birth parents are an important part of her life, as is the extended family that loves her deeply. Dane is her brother because that is his role, Tasha is her sister because that is her role. Biological designations are practically irrelevant.

There are grandparents that do not agree with me, grandmothers who would vow, "I am not his mother. He *has* a mother!" Clearly then, a realignment of terms would not be in order. Although my first instinct would be to follow the lead of the grandchild, with such entrenched beliefs on the part of a grandparent, there is little room for flexibility or compromise. And comfort levels must remain at the baseline of the grandparents' tolerance for change.

Included in this chapter are examples of what some of the grandparents in this book have chosen to do, or more accurately in most cases, what their grandchildren have chosen for them. Ultimately, a balance between the comfort levels of grandparent and grandchild must be reached in some way. The first couple introduced in this book, the Donaldsons, are called Papa-Pete and Moo-Moo by their preschool grandchildren. Their situation is relatively new and they are still working out the boundaries, both legal and emotional. The boys know and remember their birth parents as Mama and Dada and continue to refer to them in that way. They may drift toward renaming their grandparents as they reach school age, if their birth parents don't develop and maintain strong, positive parenting ties.

The Parks' grandchildren were older when ties to their father were totally severed under horrendous circumstances. Through their long struggle, Ben and Elisabeth remained Nana and Grampa, and Marion retained mother status even though she was not doing any mothering. The Parks worked at maintaining the mother-bond between their grandchildren and Marion, and work at it still, even as Marion works at it herself.

I think the most discomfiting situation presented as an example is that of Laurie and Bob Harris, grandparents featured in chapter 3. Laurie does work at maintaining a long-distance mother-bond between granddaughter and birth mother, but it appears that the real and only psychological parent is Laurie herself. Although I feel somewhat saddened by Laurie's attempts to "correct" her granddaughter when she calls her Mommy, I sympathize with what she is trying to achieve. Hopefully, the child's birth mother will more firmly establish a real bond between herself and her daughter before separating her from her "psychological parent."

It can be very useful to allow children to take the lead as to how they refer to their grandparents. If the children feel comfortable and receive comfort by calling their grandparents Mom and Dad and if the grandparents feel comfortable also, then this can be a perfectly workable arrangement. I would never suggest, however, that grandparents initiate the shift in names. I also have strong reservations about making the change if the plan calls for anything less than long-term custody. If a child is being cared for short-term and the plan is to have them back with their parents, then the terms Grandma and Grandpa and the like are not only very appropriate, but also accurate.

And, most important, clarity is crucial. Clarifying for children is so very important to their overall emotional development. They need to know who all the players are and how long they each will be playing. One of the ways grandparents can foster clarity is through "updates" on the birth parents—where they are, what they're doing, and if there is any movement behind the scenes to reunite the child with his or her birth parent.

No matter what grandchildren decide to call their grandparents, it is essential for the grandparents to be very clear to distinguish themselves from the child's biological parents. While all children need someone to call Mom, most important they need to know who is their biological Mom.

For both the Winetraubs and Randalls, the shift in naming occurred as if on cue when their grandchildren reached nursery-school age. I ask each grandparent, "What does your Grandchild call you?" and here is what they say.

Irene Winetraub explains, "In the beginning when he started to learn to talk and comprehend, the girls would say something like, 'Go ask Bubbe or Papa,' which are the Yiddish terms for grandmother and grandfather. So that's the way he would refer to us, Bubbe and Papa. Whether he knew that meant grandparents, I don't know. And he would call the girls 'Auntie.'

"And then as he became more vocal and more comprehending, and perhaps it had to do with making the connection just around the time of the adoption—I really don't remember—the girls all of a sudden started to say, 'Go ask Mommy and Daddy,' just automatically."

"At his daycare, my husband would come into the room to get him and the other children would say, 'Your daddy's here.' So it was always that we were always there for him as Mommy and Daddy and that was it."

"So it sort of fell into a pattern. When he would introduce his sisters," Irene and Bernie chuckle, "he would say this is my sister Auntie Barbara and my sister Auntie Helen. So that went on for a while, and then on his own, completely on his own, he would say, 'I have two sisters.' He didn't include her (his birth mother). He hasn't included her in a while."

Irene went on to tell me that he did, in fact, remember his birth mother, but it was clear to me that he instinctively sensed that she had a different status than being his sister, even though he wasn't sure what that was.

One of the side effects of grandchildren entering the family in a sibling role with other much older children is sibling rivalry. It is an issue that often catches grandparents off guard. Their own children are usually at least in their teens, many times some are much older, and the question of jealousy never occurs to grandparents until it rears its thorny head. Irene talked about her daughters and how they bonded so strongly with Aaron. "You love him too much!" she pretends to scold them. But she then tells me how sibling rivalry affected her youngest daughter who was in college when Aaron was born. "She was the baby in the house, and all of a sudden," Irene and Bernie look at each other in amusement, "as smart and as old as she was, how many times did we hear, 'Gee, we never could get away with that!' Or, 'You didn't get that for us!' "

Perhaps that previously solid sense of place becomes tremulous for an older sibling, whatever the age, when another sibling horns in. Whatever the reason, it is clear that age does not much temper the prickles of jealousy that sting the older child when a new child, even a grandchild, arrives on the doorstep.

> Most sibling rivalry is normal and to be expected, particularly if the children are somewhat close in age. However, if adult children become overly jealous of grandchildren living with grandparents, there are probably some other issues on the table. Families who have added grandchildren into their homes may be faced with sibling rivalry issues as well as potential issues of the first generation feeling displaced by the second.
>
> If your adult children are making life difficult because of their jealousy, tell them so! They need to hear it and you need to say it. Put a mirror up in front of their face and ask them who is the child and who is the adult? One look in the mirror, for most, gives them a whole new perspective. If this doesn't work, suggest they receive some support. Most important, make sure you still have some time left for them; they need you too.

The Randalls' grown children never demonstrated any visible signs of jealousy over Sara. However, as they begin to have children of their own, the differences in approach that Betsy and Dan have to Sara, as opposed to the other grandchildren, may cause some conflicts down the road, possibly leading to charges of favoritism.

Those differences also inhibit the Randalls from being the indulgent, doting grandparents they would like to be to the other grandchildren they don't see as often because, as Betsy tells it, "Sara lives here. If I allow the other kids to jump off the couch and get into things while they're here, Sara will want to do the same thing and she'll want to do it all the time."

A grandmother once advised me to have a family discussion with grown children as soon as possible, ironing out the details of inheritance and wills. This is excellent advice for the obvious legal reasons, and in addition, will serve to sort out and solidify formally any recent twists in the family tree.

> Grandparents really do need to sit down with their grown children and discuss their feelings and motivations for raising their grandchild. Also it can be very helpful for grandparents to share with their adult children how much they could use their support and their help.

Establishing Sara's particular branch of the Randall family tree happened gradually, over several years. Betsy and Dan started out as Gram and Gramp, but Sara now calls her grandparents Mom and Dad. I ask, "When did the switch to Mom occur?" Betsy tells me about going to pick up Sara from a birthday party a couple of years ago when Sara was just about four years old. All the children were calling out "Your mom's here!" as parents arrived to take them home. When Betsy walked in, Sara took her by the hand and said to the birthday girl, "Come here, come here, I want you to meet my mom!"

During the ride home, Betsy gently questioned Sara about it and she replied, "Everyone else has got a mom." Betsy tells me that because the adoption was underway, she felt secure enough to tell her, "I can be your mom if you want." She went on to say, "And she never, absolutely never, messes up!"

"You mean she never reverts back to Gram and Gramp?" I ask.

"No. If you refer to me as Gram, she'll look at you, but she won't say anything."

Sara found her place, is secure there, and refuses to be shaken down from it by reminders that it was once in question.

Vera Lenox works with families leveled by violence, crime, and incarceration—families whose configuration has altered with the force and destruction of shifting tectonic plates. She fortifies them, helps them to rebuild. Vera feels a powerful commitment and connection to caregiving grandparents, in part because she was once one herself. She is one of millions of grandmothers who offer short-term care to grandchildren whose parents are in trouble or flux. Grandparents have always been there, from time immemorial, to offer a helping hand, a port in a storm, and a leg up. And like so many others, Vera cared for her baby granddaughter while her daughter, a young single mom, was going to school, helping to get her on her feet. She started out as Grandma, and as the little one grew older, became Mama for a short while and then evolved into MeMa. That evolution came about because the child's birth mother, uncomfortable, and maybe a little jealous, with her baby calling someone else Mama, corrected her child. She would say, "No, Grandma is *my* Mama," and the child would reply adamantly, "No! *Me* Ma!"

Arrangements vary with each family. There are no set rules for such personal, intricate negotiations. One family I know well has a grandmother who is Mom, a grandfather who's Papa and a birth father—very much a part of the child's life—who is Dad. When Dad and "Mom" are out with the little girl, heads do turn. Another situation I am familiar with is a family who has custody of a biological nephew. His mother is in and out of mental hospitals, and the boy has been with his "alternate" family for over ten years. He also made the switch to calling his biological aunt and uncle Mom and Dad during his elementary school years. Although the family has tried repeatedly to adopt the boy, his birth mother will not relinquish her rights. This caregiving aunt, a social worker by profession, agrees wholeheartedly that this child's entire identity is at issue and welcomes, embraces the change in naming.

In the following chapter, "Mothers in Prison," we meet Shannon, whose entire family, it seems, calls her grandmother Mama. Children know where the parenting, the mothering, is coming from, and they gravitate to the appropriate names naturally.

Margaret Walker-Jackson's granddaughters also call her Mommy. It's a little startling to hear this coming from a four-year-old, directed to a white-haired woman in her sixties. But there it is, the elemental need and pull to establishing that basic linkage to place.

The resourcefulness of children is awe-inspiring. Left to their own devices, they will affirm their own identity for themselves, as long as no outside forces impose on them. And just like Goldilocks trying out bowls of porridge, the size of chairs, and the softness of bedding, sorting out where her true comfort level lies, the child finally comes home to the inner conviction, You are the parent, I am the child, this is where I belong—everything is just right.

When all is said and done, when the dust settles—and it will—all children need to know who their birth parents are. So, Mom or Dad, Grandma or Grandpa, it is really up to your grandchild and you. However, whatever you are called, make sure you convey the truth and make sure any shift in "naming" supports the best interest of the child.

7

Mothers in Prison

"...the woman raising seven children.
there are many kinds of courage & i
don't have them all.
we're all in this together."
—ALTA, "Theme and Variations"

Maybe you think this chapter shouldn't be a part of this book, that mothers in prison are only a tiny minority of people after all. I wondered about that too. But in the end, I decided that incarcerated mothers provide a condensed version—distilled down to the grit—of the many problems grandmothers, mothers, women, and children sometimes face. In their microcosm, all the inequities are made sharp and the tragedies become all too clear.

Shannon is a 29-year-old African-American woman. About eight years ago, Shannon's boyfriend Jose, after having inflicted yet another brutal beating on her in which she was punched, kicked, hit on the head with a bottle, and dragged through the streets, promised that he'd come back to kill her. When he was gone, she took his gun out of the bureau drawer where he kept it and hid it under the mattress so he couldn't find it. Later when he came after her and began to beat and threaten her once again, she pulled it out and shot him. Then she called the police to turn herself in. Shannon was pregnant at the time. She was so badly beaten, scraped and torn that her knee caps were exposed. Nevertheless, facing a second degree murder conviction, she pled guilty to manslaughter instead. She served six years in MCI Framingham for killing her batterer.

Shannon is about five feet two in her slippered feet. She has a pronounced overbite which gives her a permanent, seductive pout. Her hair is short I think; it's hard to tell because she has it tucked up into a denim cap. She's wearing jeans, a soft flannel shirt in a bright turquoise color, and a jangle of silver bracelets and rings. In her ears are tiny, gold crosses. Her nails are squared at the tips, frosted white and long, so long that she holds her fingers apart and tipped up to make room for them But why does she remind me so of a boy, an adolescent boy, sort of tough and sort of sweet, unfinished?

She has a deep husky voice and averts her eyes sometimes as she talks. She sits down in a rocking chair across from me and grabs a big, royal blue pillow off her bed. Shannon lays it across her knees—a soft wall between us—and uses it for the next two hours during the interview to pat, to hug, to stroke, to hit, and to hang on to. I think she is sincere and straightforward. I think she is brave.

"I have two children," she begins. "My son, he eventually went into a foster home, and my grandmother kept my daughter. She ended up going into a residential home, where she's at now, because it started getting rough for my grandmother. Because not only is she raising mine, but she's also raising my aunt's children and my uncle's children. She has five children now at home.

"I think it's better if you talk to her, because it's been hell for her raising children that are HIV. You know what I'm saying? And running around taking this one to the hospital, that one to the hospital, you know, trying to make ends meet. It's been real rough."

Then she stops. She tells me she doesn't want to talk about the death of her boyfriend, or her trial, or her conviction. I tell her that I want her to talk about whatever she wants to talk about. I see the wariness in her; she's beginning to balk. She slides her eyes to the right and left as if looking for an exit. I ask her, gently, what she'd like to talk about.

"I can talk about what it's like being in prison, and being away from your children, and how substance abuse affects you, my children being taken away from me, and then my grandmother raising them, conflicts, and the bureaucracy, the injustices.

"And it was rough being in prison away from your children because your head starts to become clear; you're not on any type of drugs or anything. The women in prison, *they* love their children." She says this in such a plaintive way. "But their lives are uncontrollable, you know. They're strung out. There is very little resources in the prison system as far as trying to help us get our lives together and, you know, reunite us back with our children.

"The way I was able to get reunited back with my children was when I went to MCI Lancaster, because they have the Trailer Program there. That's a prerelease center."

"You went from Framingham to Lancaster?" I ask.

"Mm-hmm. After five years I went to Lancaster. And the Trailer Program is where, they are like regular trailers and they are set up just like home on the inside, and you're able to spend a weekend or up to two weeks in the trailer and you have your kitchen and everything. The only time it's supervised is like when they do the count, they just come down to make sure you're okay or whatever. And it helps women to get reunited with their children and build their bond back with their children."

The room we're in is pleasant, sunny, and crammed to capacity with a bed, bureau, computer, and a couple of chairs. Resting on the bureau, behind a lighted candle, is a small, framed photo of a young man. I wonder if it's Jose, but I don't dare ask. On the wall there are posters of Malcolm X, Elijah Muhammad, and Jesus. I tell Shannon she looks so young. Her youthfulness took me by surprise when I first saw her standing in the doorway of the halfway house to greet me.

When I called Shannon to arrange for this meeting and she told me she lived in Roxbury, my heart shriveled. I tried limply to change the meeting to a different location, but it didn't work. Roxbury is the roughest part of Boston—crime and drugs, drive-by shootings, car jacking, and gang banging are all daily activities of, and horrors for, the people that live there.

She told me, "It's behind Sam's tavern. You can't miss it, the other houses on the street are boarded up." I wanted to ask, "Will I be safe?" I wanted to tell her, "I'm white," although I was fairly sure she knew. Of course, I didn't say any of that, but my stomach churned with lily-white fear, and long-buried bias began to seep from my pores, hot sweat.

A neighbor happened to call after I hung up with Shannon, and I began to babble on uncontrollably about my conversation with her. "She tells me to drive down Martin Luther King Avenue, past Malcolm X Park!" I related shrilly. And then, "What am I saying?" I was unhinged by misgivings, made stupid by apprehension.

My daughter Tasha brought me up short with a disparaging look, exasperated with my hand wringing. "It's daytime, you'll be fine." High school football games were often played in Roxbury, she told me, and there was never a problem. She is young and fearless; she was disgusted with me.

I tucked my cowardly head, turtle-like, back into my liberal shell and peered out with hooded, skittish eyes as I drove off. I stopped short of driving into Roxbury though. I left my car what I considered a safe distance away at a garage near Northeastern University and took a cab the rest of the way. My cabby was nice, and had trouble finding the street. He was concerned when we finally arrived and told me he would wait until I got in. I wanted to hug him, kiss him, but I gave him a tip instead.

The newly restored, peach and cream, gingerbread-trimmed halfway house looked as pretty as a Disneyland ride between two burnt-out, bombed-out, boarded-up wrecks and a hangdog tavern called Sam's. It appeared as though it might have been sucked up by a twister from the land of Oz and dropped there by mistake. I was relieved to see Shannon standing in the doorway waving me in, smiling like a young girl and looking friendly.

I ask her how old she was when she first went into prison.

"My first time going in there I was, what? Fifteen?" she tells me. "I lied about my age."

"Oh," I say, taken aback. What I meant to ask was how old she was when she went in for killing her batterer, I never thought that she may have been there before. I stammer a little and finally get out, "What were you ... ?"

"Prostitution," she answers quickly, flatly.

I am embarrassed by the gulf between us. My middle-aged-white-woman-from-the-suburbs self trying to connect with this young black woman who has struggled with demons I can only imagine. And here I sit asking her to give me a piece of herself. Why should she? If I were her, I'd want to slap my face. But Shannon is giving and I guess forgiving. And she continues on in her direct way.

"I was there about three months. And then I didn't go back until what happened with me in '89 (her conviction for manslaughter). I went in for eight months. I was pregnant with my son and they gave me three weeks stay of execution and I had my son. I left my son when he was like a week old, so I'm just getting to know who he is now. I wrote him letters and sent him cards. The foster home that he's in, that's like my second family. They sent me his first drawings, pictures, and things like that. They let him know that *I* was his mother, because it was an open adoption and everything."

"His foster parents adopted him?" I ask.

"Mm-hmm. But I see him anytime I want. He was here yesterday. It's real hard. It's real overwhelming for me because he calls me Mommy and everything, but yet I don't *feel* like his mother. Because I was stripped away from him and, you know, having somebody else raise your children, that's just hard. That's like having my grandmother raise my daughter was hard. You know because, it would be like I would ask her to do one thing and she'd say, 'Well, I'm the guardian here, I have to do it this way.' "

"It was hard on my grandmother. My grandmother raised three generations. And all due to substance abuse. She's getting old now, she's tired."

"How old is she?" I ask.

"My grandmother's in her seventies."

"And she still has children. Did you say she has five? How old are they?" I ask.

"Seven months ... ," Shannon begins, and I roll my eyes reflexively in horror, remembering the physical demands of that age.

"I know," she says to me in acknowledgment.

"Seven months to nine," she finishes.

"And what help does she get?" I ask.

"None. None whatsoever, and I tell her, 'Mommy, you need to get some help' She gets AFDC and she gets SSI for some of the kids. And that's it. And her church might donate her stuff, like during the holidays they'll send clothes, turkey, and food. And CAP (Children's AIDS Program) which has a (day-care) program for children that are HIV, that has been involved with my family for a while because of my cousin. They have helped my grandmother with a lot because my cousin was going to CAP, but she got too old to stay there, but they still keep in contact. But that's all the help she gets."

"Are there any groups that give your grandmother respite care so that she can take a break?" I ask although I really know the answer.

"No. My grandmother is up constantly. And it scares me, it really does, because sometimes I think she's going to lay down and just don't wake up. When I first got out of prison, I remember sitting in the kitchen, and she went to go bend over and she had gotten these sharp pains, had the baby on this side, bent down to pick up something, and the sharp pains just shot up through her, and we had to rush her to the hospital. She's just worn out from all this, and she doesn't get no help. We go up there and try to help her out. Me and my family members do the best that we can. But then, my grandmother is real stubborn." Shannon says this affectionately, shaking her head. "She's a West Indian woman and it's like, 'Don't worry about me, I can handle this. The Lord put me to here take care of these children, and I'll take care of them.' And she has her masters and she has all types of degrees and we call her the professional babysitter." Shannon laughs out loud.

"So her church organization gives her some help. What church is that?" I ask.

"Holy Tabernacle. She needs a break. A lot of my family members think she should give the children up."

"For her sake?" I ask, and Shannon nods yes, rocking silently in her chair, clutching her pillow.

"And my grandmother is like, she's tired of seeing all her grandchildren being placed in foster homes and stuff, and if she can prevent that from happening she's not going to see them go into foster homes."

Shannon fills me in on some details. Her sentence was eight to fifteen years, she was incarcerated for six before she was released for early parole. Shannon's mother is now dead from "complications of drug abuse." Shannon was bounced around to several foster homes as a child. DSS would not allow her to live with her grandmother because "my mother would keep coming around."

> One of the tools that can be used for working through unresolved issues involving a parent who has passed away is journal writing. Keeping a journal, writing down thoughts, feelings, and what they wished they could have said while their parent was alive, is a helpful tool for some to begin to come to terms with a troubled past.

"That's how the crazy cycle started anyways. My mother was in a body cast for two years, and her addiction started with legal drugs, and then she turned to substance on the street. And so we were taken from my mother—I have seven brothers and sisters—and placed in various foster homes. Some of them were placed for adoption. I kept on running back and forth to my grandmother's, running away from the foster homes. There was a lot of things that were happening to me in foster homes. And eventually they gave custody to my grandmother. By then I was 12 years old."

> Foster care is a horribly underfunded, understaffed, underprioritized system. Because of the overwhelming numbers of children in need, the num-

bers of children needing temporary care far out-number the amount of safe, reliable homes. The need for foster families is so great, standards are frequently lowered with the hopes that with social service support and guidance, the foster family will be at least adequate. Having had the opportunity to be involved with the system as a foster parent, the question I found myself constantly asking was, "Of the many foster parents I have met, are there any whom I would feel comfortable about raising my children, even short-term?" The answer was always, no.

Shannon represents another victim of the foster care system, a system that, at one time, directed foster care parents, "Don't let the child get attached to you." Thus, children were constantly moved so that an attachment did not take place. Foster care professionals now recognize that attachments for children are not only important, but necessary for the child's emotional well-being. Shannon's emotional well-being diminished with each move, each disappointment.

Although Shannon has been a victim, she is also a survivor. Anyone who has gone through such a painful and abusive childhood will need a great deal of counseling and support. Survivors need to learn to recognize that they are good people with much potential.

"But by then I had already turned to the streets. I was on the streets at the age of 11. Prostitution, you name it, I was doing it. I rebelled against my grandmother. She tried, she tried to instill the proper morals and everything in me, but I was just so angry about the way things were, and I felt that everything was *my* fault ... because of what was happening to my mother and everything else ... me and my brothers and sisters being separated. I would run, run, run."

> So many children, regardless of age, gender, or background, feel deeply responsible for the problems that their parents or family have. Most children are unable to see themselves as victims, instead they see themselves as problems. So many children like Shannon grow up believing they are not good enough, not capable enough, not deserving of love and affection. This may pave the way for an abusive relationship later in life.

"Eventually, I came back home (to her grandmother's). I went back to school. Ended up getting pregnant with my daughter. My grandmother took custody of my daughter because I was still a minor." She tells me with her head hanging down. The rocking chair creaks slowly, and she is silent for a while.

I know what happened to Shannon in foster care because I've seen the

Academy Award-winning documentary, "Defending Our Lives," about eight women incarcerated at MCI Framingham for killing their batterers. Shannon was one of those women. She doesn't want to discuss it now, but she tells it in the documentary, while tears rain down her face and slide into her mouth, "I come from an abusive background. I always thought it was okay to accept this abuse, you know, as a child." Her head cast down low, chin to chest, heavy with grief, burdened with sorrow, just as it is now.

Fully 100 percent of women incarcerated at MCI Framingham have been either abused physically or sexually as a child, raped, battered, or forced into prostitution. Women generally commit nonviolent crimes against property. They face a gender-biased judiciary when they come to trial and when they do fall out of stereotype and commit violent crimes such as the one Shannon committed, they are sentenced more harshly then men. Women are convicted of crimes that men never serve time for, like prostitution. Because there are so few women's prisons, they are remanded to centralized, overcrowded facilities far from home that make it nearly impossible to have contact with legal counsel, family or, most important, their children, and they are detained longer and have longer probationary periods than men. For women like Shannon, incarceration is just another stop on the endless road of victimization. And because most women in prison are single mothers, their children inherit the same potential route and destination.

A few of the more fortunate inmates have the benefit of family members to care for their children while they are incarcerated. But DSS is mandated to place the children of inmates under the state's care and jurisdiction, for adoption after two years. They are supposed to take the length of an inmate's sentence into careful consideration, but that doesn't always happen. They are supposed to notify the women when their children are placed in the adoption pool and counsel them, but that doesn't always happen either. Shannon was lucky to have her grandmother and she knows it.

To say that it's been terribly difficult for Shannon's grandmother is a gross understatement. After a while, Shannon's daughter started rebelling, and the grandmother decided to place her into a residential facility for teens.

"She comes home on weekends, holidays, for doctor appointments," Shannon tells me, shaking her head. "It's like a crazy cycle, crazy."

Shannon's grandmother relies heavily on her bishop's counsel, but Shannon urges her to seek outside help as well. "My grandmother does not believe in nothing that we believe in; things that might have saved our lives—you know what I'm saying—things that were helpful in our lives. My grandmother is strictly church. 'The Lord will save everything.' And I tell her, 'You know, God works through people. You've got to get some help for yourself.' There are times when she gets real stressed out. Sometimes I might call and I'll say to her, 'What're you doing?' And she'll say, 'I'm so tired.' And she'll be laying in the bed and all you can hear are the babies."

"HIV babies—they must be so demanding and so needy," I say.

"When my grandmother brought my little cousin home from the hospital, it was just the saddest thing. A baby that's kickin' off of heroine and cocaine, plus on methadone. In so much pain ... it was like ... oh my God! And I remember we used to all just cry and cry, and my grandmother would be like, 'Listen, don't worry about it. Everything's going to be all right.' That's when HIV just came, they really started talking about it and stuff. She's all right though, the baby's all right. She's not no baby, she's a big girl."

"So your Grandmother took an HIV baby home from the hospital and raised her up to be nine years old," I say with admiration, "All by herself."

"All the babies that my grandmother raised, just about ... only mine and one other, they are the only ones that weren't drug addicted. I was smoking reefer and drinking beer, but when I got pregnant with my daughter, I stopped everything. All the rest of the kids my grandmother brought home, they were crack babies, heroine babies."

"And she raised them all, on her own," I confirm.

"Me and my oldest brother, we weren't drug-addicted babies. But years later, the rest of them were drug addicted. And my mother couldn't care for them and we got put in foster homes."

"So what help do you get when you're raising a drug-addicted baby?" I ask. "Is there any organization—?

"No. No." Shannon gives me a look like I'm from another planet and I have to laugh. "No one helps you. The only help you get is in the hospital when they got all the tubes in the baby, and then they're withdrawing them and stuff. But then they come home, they've still got the shakes, they cry, they shit all over the place, you know what I'm saying. Nobody helps you." She mutters bitterly.

Shannon calls her grandmother Mommy. "She always has a house full of grandkids, and all of them call her Mommy. She only has a four-room apartment, but it's always been like that where all her grandkids always came to her." Shannon is the oldest grandchild.

Shannon confides that she is writing her own book about her experiences. I notice a note resting on her computer that reads, "Who I was, Who I am, Who I want to be." I ask her about it and she says, "I'm working my steps. I go to AA. My counselor gave me those three things and I'm supposed to write 15 pages on each one. And I've only gotten to, 'Who I *was*.' That's it!" She laughs.

"Going through the Twelve Steps is real hard, because you have to take it a little bit at a time. And then I had somebody tell me, 'Well, just think of the small things that happened in your life.' And I'm like, 'Everything was *tragic*! Please!' " She harumphs. "I cannot sit up here and tell you that I am going to take small things when there was never nothing small that happened in my life. Everything was major. It was major and it was a tragedy."

"For the first two years (of her daughter's life), my grandmother showed me how to do some mothering. And I wasn't using 'it.' And then when I started using, it came to a point when I was neglecting myself and my kid. And then when you go to jail you realize that the smallest things mean so much to you. Some people do, some people don't. You've really got to hit your rock bottom to realize how much you love your children, how much you miss your children, and how much you want to see them. I mean, that is like the *hardest* thing for women in prison. You know because you have this system that just doesn't care about anything. You're not supposed to show your emotions, or you're not supposed to show how you're feeling."

She talks about some of the organizations that come to the prison to help the women—groups like "Aid to Incarcerated Mothers," "Social Justice for Women," and "People to People." The last two programs have been "booted" from MCI Framingham recently.

Shannon says that when DSS places the children of inmates up for adoption, those organizations would "give you support around that because a lot of the women would have hard times."

"Hard times?" I question, not quite sure which hard times she's talking about.

"As far as giving your children up. That's hard to do! That's ... that's *real* hard to do. And some women, they did it because they didn't have no place else for their children to go. Some of them, they just didn't have no choice, because they would come back and forth through the prison system. It became a revolving door for some of them."

She tells me that Aid to Incarcerated Mothers provides help and support to women inmates with children. "If your children were from out of state, they would fly your children in, put them up, and have your children come to see you every day. Like if your children were here for a week, they'd come up every day of the week. And they gave us (mothers and children) Christmas parties and gifts for our children and Halloween parties. They were just there, you know, for everybody. And I think that program there kept us *sane*. If it wasn't for Aid to Incarcerated Mothers, I don't know what would have happened to me." Shannon says that Social Justice for Women provided parenting, and self-help groups.

Women's needs in prison center primarily around children and family issues; men, who are far more litigious and aggressive—and successful— regarding their needs and demands, have issues that center mainly around their personal comfort. Men and women both require drug counseling and rehabilitation, but there are fewer programs for women, the lack of which impacts directly on their children when they are finally released.

I ask if she knows why some of the programs aren't there anymore. She shakes her head no. "It's just like they started coming in and snatching all the programs out.

"It's pitiful!" she relates in a disgusted tone. "There should be other alternatives for women with children, you know, because when women go to prison, most of the times they don't have nobody to take care of them. Men go to prison, they have women at home. If they don't have a woman to take care of them, their cellmate will end up hookin 'em up with another woman, you know what I'm saying? That's how it happens. So men always ... they have women that come see them and take care of them and stuff. We don't. We end up losing our children in the process, there's no one there to support us, and hoping on the system to give us the proper programs for us to go to, and that gets taken away from us. When they sentence us, they also convict our children."

I ask her what she would say to another incarcerated mother if she could.

"It's never too late to change. Although it's hard. I've been through the wringer. I've prostituted, I stole, I did whatever it took to get my fix, what- ever it took for me to survive ... sleep in a motel for the night, but that would be my home just for the night, but I knew I would have to go out and get more money to find that second home and to get that fix. But you know, I mean, for me I would say that what saved me is connecting with the right people. I go to Dimock Community Health Center for my treatment, and dealing with Aid to Incarcerated Mothers, and just getting involved in the community's different organizations. I go to my women's group on Sunday."

I encourage Shannon to tell me about her women's group.

"Women come from all over to this meeting—Boston, Springfield, Lowell, sometimes New York."

"Women who have been drug abusers?" I ask.

"Some women have abused, have *been* abused, prostitution—you name it, it's there. We're all in recovery. Women of all colors, and it's a very supportive and powerful group."

"So you empower each other," I confirm.

"Yeah, we empower each other. And that's what's important. It's about change. Because when I was in prison, I would always see women coming back and forth. And that's just like the cycle of violence. The people ask us why we continue to go back and forth into these relationships. Because we know nothing different. And I'd say, 'Why do these women keep coming back and forth?' Because they know nothing different. If there were more people out there to show them a way to do right and to do different, you know, more programs like the house I'm in here. This is for seven homeless women who are trying to reunify with their children. And I came here because I knew I needed structure in my life. And I knew I couldn't go back out on the streets because the streets are going to kill me. So I had a choice, either it was going to be them streets or me getting my life together. Just because I did them six years, that didn't mean my life was together, you know? I still had a lot of old behaviors and I knew I needed some type of structure, counseling, and to be around people who were in recovery and people that I knew that could help me to empower myself. And that's what I did.

"It's hard to get out of that cycle, because I was trapped in it for a long time. And sometimes I mentally get trapped in it and I might have to pick up the phone and talk to somebody. Because sometimes I feel like, what is my purpose of doing what I am doing? Why do I have to wait for housing? If I go out there and make some fast money, I can get housing. You know what I'm saying? I can go get me my own house and not have to worry about anybody telling me, 'Well, you're number 66 on the waiting list.' I know how to get that money real quick, but it's not about that today. It's about me saving my ass."

"I used to say to a lot of the women who came through Framingham, 'Why do you keep coming back here? What is here that you *like*?' I used to get real angry with them. I'd say, 'Jesus! If they'd just give me a chance ... just give me a chance.' But see, what I did when I was in Framingham ... I had a rough time at Framingham, but years later I started to realize that I could not continue to be angry and bitter. Because we do become angry and bitter. I had to connect with the women that were coming from outside the communities into the prison that were willing to help us. And that's what I did, I connected with them women and they connected me with different organizations out here, and that's why I am able to stand on my feet and go on. It's about women connecting with women.

"I mean, we can be our greatest inspiration, you know. We don't have to connect with men today, we need to be able to empower ourselves. I remember years ago, you couldn't get me to talk to a woman. You know what I'm sayin'? Because they were snakes, and they wanted my man," She laughs. "You know how we think crazy and stuff, right? But today, I have women call me all the time just to tell me that they love me. And not because they might want something from me, it's just because they love me and that gives me the motive to move on. And when I'm feeling bad, I can pick up the phone and say, 'Listen, I need to talk, sit up if you in the bed, sit up and listen to me because I need to talk.' So that's what I do for me, and I see a lot of other women doing it that come from the same places I come from. They've been to Framingham, some of them have been to the Fed's joints and they've turned their lives around. What I do is I look at other people's situations and realize that my pain is not unique. My pain is not unique because there's other people that are suffering just like I am, maybe worse than I am. And I look at their situations and say that I am more fortunate than this person so let me reach out to this person and give them what I have to offer. My connections, my connections are your connections. And that's what I do. I love fellowshipping with women. We have brunches here and just tell the women, 'Come on over.' We talk, recovery, recovery, our children, making connections, and we advocate for each other, we advocate for each other. It's about everything—children, relationships, not just with men but with our family, and how some of us had to pull away from our family because there are active people in our family."

"There's what?" I ask stupidly.

"*Active* people, people that are using. And like me, I had to pull away from some of my family because I can't be around them. And like I said, I've got to save my ass. Tomorrow I celebrate seven years clean time. And you know any given day that can be snatched away from me. If I choose to be around people that are active, I become vulnerable, and I end up picking up. That's not what I want to do. I want my children in my life and try to break the cycle in my family. I don't want my children to become a product of the system. They have been for a little while, but right now I'm working on that. I don't want my grandmother having to raise my children, I want to take care of my children."

"So that's your goal?" I ask.

"That's my goal. We go to family counseling together. For the first time, DSS is on my side. God is like really moving in my life."

Shannon believes the residential program that her daughter attends on weekdays is, "basically saving her life. We're in Roxbury. I love Roxbury, I grew up here, but you hear about it every day—teenage homicides, crime, teen pregnancy—it's rising rapidly. At first I was angry when my grandmother put her in the residential school, but today I am grateful for it, because the school she was going to, it wasn't about education. It was more or less about who's bringing the drugs in and who's bringing the guns. Young kids her age getting shot down. So basically my grandmother placed her there so she wouldn't get caught up. She's an honor roll student, she's got a good head on her shoulders, very outspoken. She's able to explore life. Things that she's doing there she wouldn't be doing here because of how screwed up the school system is here in Boston.

"She goes skiing, she goes outdoor adventuring, she goes skydiving," Shannon tells me smiling. "And when she tells me these things, it makes me feel so good that she's able to do these things, because I know damn well she wouldn't be able to do these things here. Cause they're not thinking about that here, they're not thinking about educating our kids, that's the least thing on their minds. It's about guns, who's using, who's selling, who's pregnant, and I don't want that to happen to my baby. I don't. I'm trying to break this cycle—this insanity. I'm really trying to break it."

Whenever I think of Shannon, I am reminded of a line in author Maya Angelou's book, *Wouldn't Take Nothing for My Journey Now*. In it, Angelou tells about the grandmother who raised her and who, recalling a time when as a young woman she was faced with difficult choices, said, "I looked up the road I was going and back the way I come, and since I wasn't satisfied, I decided to step off the road, and cut me a new path."[1]

> Of all the people one may need to forgive, often the most difficult to forgive is oneself. We need to let ourselves off the hook for decisions and consequences in our lives.
>
> To overcome the struggles of the memories and challenges faced by those who have come through traumatic childhoods, it is essential to see yourself in a new light. Like Shannon, you must see yourself as a survivor.

8
Guardianship— Adoption— Letting Go

"... But there is no erasing this:
the central memory of what we are
to one another, the grove of ritual.
I have set my seal upon you."
                    —Robin Morgan, "The Network of the
                    Imaginary Mother 4 The Child"

The voice on the phone line is incongruously cool, and dry as fallen leaves while saying, "I am in a horrible situation." She found my name and number through the grapevine of grandparents involved in this issue and called; one of many calls I receive—we all receive. Calls from grandparents, predominantly grandmothers, looking for information, for direction, some-

165

times just wanting to tell someone their story. I ask this grandmother to tell me hers.

Ever so calmly, she tells me that she had raised her granddaughter for eight years, since infancy, and now the birth mother, her daughter, wants her back. Her daughter is going to court with "her high-powered lawyers" to dissolve the eight-year-old Permanent Custody decree. Everyone this grandmother spoke with—every lawyer, every social worker, every counselor—shook their heads and told her there was little that could be done to stop the tide. She asks me for advice, a good lawyer's name, and encouragement.

I give her the name of a good lawyer, but I cannot encourage her, and this is the advice I offer.

"You will want to try," I sympathize, "but when it becomes clear you cannot retain custody, step back." There was silence on the other end of the line. I wait for a response and think, of course you will want to fight for your granddaughter, rail against the system, argue for sanity. But it won't work, and when it starts to look like the sun will not rise that day, and you can feel the empty spaces in your heart elbowing for more room, and the bonds you wound so tightly are slipping away like cobwebs on the wind, step away. Step away from the wall and go around and come back at a different angle. Gather your energy, pick up what's left of your heart off the floor, and begin again.

Still, there is silence. I implore, "Look at the larger picture. Put your energy into preserving the bond between you and your granddaughter and keeping your family intact at all cost. Work toward mediation, compromise, and healing. Plead the case that you are the child's psychological parent, that you have her best interests at heart, and that all you want to do is share in her life. Keep the lines of communication open between you and your daughter." Hide your anger, I think to myself, pocket your disappointment, fold away your pain. "Don't rile the birth mother, don't push the judge. Try to patch together a workable arrangement that will include you in your granddaughter's life."

The grandmother says she understands, but worries that because the daughter is now married, she could prevent her from seeing the child at all, ever. She's right of course, that could easily happen. I coax her again, "Try to make some sort of peace with your daughter for your granddaughter's sake."

"But my granddaughter doesn't want to go with her mother," she tells me, and my heart sinks, my stomach turns. I think of "Baby Jessica," "Baby Richard," and the judiciary that considers the best interests of the child "irrelevant" in custody disputes of this nature. "Work hard," I tell her, "very hard, at making the transition for your granddaughter as smooth as possible, for her sake. Make it a priority, make it your new goal."

Finally, I have to ask her—I shouldn't, I know, but I do. "Why didn't you adopt her when you had the chance?"

"Because I didn't think I had to. I didn't think she would ever want her back. I never believed she would fight to get her back after all these years!" Her voice leaves its even plane and rises with frantic energy. I feel guilty about asking.

I recognize the familiar train of thought—the "grandparent drift," the "Don't-rock-the-boat" syndrome, the "I don't want to muddy the waters" philosophy. I used to become impatient with grandparents at support group meetings who expressed variations of those themes. Sometimes I would ask them—bait them really, it wasn't nice of me, "What happens when Daughter X or Son-in-law Y comes back between rehabs and wants to take your grandchild to live in a tent at a nazi-biker, free-love commune in Alaska?" That usually elicited some laughter, but there was a grain of gritty, scary truth in that dumb joke. Just enough grit, I hoped, to force a kernel of recognition to grow, one that might nag at them periodically like a pebble in a shoe and wake them up to the hard potential for disaster before them. While not perfect, as recent much-publicized adoption dissolutions have shown, an adoption is much less likely to be disrupted than a guardianship.

Permanency, stability, security—these are the reasons grandparents march through courts in droves, costly attorneys in tow, to win the documents that will keep their grandchildren safe, if only for a little while. Grandparents frequently start off with a temporary guardianship, normally granted for a 90-day period and then reassessed by the court. If situations with birth parents don't improve, grandparents may move on to permanent guardianship in which the courts grant sole legal authority for the child until and unless the birth parent feels they can prove the case to the court that they are now capable of parenting. And sometimes grandparents choose to adopt.

We adopted because we believed that Sabra deserved a mommy and a daddy to be there for her then, now, and always. She is part of us. Nothing can change that. But we wanted her place in the family to be firmly secured, inviolable. We wanted her to always feel it to her core, to never feel tentative or vulnerable. We planted her roots as deeply as we could.

Economics plays a major role in determining whether or not grandparents adopt. Grandparents whose grandchildren are in the social service system may receive foster care payments (if they qualify as foster care parents) and services such as day-care, health care, educational grants, and clothing allowances. But they must relinquish control of the children to DSS in the bargain, a prospect which makes grandparents shudder and is usually avoided by them at all costs. Grandparents who have legal guardianship and whose grandchildren are not under the foster care umbrella may qualify for AFDC (Aid for Families with Dependent Children) but generally at a rate which is approximately one-third of what is available to foster care parents. In addition, there is little or no access to day-care, health care, or educational grants.

Once a grandparent adopts a child who has never been in the "system," the state washes its boney bureaucratic hands of the arrangement altogether, and intergenerational families are on their own—fixed incomes and all.

The most emotionally fragile children, the ones whose lives have been in constant upheaval or torment, the ones most in need of a permanent, stable, and loving home, are often the ones whose grandparents cannot afford to give up welfare benefits nor pursue an adoption through the courts. When families must weigh basic, gut-level needs such as having a roof over your head and food in your stomach, against the slightly more lofty goals of permanency and security, guess which wins. Once more grandparents are left with nothing more than a choice between one pain or another, in this case, the lack of economic security versus the absence of emotional stability.

Margaret Walker-Jackson

Margaret Walker-Jackson is a woman who has been through it all and has survived with grace and style. She has come full circle with custody arrangements for her grandchildren, from informal physical custody, to temporary legal guardianship, to permanent legal guardianship and now toward adoption. She talks about a grandmother in her support group raising six grandchildren and says, "I'm sure she doesn't want to adopt." The unspoken reason is, of course, financial. Margaret's finances are tenuous, meager, but she has come to a place in her life where she wants, more than anything else, to give her granddaughters that one final precious gift, security—a legacy of love.

Margaret has all the "Ws" covered; she's wise, warm, and witty. I liked her instantly when we first met at the State House a year ago. She is another member of the Grandparent Support Group Network panel that meets monthly trying to rally other support groups, connect them with local councils on aging, keep abreast of and support favorable legislation, and try to find and, in some cases, pull together new services for grandparents such as respite care, wellness conferences, and stress management seminars. Sometimes there is even time to offer one another much-needed support and sharing. We have come to be friends and I look forward to seeing them all.

Margaret has a dignified demeanor and an easy laugh, full and throaty. Her white hair reminds me of milkweed seeds that puff out from dried pods in autumn, spikey-soft; it frames her walnut-brown face like a halo. She is partial to very fancy, drop earrings.

I've learned a few other things about Margaret over the last year. I know she has six children, 14 grandchildren (including the two she is raising), and three great-grandchildren. I know that she has cared for both her 13-year-old granddaughter, Tamika and her four-year-old granddaughter, Charlotte, since they were babies. I know she is 68 years old.

She has agreed to meet me at the Dorchester Square Health Center where she works, to tell me more.

The Health Center sits like an old queen on the corner of a busy, inner-city intersection. Thick, Doric columns flank heavy, carved oak doors at the front of the red brick former library. Mullioned, gable windows trimmed in cream reach out from all corners giving a faceted, hexagonal impression. Her neighbors are a cubbyhole pizza joint, a dingy drug store, and a flat-topped beauty parlor; she looks out of place, out of time here. The building takes up the whole small corner, and I wind up circling and circling the little oasis for a place to land.

I walk up the wide, curved back stairway and meet Margaret who tries to scare up a quiet room so we can talk. The place is bustling. People are in noisy meetings around large, vintage, wooden tables, grouped around desks talking privately, marching through corridors carrying manila folders. A few are toiling alone bent over typewriters or a stack of papers. There is an incongruous mixing here of Formica and chrome, with wainscoting and old oak. She finally finds a tiny cubicle with a very high ceiling; one of those mullioned windows is perched way at the top. Its a tease; you can see the bright blue sky and the cotton ball clouds that roll by, but you can't get a breath of fresh air to save your life.

I notice a fairly comfortable-looking upholstered office chair by the lone table in the room and plunk down in it. Too late I realize the only other chairs available are chrome and electric-blue vinyl, straight-backed things. I curse myself inwardly and quickly try to switch my chair for the one in which Margaret is about to sit, but she will have none of it; she turns me down flat.

Margaret sinks heavily into her chair, rests her elbow on the table beside her and leans her cheek against her hand—a weary gesture. Her hands are large with long, thin fingers—pianist's hands. I notice that her light brown eyes have a corona of blue—mysterious and exotic—and that she is wearing snazzy, dangle earrings; blue beads dip and swing alongside silver moons and stars. I admire her blouse, a forest print, brown with leaves and ferns, also very exotic. It suits her.

She speaks softly and low, so I turn my recorder up to the max and listen carefully as she begins slowly.

"My 13-year-old began to come to me in small doses from infancy. Her mother is an addict; she has that problem. I was living in Waverly, Virginia. Had a little catering business there. Received a call from a social worker and was informed I had a beautiful granddaughter—which she is." This last statement she says smiling proudly. "But my daughter still needed help. The social worker was very empathetic toward my daughter. She felt that if I would say that my daughter could come and stay with me, that she (the social worker) could prevent the Department of Social Services from taking the child away from her.

"Now, mind you—and I am being very candid—my daughter has six children. She did not raise them. The paternal grandparents raised her two older boys, and a third boy was adopted out. When he was born, the circumstances weren't good (for Margaret), and he went to a loving, very caring family. And when I had an opportunity finally, I just thought it would be too heart-wrenching, after he had been there from infancy to three-and-a-half years old, to take him out of that home. So I opted not to and just requested that, from time to time, we stay in touch so that he will always know that he has brothers and sisters. And they allowed that and that works out fairly well.

"My daughter came to live with me. I told her, 'Now you have nothing to do but take good care of the baby,' and they were with me until the baby was almost a year old."

Meanwhile, Margaret had a number of personal setbacks. Her father took ill back in Massachusetts, and she left Virginia to tend to him. She had to close down her catering business. Then her father died and she was left to settle his estate. She and her youngest daughter, Jessie, as well as her baby granddaughter, Tamika, and the baby's birth mother, Rhonda, all had to move back to Boston.

Amid all this, Margaret's brother was advising against allowing Rhonda and Tamika to continue to live with her. He pointed out that Margaret was (at that time) in her late fifties and had many other responsibilities. He cautioned her about taking on too much. So when Rhonda found an apartment in the South End, Margaret decided the best thing to do would be to help her out financially and get her on her feet and on her own.

"Everything seemed to be going well for her. Then Rhonda began to say, 'Tamika misses you. Could she come and stay on the weekends?' Well, she was accustomed to being around us—Jessie (who was just turning 18) and I—and we saw no problem with that.

"We would go down and get her on a Friday, and we would go back on a Monday and nobody would be home. Tuesday, nobody would be home. And then it just got to be a week or two would go by. So the handwriting was pretty much on the wall.

"After about two months, I was advised by friends to go to an office on Morton Street for assistance. I didn't know at that time that it was the Department of Social Services." The baby was about 18 months old, and it had become clear that she was with Margaret to stay. It was also clear that Margaret needed some assistance.

"I went over there to DSS—this was approximately 11 years ago—and they had very rigid rules. I would definitely have to go into court and declare Rhonda was a negligent mother. The language really sounded very bad at that time—I am using the language they use today—the language then was almost making them sound like a criminal. I said to the social worker, 'I can't really do that because she needs help. She is more sick than she is mean or deliberately insensitive. They live in a whole different world these people (addicts).'

"I did not pursue it. I just *could* not. So I fell on some pretty hard times. I did bus monitoring and I would have to take her around with me on the buses early, early in the morning. It was really pretty rough."

"Where was Tamika's father?" I finally ask.

Margaret closes her eyes and covers her mouth with her hand for a moment. "We don't know," she answers softly, sadly. "I tried to find out because I think it's so important, because sometimes there may be a sympathetic relative there. And you're not looking for physical support, you're just saying, 'Be there for the child, so the child will know that there are other people out there that care for her.' But I met with no success."

> Girls obtain much of their sense of self from their father figure. That sense
> of self may go undefined because of feelings of abandonment created by a

birth father's lack of involvement. Children will question their own self-worth because of a birth father's lack of commitment or caring. The child may internalize, 'If I were good enough, pretty enough, or smart enough, my birth father would want to have a relationship with me.' Sometimes even though children may try to rationalize some of these feelings away by concluding, 'He's a bad guy,' they will remain vulnerable to believing, at some level, it's really their fault. If not addressed, this could leave a lifelong legacy of insecurity, difficulty in relationships with men, and a constant, yet subtle, quest for a father figure.

"Subsequently, I was able to land a fairly decent job with the First American Bank. I was able to have family health insurance—it makes a big difference—and made a good salary.

"Unfortunately, my daughter Rebecca's marriage wasn't working out, and she came out to Boston. She and I took an apartment together about nine years ago and," she laughs, "we've been buddies ever since. We were a *family*," she says joyfully. "There was Rebecca and myself, her daughter Adah, and Tamika; there were the four of us and we were a family unit. And it was a Godsend for me."

Margaret's younger daughter, Jessie, had moved out, married, and had started a family of her own by this time.

"I took many jobs after that because Tamika had many emotional needs. Now I don't want to convey that she's knocking out walls and all that sort of thing. She isn't that kind of person, quite the contrary. She is very sweet and lovable, takes all the world's problems on her shoulders, wants to make sure that anything that goes wrong isn't her fault.

"I left First American Bank to take a job out in the town of Sudbury as a teacher's aide and bus monitor because I could get her in a special program out there—it's a very small school setting—to give her the kind of tools that she would need. And I stayed out there until she finished the fifth grade. We were up at five o'clock every morning. I don't always recommend Metco for everybody. All that traveling, and you are sending mixed messages (to the students). But that was the best I could do at the time having limited funds.

"Then I heard there was an opening here at the Health Center—it was much smaller then. And I became a patient clerk and ultimately created the role of telephone operator as the Health Center began to grow. It was so convenient because I only live a block away and the girls' school buses would stop right here at the corner. I could take five minutes here or there and leave my duties, because it was informal here, and someone would take over. So I could greet the children or they could come in and stay a few minutes and I could check with them; it worked out very well."

At this time, Margaret still had not made legal arrangements for custody. She learned through friends that she might be eligible for Aid for Dependent Children (AFDC) and went to apply. She was turned down, in part, because she could not obtain Tamika's birth records.

"My daughter was seeing a social worker that she had a fairly good relationship with. This social worker said to her, 'You must do something to help your mother get some assistance for your daughter. You know that you still need help yourself.' So my daughter wrote a letter that was notarized saying that she was not well, and that, until she was well, she wanted Tamika to remain in my care and custody. It was very well written and covered all the bases about school, medical care, and it was accepted, and that is what's in Tamika's file to this day.

"So that was fine, and I just saw Tamika and I going down through the years together. I got to be 65 and I thought, I no longer want to be a telephone operator. I would like to go back to school and I would like to do something part-time. And there were some other things that I wanted to do that would still insure me an income, but I wanted to have more time to spend with Tamika, and I just wanted some *freedom*." Margaret was accepted into Harvard University's graduate program.

"But then I heard my daughter had a set of twins. Tamika and I went to the hospital to see Rhonda and the babies. Six months later, one of the twins died. Because of my daughter's background, there was an investigation and an autopsy was done. They determined that the baby died of Sudden Infant Death Syndrome (SIDS).

"Again, this very good friend of hers that was a social worker and I tried to encourage her to go into full treatment for a year, to let us take the baby, the remaining baby, during that time and give her time to bring her skills back and her self-esteem back—all the necessary things that need to come back after a 20-year habit, for *yourself*, before you can start child-rearing.

"Of course, she wouldn't hear of it. She is very dramatic and very bright—very, very bright—and she was very convincing. She could 'do this alone,' there was 'nobody but she and Charlotte' (the remaining twin), and 'nobody had ever given her a chance'—all those things. She found another apartment, and things began to go downhill. She wasn't even in the apartment a year, and I could see the signs.

"Just before Christmas two years ago, I had been out shopping, and I received a phone call. It was my son-in-law and he said, 'I've gone to get your grandbaby. The police gave us 20 minutes to get there, or they were going to turn her over (to DSS).' The police had come and arrested Rhonda for something to do with possession or allowing her house to be used for drug trafficking. Doors were kicked in. The baby was not quite 18 months old."

"By then I had begun to learn a little something. I went immediately after the Christmas holidays straight to Superior Court," she laughs sardonically, "to find out what kind of rights I had." Margaret sits up straighter in her chair and clips the last six words out forcefully.

"I talked with a very good clerk of (probate) court. He said, 'Now, there is a lawyer up here. You go to him—that's what he gets paid for—and he will advise you on how to write your deposition.' So I went to the lawyer. I didn't think he asked me very good questions, but I filled out the paper and took it back to the clerk. He looked at it and then he looked at me and he said, 'You are going back into court in about 20 minutes. Take this paper, and go over there and sit, and *you* write why you need temporary custody of this child.' So I did. I just said the mother was a (drug) abuser and was unable to take care of herself and therefore she could not take care of this child. I appealed to the court. The clerk looked at it and smiled and said, 'Now you just wrote your own deposition, and you didn't make your daughter sound bad and you didn't make yourself sound like too much of a hero.' " Margaret laughs appreciatively.

"This is who you go to! And you win them over and you say 'Thank you!' And if they look a little harassed, you know they have had a bad day. Say something kind to them, and they respond. They will respond to you in kind. I advise everybody, 'Go to those clerks. Have patience and do not be snappy with them, because they have been there.' "

This has been my experience as well. Very often the most helpful, most knowledgeable people one comes in contact with during these legal custody and adoption proceedings are the clerks at probate court.

"I got immediate temporary custody. The judge just said, 'Thank God for grandmothers.'" Margaret obtained legal custody of both Tamika and Charlotte.

"Here is what happened next. I didn't know anything about DSS. You see, I was terribly ignorant about how they worked, except that I was terribly afraid of them having heard all those tales. My daughter had never told me why she was getting all this free day-care. She never told me there had been a 51A filed on her. She told me it was because Charlotte was so bright, which she is. And I would never have known if the day-care provider hadn't called me and said, 'Mrs. Jackson, I look forward to meeting you because I've heard so much about you. But you know they will no longer be funding Charlotte's day-care as of the thirty-first of this month. And I said, 'Who are *they*?' " She tucks her chin into her chest and laughs at herself, her naiveté. "She said, 'Hasn't the social worker been in touch with you?' and I said, 'Nobody said a word to me.' "

Right after that conversation, a social worker contacted Margaret. She explains, "He said, 'I recognize your voice,' and I said, 'I used to work at the Dorchester Square Health Center, I recognize *your* voice, and I understand that you stated that nobody in this family would be allowed to take Charlotte!' What had happened was when DSS investigated my daughter, she was saying the people hanging around the apartment were her sisters and brothers."

It is a mistake to assume that an entire family is dysfunctional or drug-involved because of the behavior of one of its members. In a recent publication of the Child Welfare League of America, it was stated, "The majority of kinship care families ... were poor but stable and hardworking families who cared about each other. In many cases, the problem parents appeared to be the only dysfunctional member of the family."[1]

"Well, when he came to meet me, he just parked outside of the house, saw Charlotte come out of the (day-care) wagon, came to the house, and said, 'Oh what a nice, loving home,' went back to his office, hit the computer ... and I lost *everything*."

There is a long pause. Margaret just sits looking at me, and I at her. The room is quiet except for the noise of traffic outside the claustrophobic cubicle we are in. "You lost everything?" I repeat, puzzled. Surely, that couldn't be the ending to that little story. But it is.

"I *lost*," she says quietly, with finality. "I didn't get a check, I lost the day-care, he never sent me a letter advising me what to do. But in the meanwhile. ... "

" 'Oh, what a nice loving home,' and you lose everything?" I interrupt her again. Now its my turn to be naive. What do I expect? The children, now under Margaret's capable care and not their heroin-addicted mother's, were no longer the concern of the social service department. And they, in all their wisdom, saw no reason or way to help them further.

"Just like that. He hit the computer and went on vacation! So I went over to the Columbus Family Day-Care Center just up the street, and I said, 'I need help.' I met a very nice woman, Nora Niles, who was familiar with the case." Nora is a social worker who helps in family placement. "Nora called everybody she knew. And everybody was 'very, very sorry,' but I had 'no recourse.' She even wrote to the commissioner of DSS and told him that 'the appropriate steps were never taken in the case, and if all grandparents were handled in this fashion, what would become of these children, because many grandparents were on a fixed income, and it was not a matter of being greedy.' They portray you as being greedy to cover their own tracks.

"Nora eventually introduced me to people at Family Services of Greater Roxbury, and I was able to get a sliding-scale-type fee so I could send Charlotte to day-care because I had to work.

"Once I realized that Charlotte was going to be in my life, too, I needed to talk to someone about it." Her plans to attend Harvard quashed, Margaret went into a depression. "Couldn't get out of my bathrobe," she says.

"I came here (to the Health Center) because I had friends here. Someone suggested that probably what I needed to do was start seeking mental health counseling. I said, 'No I Don't!'" She stiffens as she states this indignantly. "I need to talk to people who are doing the same thing.

"Because I worked in that clinic, I saw so many grandparents who did this—sometimes with *ease*, sometimes *not* with ease—and I needed to talk with *these* people for help and support. That's actually how Raising Our Children's Children (ROCC) came into being; I just started talking to people. I didn't have any pamphlets. I told them how *I* felt, asked them, 'How did *they* feel?' and we began to meet by twos and threes and we are up to 66 members now." She says this beaming with satisfaction.

Margaret has perked up. She is sitting up taller and speaking up louder, talking at a fast clip, animated and enthusiastic. "We meet in each other's homes, which is why I meet twice a month, so that nobody feels as though they missed anything. One meeting is usually more structured than the other, but all of it is for *ourselves*.

"Many people ask if we involve the children. Only once a year, I tell them. Maybe we'll do a picnic or a barbecue. My needs are now, as we expand, to have someone help me with special events like that, or Christmas parties, or preparing Thanksgiving baskets."

"My theory behind ROCC is to bring things *to the people*, as opposed to always bringing them out. That's one of the reasons we meet in the home. The second is confidentiality, particularly for new members. When I know there are two or three people that are going to attend that have never been before, I say to them, 'Well, we're going to meet at so and so's home.'

They will come, and they feel warm and they feel welcome and they unburden themselves. And we are just there for each other.

"The group is dynamic!" Margaret laughs, her eyes twinkling. "There are so many really great people within the group. Some of our children are also beginning to help us. One of my hidden agendas to have these meetings on Saturdays was to get my own family more involved. To establish the fact that you have got to have your own time to do things for yourself. So that if the children know that grandma is going to be out for these two or three hours, 'please help to make arrangements to see that the rest of the household runs smooth,' and so far its been working." She smiles, pleased and proud.

"Some people ask, 'Why don't you provide baby-sitting services?' I am going to stay as far away from that as I possibly can! If, further down the line, some of the younger grandparents feel as though that is something they would like to do, I will help them in any way I can. I will help them get set up, I will make the contacts, I will network and advise. But no, this is for ourselves." Margaret laughs.

"Also, the other part of this is, we no longer have the *neighborhoods*. I was describing to Tamika the other night, as I sat on my back porch, that after supper in the city, you could wash your dishes and turn and say to the kids, 'Lets walk 'cross town into the South End. I think we'll go visit Great Aunt So and So. And you could walk! And get back home at around nine-thirty or ten o'clock. It was a neighborhood. Sometimes you wouldn't get to your destination ... you would meet so many people you knew ... you'd stop and get an ice-cream cone. I can't re-create the old neighborhood, but I certainly can re-create the atmosphere and some of the feeling. Sometimes members have known each other 10 years back from the old neighborhood. So old relationships have been rekindled. That's been really great."

"We serve lunch." Margaret says this seriously at first, and then slyly with a chortle. "Yes, I always make sure we have a nice lunch." We laugh together, we both know how good it is to have something to look forward to during those long, same old, same old days of child care. These group times—play groups, bridge clubs, even League of Women Voters and Friends of the Library—serve this function and play an important role in the lives of women. Connections, a few hours freedom, small talk, or deep talk, but no "little people" talk, food, commiseration, advice and affection—an occasion. Margaret knew the importance of that and was able to turn her support group meetings into a "good time," a social event with a sense of community. We laugh together, conspiratorially, because we both inherently understand the need.

"We dress up a little, put on make-up ... but we tackle issues!" She says the last firmly, adamantly.

"I have two retired nurses who are part of the group," Margaret goes on.

"Are they grandparents raising grandchildren?" I ask.

"They just come to lend support ... and because they like the *feeling*."

"They like the lunches," I tease.

"They like the lunches and the camaraderie," she tells me with a warm smile.

"I also have a number of good friends, I consider them friends now, who are willing to come out and run seminars for us on (things such as) Medicare, health issues, our own personal health ... a young pediatrician who will run a seminar anytime we ask, in terms of advice on children's health, children's issues. And I have just now been approached by someone from the school committee who would like to become a part of our group and talk about school issues. The majority of our children, of course, attend the public schools here in Boston, and so we need to know these things."

Margaret tells me that there is someone that wants to talk on "parenting" issues, but she hesitates. She feels the need to "screen very carefully" what this person has to say. Margaret doesn't want her members to feel preached to, as if there is only one way to do things, or to feel that what they have done may be wrong. She is sensitive to needing to "blend the old with the new" ways of parenting.

"The philosophy of the support group, as I see it, is that no one person has all the answers, we all have different answers!" she says.

"I do a lot of networking, making sure my grandparents who have diabetes, or high blood pressure, or heart problems are all right. I stay in touch with them, and I am in constant touch with the medical community. I have a young nurse from Northeastern (University) who I call on to come to meetings and talk to people separately."

"You are a true support group," I tell her admiringly, "in a deeper sense of the word than most support groups I come in contact with." Margaret seems a little surprised at that. "And you really lend a wide range of support," I add.

I ask her what percentage of her group members have custody, and what percentage adopt.

"That's a mix. The majority of my grandparents do have custody. It helps because the (birth) mother or father of these children is still your own child. If all else fails, once you have legal custody ... or if it hurts too much to say no (to the birth parent) ... or if you don't want them taking the child, it helps. There have been times when I wouldn't allow my daughter to take her girls because it wasn't good for them or her. But I felt much stronger once I knew I had the courts behind me.

"Now, I am personally going to file for adoption because I *am* 68." She laughs as if her old age were absurd. "I'll be fortunate if I see the older child come of age to make her own decisions, the odds are that I'm not going to see this four-year-old become 21." She laughs again and then becomes very serious as she continues. "And if I do (live that long), what kind of condition would I be *in*?" she asks. "So I want to make sure ... I have *little*, but what I want to insure is my social security benefits (for Tamika and Charlotte to be eligible to inherit).

"Family welfare is sometimes not much kinder than public welfare. So the least dependent that they have to be ... that's my reason for adoption. The majority of the grandparents do not adopt because you live in hopes— you *live* in hopes—that even if you share the parenting, you just hope that they (the birth parents), ultimately, will be able to heal themselves.

"I have a grandmother (in the support group) that's 65 years old and is caring for six grandchildren, and the oldest is 10. And I am sure *she* doesn't want to adopt. She is just fortunate that she has a large family herself, so she has a couple of daughters and daughters-in-law who help. One comes in from Springfield and takes over for a week or two. She is a very fortunate person that way. Many of us don't have that kind of support.

"The other pitfall, if you have a good-sized family of your own, is that you have to get beyond that "sibling rivalry" and jealousy. We all have to live through it and deal with it in some sort of way. Because you're the other children's grandmother also. I have 14 grandchildren in all. And after all these years, I can see some of my daughters-in-law and sons-in-law and some of my own kids starting to say, 'You know, Ma's getting old and didn't *have* these babies, and it is not because of any desire on her part.' So I can feel attitudes changing and they are becoming more helpful as they get older and more understanding. But, you know, it takes a few years to wade through that!

"My oldest son is a psychologist in the Boston Public Schools, excellent with young people, does crisis intervention, is on television, he is a doctoral candidate at B.C., and he is just *beginning* to ... " She begins to chuckle and it overtakes her; she laughs raucously, rocking forward throwing her hands on her knees, her earrings swinging wildly. "just beginning to understand." She wipes at her eyes with the backs of her fingers and becomes serious again, "This is a unique position, so it isn't always easy.

"We are portrayed sometimes as 'these great valiant women.' Particularly in the black community, 'Oh, black women are so strong.' " She says this sarcastically. "We are as human as anybody else. We cry, we get depressed, we don't know when it's going to end from one day to the next ... and this is not our choice!

"It was lovely when I had four of them (grandchildren) come visit me for two or three weeks, or maybe a month ... and go home. It's not easy at 24 hours a day, seven days a week. These children have needs.

"When I address young women, I say to them, don't ever think that what they do to themselves doesn't have that shock-wave effect. Because it affects everybody.

"When that little one (Charlotte) looks at me and says, 'Mama, can I have a Daddy?' how do I answer that? That's why I get angry with these young women. Whatever their motivation is, whatever their problems are, whatever their rationale, take one unselfish moment and think about the child, about that *life*!

"She (Tamika) is the one who has a goal in life, and I think her goal is to be with her mother and take care of her mother. She feels as though the family treated her mother badly. This just began to surface in adolescence.

> Children of alcoholics and addicts, because they see their parents so out of control, often attempt to give their parents and themselves stability and control in their lives, even if it means sacrificing their own childhood. They struggle with ambivalence regarding the afflicted parent, torn between anger and disappointment with their parent and their urge to be protective of them. They try to parent the parent.
>
> Conflicting "good parent, bad parent" issues may surface as confusion between loyalty and fear that, 'If my mother is bad, than I must be bad too.' At times, the child may see both themselves and their parent as "victims," and may feel that they are "united together against the world."

"If she (Rhonda) is broke, and things aren't going right with her personal life—and she is beginning to have health problems now because she is 45—then she is in touch with us. Although I know where she is, and I know her phone number, I no longer bother to even encourage the girls to call her. The older girl is now beginning to say, 'Do not give my mother any more money.' I say, 'Well, Tamika, I think I understand why you are saying this, but you have to remember that your mother is my daughter the same as the rest of my children. So I would never see her go hungry, I would never see her in real pain. But you don't have to worry, I'm not going to give her big money.' " She says this with a short, rueful chuckle. "Tamika says, 'She never calls you and asks how you feel, and I am really getting sick of her.' So, I just let her vent her feelings.

"There have been a couple of divorces among my children, but the parents are still around. And they (Tamika and Charlotte) see that, and it's different. Rebecca and her husband have been divorced, and he's remarried, but he comes down from Framingham once or twice a month and picks up his daughter. She knows his other family. And that's the way it is throughout the family. We have family gatherings. We sent one of my grandsons off to college, and everybody pitched in, which included the divorced ones with the ex-in-laws, because we were all friendly. The divorce happened between my son and his wife, it had absolutely nothing to do with our wanting to make sure this young man got off to college, so that he knew he had family support. We all pitched in and gave a big gala for him and nobody was fighting or arguing. But (Tamika) sees these things, and she feels the loss."

As author Hope Edelman explains in her book, *Motherless Daughters*, "Like the child whose mother dies, the abandoned daughter lives with a loss, but she also struggles with the knowledge that her mother is alive yet inaccessible and out of touch. Death has a finality to it that abandonment does not. A daughter whose mother chose to leave her or was incapable of mothering may feel like a member of the emotional underclass."[2]

Margaret continues to talk about Tamika, "She is an insecure kind of person so its really hard because you will reach out for her and she'll draw back sometimes. She has her own type of special needs."

> As they emerge into adolescence, most teens become reluctant to openly talk about feelings. While this is normal, it is important for caregivers to continually provide outlets for sharing feelings.
>
> Abandoned children may formulate that they don't deserve to have people care about them. Moreover, they may also feel that they don't deserve success and therefore don't create any in their lives. They may have doubt about their abilities to succeed, thus only allow themselves to fail. Caregivers must watch for signs of self-defeating behaviors, actions, or words; an inability to give or accept compliments; self-critical behavior, or a reluctance to try something new or join in.

Margaret and I commiserate about raising teenagers again, coping with it as grandparents. She tells me, "It's no longer that you know the boy down the street and you know his parents. You don't know anybody anymore. When do you say yes, and when do you say no? I don't envy you." She is teasing me now. I laugh.

"And I don't envy you," I tease her back.

"I used to say that to my children, 'I don't envy you having to raise children in this day and time.' Boy, I never thought it was going to come back and haunt me!" She laughs. Then she says wistfully, "That's the least of what I wanted to do."

Margaret's thoughts drift over to her daughter Rhonda, and she begins to talk about a meeting she had with a drug counselor at one of the many rehab facilities her daughter attended. "I challenged him. I said, 'How dare you decide that I have had no pain! How dare you! How dare you indicate that I have had a life of roses! Let me explain something to you. When she decided this was what she was going to do, or was led into it, she was a grown woman and out of my house. And you don't know anything about my life so you can't make suppositions because I smile on the outside. You can't see the pain on the inside. You don't know what I went without, or what I've done, or what my philosophy of raising children is. She did not have to baby-sit her brothers and sisters; I didn't believe in that, that was *my* responsibility. But she, ultimately, 10 years down the road, has to make up her mind that she's not going to put that needle in her arm or her leg. I have nothing to do with that decision. That is her decision.

"I encouraged her to get out of that program. I told her, 'Until the day you can look yourself in the mirror, for better or for worse, and say "I am really sorry, but I did this," then you can move on.' I don't see how you would have the ability to get well otherwise. We have to forgive ourselves. I can't tell you how many things I have had to forgive myself for in order to move on, in order to be a better person."

Margaret begins to laugh and confides, "They wanted her out of the program after they met me anyway."

"You were too much for them," I kid her.

"Well, I was just shocked that those people didn't talk about responsibilities. That when you make your decisions, there's going to be subsequent actions after these decisions—so be careful.

"You know, the government's wasting tons and tons of money. I'm not too sure that they don't try to keep these people addicted so they can keep a certain amount of mediocre people in jobs!" She laughs when she says this, but her eyes are hard as stones, and I can see she really means it. "Because you wonder. Drugs are still in America, Noriega's in jail—or wherever, and all this mess is still going on. Why aren't we curing these things? Why don't we care about our children?"

Margaret and I talk about the "War on Drugs" and how so much money is pumped into the cops and robbers game the government is playing. I remark that it's too bad some of that money couldn't be spent to help the children that are the ultimate victims of the drug epidemic. In a recent *New York Times Magazine* article entitled "It's Drugs, Stupid," Joseph A. Califano, Jr., former Secretary of Health, Education, and Welfare, pointed out, "Neither party gets it. Crime, poverty, health care costs—America's biggest problems lead back to drug abuse." It is clearly the primary cause for the meteoric rise in numbers of children being raised by grandparents. However, the only mention of the children of addicts was, "Put children of drug- or alcohol-addicted welfare mothers who refuse treatment into foster care or orphanages."[3]

I do not know Mr. Califano, nor am I familiar with his views. Perhaps I am assigning too much weight to this one brief article, but I can't help feeling disappointed with it and thinking it epitomizes the absence of consideration for the children fallen prey to the addictions that consume, kill, and imprison their parents. Do the children of addicts have a more-than-even chance for succumbing to the same spiral of abuse? What can we do to stem the tide of the next generation of addicts? Stopping the cycle of hopelessness, rootlessness, low self-esteem, and the need to medicate your dreams into existence or numb your nightmares away—making the children a priority instead of uniforms for drug enforcement SWAT teams—perhaps that will turn tomorrow's tide. Prevention: does anyone out there get it? Margaret points out that in order for that to happen, the whole country would have to change their way of thinking—a sobering thought in light of a recent *Boston Globe* article about the Christian Coalition's "Contract with the American Family." This organization, with over 1.6 million members, supports a "Parental Rights Act" which includes a proposal for the defeat of the UN Convention on the Rights of the Child.[4]

Margaret says, "As I get older, do you know what I see? I don't see a country that actually cares about its children. And that has nothing to do with color. The court system, the educational system—where do we stand in the world today? The court system only reflects the mores of the country. And we (grandparents) have to be pushed down because we shouldn't be doing this. We shouldn't be saving these children. We shouldn't be giving them love and saying that all things are possible. I wonder why I had to get so old to realize that?

"I had ultimate faith, that in the long run, if you kept on working and kept on trying to do the right thing and gave your kids a lot of love and always looked out for the advantages, you would get them (the children) going in the right direction. But the country, I found out, does not care! Because, if it cared, these poor educational systems would not exist.

"I heard Dr. Jocelyn Elders speak recently. She said something I thought was really significant. She said, 'Our lawmakers seem to be consumed with giving our children sex education. I want you to examine this. Who needs to be educated about sex? You know what sex is. They know what sex is. But look at our reading scores. Look at our math scores. Look at our literacy rate. Now if I want to pass a bill that has to do with condoms and sex education in the public schools, I could have the money in no time. But if I were to say that the literacy rate is really bad in this county or that county, they would tell me, 'We'll have to have a conference. We will take it to committee.'"

"Those men in suits love committees, don't they?" I say.

"Well, did you hear that the city council in Boston wants to accelerate their salaries by 10,000 more dollars a year?" Margaret tells me.

"Oh? No, I didn't hear that, but I'm not surprised."

"Is that *scary*? 10,000 more dollars a year!" Margaret laughs.

"I'm telling you—those men in suits. ... "

"Yeah, they're really good at what they do," she says sarcastically.

"Buying those suits ... they need that money to buy those suits," I say and we snort with laughter.

It has been two hours of sitting in that hard chair for Margaret, and I decide it's time to call it quits. We agree on a time to get together again, so I can meet her granddaughters. Margaret chuckles and says she can just imagine how her four-year-old will love that, "She'll just try to take over. She's a professional."

Margaret tells me that Tamika has a weight problem and says, "I try not to say anything (about her eating) because I know why she does it. She does have a lot of emotional needs. For a long time, she had Attention Deficit Disorder (ADD), but she seems to have overcome that now."

ADD is present in about 5 percent of the general school-aged population. I would be willing to conjecture, however, that the figure is higher among children who have come into grandparent's care from very rocky beginnings. In the book *Driven to Distraction,* it is pointed out that ADD "remains poorly understood by the general public, often going unrecognized or misdiagnosed. The hallmark symptoms of ADD—distractibility, impulsivity, and high activity—are so commonly associated with children in general that the diagnosis is often not considered. Due to repeated failures, misunderstandings, mislabelings, and all manner of other emotional mishaps, children with ADD usually develop problems with their self-image and self esteem." The authors go on to say that afflicted children are often "labeled lazy or defiant or odd or bad."[5] There are many ways to deal with this disorder—therapy, counseling, behavior modification, and medication, but the first step is knowledge and understanding.

"It's all about self-esteem. I've been trying to get some counseling for her, if I could find the right person, but that's not always easy. We were told that we were doing pretty good, so we wouldn't be top priority. That's all very complimentary, but that's not the point! The point is that she's 13 and I know that I have limits."

> Weight problems, poor eating habits, and, in some instances, eating disorders develop in children who have been abandoned, abused, or neglected. For some children, food becomes a way to "feed the soul," to fill up the emptiness they feel. Food becomes a form of self-nurturance, and children tend to nurture themselves with high-sugar, high-fat foods. For many of these children, food becomes a safe, reliable friend, a friend who never lets them down, never abandons them, and never hurts them.
>
> Children with eating vulnerabilities should receive appropriate psychological support to face and resolve those issues of abandonment, rather than feeding the void they create.

As I pack up to leave, I remind Margaret that we have a Grandparent Support Group Network meeting at the Executive Office of Elder Affairs in a few days. "We missed you at the last meeting," I tell her.

"I'll be there," she promises. We are expecting several DSS officials to attend. They are going to be filling us in on how the "system" works. But Margaret fears the meeting will turn into nothing more than a "love affair" with DSS.

She needn't have worried. The meeting at the EOEA is very well attended, and Margaret is there as promised. Most of the panelists are grandparents raising grandchildren, and some have had unpleasant experiences dealing with DSS throughout difficult custody proceedings. They are not won over by the "Ombudsman" in attendance along with a couple of her assistants, although we are all surprised that this Ombudsman exists, that there is a branch of DSS that actually mediates disputes both with and within the system. Is this a secret, we wonder? There is a lively discussion The DSS officials are oddly tentative, somewhat patronizing, and lend no new information.

Toward the end of the meeting Margaret speaks up. She implores DSS to "treat the grandparents with respect, give them answers to questions, be patient." And if decisions are made *not* to place children with family, "Please, tell us *why*!" She asks for "understanding." She tells them finally, "Because ... this is flesh of our flesh!"

Margaret and I meet once more a week later at the Health Center. The plan is for me to pick her up there and drive her home when she's done working, so I can meet the children. When I arrive, she meets me at the back stairway again, and we walk up to her tiny office space. Charlotte is there. She dashes around, a little pink and blue plaid blur, a dynamo. She is obviously well known and loved in this place. She flies from one office space to another, greeting people, asking for pencils from one, paper from another. She finally settles down at a large wooden conference table and begins to draw.

Margaret doesn't look quite as sharp today. Her eyes are tired, watery pale. Gone are those wonderful earrings. And she's moving very slowly.

She begins by apologizing, in advance, for her messy house. I tell her, "Please, don't worry about it Who cares!" I say and mean it. "You should see the condition I left mine in today," I tell her. But she still frets. She tells me she just can't get going lately, she's been depressed. Money problems.

I sit squeezed into the cramped space next to Margaret's desk as she fills out time sheets. She talks to me, slowly, mechanically—as if she's reciting a grocery list to herself. She speaks so quietly, I lean forward across a pile of papers and strain to hear.

"I get a check for $512 a month from Social Security. It's really $525, but they take out $12.50 for Medicaid. It's really funny, they say they are *giving* you Medicaid, but you're really *paying* for it. My rent is $525 a month." She also receives $200 every other week for her two granddaughters. She would receive more if her grandchildren had problems or if she were a drug addict, or if she didn't work. She works part-time at the Health Center. She doesn't mention what she makes there, but I imagine it's not very much.

"Shall I buy Tamika the shoes she wants, or pay the electric bill?"

She tells me she tries to do everything right. She shops at the second-hand stores. She tells me people don't treat her with respect; they make her feel like she is begging. I ask her who she is talking about, and she says, social workers, people at the welfare office, lawyers, politicians. One politician told her she must not be budgeting properly.

Margaret finishes up her work, and we go hunt for Charlotte. We find her still at the table, her head bent over her drawings. Her long, puffy braids, all six of them, are secured top and bottom by elastics threaded through royal blue beads. They bounce as she colors. She is wearing a too-small, but pretty, pink and blue plaid dress, pink ruffled socks, and ancient saddle shoes—I haven't seen the likes of them in years—one with a floppy sole. I sit down next to her and look at the bottom of her foot, trying to gauge shoe size, as she sits cross-legged on her chair, drawing.

"What a little foot," I say.

Charlotte jerks her head up, her braids swinging furiously, and gives me a defiant look. She has creamy, coffee-light skin, and wide-set, watchful eyes set into a soft, baby face.

"No," she protests, pouting. "I'm a *big* girl."

"You sure are!" I try desperately to redeem myself. She does have a small foot, I think to myself, smaller than my four-year-old's. Could I hand some shoes down? Some clothes? Or would it cause discomfort between Margaret and me—be awkward?

Charlotte takes a shoe off and Margaret patiently wiggles it back onto her foot, ties it securely, and we are off. Charlotte refuses to put her raincoat on—she is clearly a force to reckon with—and we step out into the warm drizzle without an argument.

Margaret's street is only a block or two from the Health Center. We drive up to a "triple-decker," a turn of the century, wood frame house built for economy. Dorchester is filled with them. Three levels, three porches, three families. The rule of thumb used to be that when you bought the house, you lived in one apartment, the second apartment covered your mortgage payment, and the third was income. It was your home, and you had a vested interest in upkeep, in the neighborhood. Now, absentee landlords own them for profit only.

This triple-decker will need a coat of paint soon, but it is solid and in good repair. Most of the modest homes on this street have been kept up fairly well, but the yards remain forgotten, untended. The tall houses stand all lined up like the old guard, somber and plain in dull brown coats, the overgrown grass and hard-scrabble weeds taunting them from below. At the end of the street, I can see a playground. Impenetrable, chain-link fencing chokes in a dried-up ball field and gun-boat gray, metal swing sets. It's midafternoon, but no one is playing.

Inside Margaret's apartment on the first floor, the walls are painted off-white, the trim, salmon pink. She begins to fuss about as soon as we enter, still apologizing for what turns out to be minor clutter. I take my raincoat off and settle into a soft terra-cotta colored couch next to Margaret's over-flowing desk.

"This is my Tamika," Margaret introduces her granddaughter to me as she enters the living room. I see that she is very overweight. She does have a beautiful face, purely dark, with lovely almond-shaped eyes that tilt up at the corners—cat eyes. I tell her so. I ask her if anyone has ever told her what beautiful eyes she has, and she says, "My grandmother tells me that." She is very sweet and painfully polite.

"I look like my mother, except my mother's face is skinny and mine is sort of round," she says, drawing her finger around her chin.

Margaret tries to shoo Charlotte away, and I tell her she's fine, not to bother. Charlotte brings me a plastic-covered toy that came in the MacDonald's kid's meal she had for lunch, and I unwrap it for her. It's a miniature "Ken" doll with egg-yolk yellow hair. She asks me what he does, and I tell her, "Nothing much."

Tamika speaks whisper-soft and enunciates with precision. She sounds like Marilyn Monroe. I ask her what it's like to live with her grandmother and think that it's a stupid question the minute it leaves my mouth. She answers, "Sometimes we don't get along, but my grandma says that when I get a little older, it will get better."

"Do you see your mother often?" I ask.

"Not really. I sort of get along with my mother, I just didn't understand why she didn't take care of me. But I don't ask her because I really don't know how to say it."

"And she might not know how to answer you," I respond.

"She might say she couldn't, but ... She has always told me that she regrets she didn't, but there are some things I probably wouldn't understand now. When I get older, it will probably be better for me to talk about it then, because I'd probably understand more."

"You're right," I tell her.

"I don't think I can understand at my age," she says.

"It's hard to understand, even when you're a grown-up, why people do the things they do."

"I know she says she made a lot of mistakes, but I just don't understand why" she repeats with a big sigh.

> While a mother's addiction is difficult to understand, with assistance, someone Tamika's age is old enough to begin to process much of the infor-mation that will help her put into perspective why her mother is unable to care properly for her.

A teen will need help wading through the maze of passionate, conflict-ing, and confusing emotions. Once this occurs, she will then have the opportunity to deal with her unresolved feelings of loss and abandonment. Children need to have that opportunity so they can understand who their mother is and why she behaves the way she does. These questions, and the need to understand them, make up the very fabric of who that child is and who she will become.

Margaret comes back toward the living room from the kitchen where she has been puttering. "Ken's on the floor," I warn her. "Don't step on him."

"Ha! I'm sure it'll be worse for me than for Ken," Margaret says, as Tamika leaves to go back upstairs to Rebecca's second floor apartment to watch a movie with her cousin Adah. She shakes my hand shyly and sidles off.

I ask Margaret how Tamika feels about her plans to go forward with the adoption, and she says Tamika really loves her mother and she thinks that Tamika feels "way deep down inside of her that it was her fault that her mother is the way she is, and that maybe no one ever really gave her mother a chance. What I had to do is explain to her that my adoption was out of love and protection. I didn't get into the other reasons."

The other reason Margaret is driven to adopt is her fear that Rhonda could step in at any time and take the children back.

"I think DSS really bore it (that fear) out, believing that the birth moth-er has the ability to make decisions over someone that has loved and cared for these children. I did explain to Tamika about the Social Security bene-fits, and that as my children, they would receive that support, and I think she accepted that. And also that it had absolutely nothing to do with—after she reached a certain age—of being with her mother."

"Is that what she wants to do?" I ask.

"I think so. I tell her when you are old enough to make choices, I won't try to stop you—advise you, but not stop you."

Tamika barrels in to tell her grandmother a tale about a broken VCR, and who did it, and when, and why, and what she did to try and fix it. "So did I do something good?" she asks jokingly, but she holds her breath and waits for an answer. Margaret smiles and replies, "Yes—you're always good."

Although teens may not reveal their emotions, internally they are often overwhelmed by the magnitude of their feelings. Adolescents like Tamika need to receive continued support and guidance both at home and from individual therapy in order to help address unresolved feelings of loss and abandonment. In addition, issues of "fault" and "guilt" must be addressed. Children in this situation need to realize that a child cannot ever cause parents to do harmful things or influence a parent's poor choices, and that they do not have a responsibility to take care of their dysfunctional parent. Children need to learn that they are bystanders in the parade of poor choices and consequences created by dysfunctional parents.

The "Big Sister" and "Big Brother" type of programs are wonderful assets for children like Tamika. They offer safe, reliable adults with whom children can form a bond, have fun, and share feelings and thoughts.

With help and guidance, children are able to recognize that they are capable of making positive choices, and that they can orchestrate their lives so that those choices have favorable outcomes.

The Genarros

Grandparents long for, pray for, and fight for three things: to keep their grandchildren safe, to see their adult children come through their bad times to emerge as healthy, responsible people, and to come together as a family, healed and whole.

Jeannie and Vincent Genarro are as tenacious and valiant as knights on a crusade. They never gave up on their quest for their grandchild's safety, their daughter's maturity, and their family's preservation. Watching their story unfold provides some guidelines for grandparents embarking on their own harrowing crusades. In this chapter, we see an example of developing that vital transition period between birth parent and child, as well as a few potential pitfalls to watch for while dealing with adult children.

It has not been easy for the Genarros to let go of custody and control of their grandson, Alexander. They work at it, agonize over it, talk it over endlessly. And they grieve. They do it all for the sake of their grandson, their daughter, and ultimately, their family.

Teenage pregnancy, drugs, rebellion, irresponsibility—all common ingredients in the simmering pot of turmoil the Genarro family tried desperately to keep the lid on. Inevitably the volatile mix boiled over, and Vincent and Jeannie were left to clean up.

"Her teenage years were really tough," Jeannie Genarro tells me shaking her head. Rose had been running away, staying out all night and partying since she was 14, and no matter what the Genarros did to curb her wild side, she continued to act out. They anguish over the fact that their son, Gary, a few years younger than Rose "lost out" because "she took up all the energy and attention." Then at 16, she became pregnant.

"This was like one more thing. She did want to keep it. Of course, they think they're toys. So she lived with us. Her pregnancy was great. It seemed like she changed overnight from being rebellious and not coming home and things like that. She seemed to grow up a lot."

It was a short-lived reprieve.

Jeannie is in constant double-time motion. She fiddles with the peaks of her auburn hair, the color of dark-rubbed copper pennies, cut in a shag. It feathers down her neck and around her youthful face. She jumps up and down constantly to check if the tea water is boiling yet, to get milk, sugar, napkins. She is a bundle of nervous energy—cute, quick, busy—and talks at Chip-and-Dale speed. Jeannie is a young grandma, in her forties, and is dressed for a jog—pink "Bermuda" sweat shirt, gray leggings, white socks, and sneakers. She looks more like a teenager than a grandmother.

"When the baby was about three months old, she (Rose) started going out, and we would allow it to happen. I don't know ... my husband and I are very ... we're enablers I guess. When I think back on it now, I think I would have done things very different in those early months, maybe. I don't know. It was hard to let her make her own mistakes. I think I interfered too much."

Jeannie stepped in to care for the newborn when she felt that Rose wasn't doing things right.

"I think I should've stepped back," she tells me, popping up to get honey from the cupboard, banging doors, shuffling contents to find the right jar.

"We were in close quarters here," she calls out from behind the refrigerator door, still looking for honey. The house is a small "Cape Cod cottage," all blues and greens and wicker inside, absolutely pristine and newly built. Squeezed into a tightly packed, motley neighborhood of much older homes; it sits on the end of a cul-de-sac like an exclamation mark. This is an old fishing community, with deep ethnic roots. Stacks of lobster pots are as common here as swing sets in back yards, and cement Madonnas bless dark squares of freshly tilled earth that promise lush plots of tomato and pepper plants. You can almost gauge the health of the fishing industry by the number of homes with peeling paint and the expansion of vegetable gardens.

You can't see the ocean from the Genarro's home, but you can smell it the moment you step out the door. You can feel it in the air and see it in the sky, gray and melancholy, heavy with moisture and salt. It makes the grass extra green and the hydrangeas as blue as the sea.

Rose was so young, Jeannie tells me. "So when she started asking to go out, we felt bad. But she started bringing home friends that were completely different. Then she started saying she would be home at a certain time and she didn't show, and it kept getting later and then not showing up at all. And it just got out of hand, and I didn't know how to stop it. I couldn't stop it.

Jeannie tried to be firm with Rose. She told her she would not baby-sit while she partied. "Then she started to come and take the baby out of the crib, taking him with her wherever she was going, riding around in cars, whatever. I just couldn't let that happen. I probably should've. I don't know. You tell me what the answer is."

She leans toward me with an intensity I hate to disappoint, her brown eyes boring into mine.

"I have no idea," I tell her apologetically. I have no answers to give her. I don't know that anyone does. All of us paddle our own way, panting and sweating, down uncharted rivers trying to avoid the rocks and undertow.

She continues somewhat deflated, "I lost the control of it, and I let her go."

After a few months, Rose heard of an apartment and was determined to live on her own.

"In a way I was sort of relieved. I don't know whether I was dreaming or what."

Jeannie hoped that this would be the start of a new life for Rose, that she would get her life together and prove that she was capable of being a mother to her young son. But the evening before the Genarros were to leave for a long-awaited vacation to the Bahamas, Rose came to get the baby in the middle of the night to bring him with her to her new apartment.

"There was no furniture there. The baby would have to sleep on the floor with her. Which, I suppose, looking back on it now, is probably not the worse thing in the world. But he had a bed here, and I guess I just couldn't see them coming in and taking him out ... and I knew she had those friends at the apartment. I got hysterical. I remember calling my girlfriend and saying, how could I leave tomorrow? I was just so stressed out, I cried all night."

"When I came home a week later, she was sitting in the house and she had all those stray kids in my house—no baby. She had left the baby at my mother-in-law's, thank God! But I could tell the house had been partied in.

"I had to go see the baby. I wanted to get the baby. I swear to God when that baby saw my face—eight months old—I could see the excitement that I was home." Her voice breaks and tears come to her eyes. It is the only time she cries during the interview, from the memory of her baby grandson and the joy and recognition that lit up his little face at seeing her. She places her fingertips at her lips and lowers her head a moment to stop the momentum of emotion.

"Don't mind me," she apologizes and then continues with a quavery voice. "I took the baby and went home. It just got worse from there. The partying got worse."

Jeannie had just started a new career, one that she had worked hard to achieve, and had put on hold until Rose was settled.

"I would come home from work, go to her house, pick up the baby, bring the baby home because he slept at my house. I would go back in the morning and drop the baby off. I did all his laundry. If my husband got out from work early, he would pick the baby up. So the baby was only with her three or four hours." Unfortunately, it gave Rose more time to party.

"Somebody filed a 51A on her. I was flipping out because I thought, Oh my God! I've heard about these kids that get taken by the State and get put in foster care." She says "foster care" as if it was prison, or hell.

Jeannie explained to DSS that she had care of the baby at night, so he was not effected by the partying, but that Rose needed help. She needed counseling, she told them.

"I remember going over one day—the baby was about nine months old, and the baby was in the tub, and she was somewhere else. He was standing up naked. He was happy to see me, and he was jumping up and down. She was nowhere to be found. I said to her, 'Rose, you can't leave a baby in the tub. In one second they can drown!' "

"Did it surprise you that she had no mothering skills?" I ask.

"In a way it surprised me, because I just didn't think it would be possible that somebody could do that from the way I was brought up and the way I brought her up." Jeannie says that it was as if her daughter "stopped growing" after the age of 15 when she dropped out of school. She seemed to be perpetually stuck in an adolescent loop of self-absorption and partying.

Then she was arrested.

"One night she called me from the police station. There had been a raid at a party where there was LSD. She wanted me to come and get her. I said to her, 'I will come and get you, but I want you to give me legal custody of Alex. I am not going to take any more chances.'

"I had threatened before that, but I could never do it. I don't know if it was just because I thought that she was going to get her act together. Plus, it was my *daughter;* I didn't think she'd be this way her whole life! But something like this could ruin her whole life, if I was to take the baby. There was just so much going on emotionally—the ties that we had with my daughter, and then the ties we had with Alexander."

When the Genarros began their custody pursuit, the birth father and his parents blocked the proceedings. The paternal grandparents became alarmed because they had become involved in the baby's life by that time and wanted to ensure their visitation rights. They advised their son not to sign over custody until a lawyer looked over the agreement. Their lawyer then drew up an agreement solidifying visitation rights for the birth father and the paternal grandparents. At the time, Jeannie says she was "so stressed out, and needed this to happen quick," before Rose changed her mind. The delay cost them six months of time, legal fees, and aggravation.

"Any little drawback or stall, I thought, This is it, we're going to lose him! I was like a mental case."

Thankfully, all custody issues were combined and heard during one court hearing. The Genarros were awarded temporary legal custody, and the birth father and paternal grandparents were awarded visitation rights.

The delay was stressful for the Genarros, but the paternal grandparents and birth father did the right thing under the circumstances. Although Jeannie welcomes them into the baby's life and describes them as "nice people," in a more contentious situation, grandparents on the other side could lose their visitation rights if they don't take the initiative and step in to secure them.

Jeannie says, "I never thought it was going to be permanent. I was just thinking we would have to do this until she gets her act together. I didn't think I would raise him forever. She did love him, and I knew that she loved him. But she just wasn't ready to give up her lifestyle."

Visitation for the birth mother was left up to the Genarros. "I allowed a lot of things that I shouldn't have allowed. Like she would come with her friends, and she'd say, 'I want to take the baby for a walk.' She'd never show up on time, or she would show up in a car full of friends, and we'd have to jam the car seat in between them. I should have been stronger. I should have said, 'Look, if you want to see your son, you come by yourself.' Sometimes I did say no, if I thought it was a dangerous situation. But sometimes I would let him go, and then worry after. I wasn't making good decisions sometimes ... in regards to being a strong person and just saying, No."

"Why do you think that happened?" I ask.

"I think I was just feeling guilty. I think I felt guilty about taking him from her. I felt like I *took* him."

> This grandmother needs to cut herself a break. She needs to recognize and take both pride and satisfaction in the fact that she and her husband made positive decisions for the sake of their grandchild. It is not easy for people to let themselves off the hook. If it remains difficult to do so, caregivers may benefit from short-term, focused counseling to address the unwarranted guilt.

Over the next couple of years, the Genarros grappled with their ambivalence, as well as with their daughter Rose's inability to parent successfully or get her life going on an even keel. "She was going from apartment to apartment, and some of them were lousy. She never had him overnight, never; I wouldn't allow that. She had him two hours at a time. Sometimes she might do something good, like go with friends and walk the baby carriage down the boulevard and have lunch. And I thought, Oh wow! But then, the next time, even if she took him with one friend, she'd come back in a car with a bunch of other friends, they're all smoking in the car, the baby reeks of smoke, it was like ... akkk!" Jeannie holds her head in her hands in disbelief and frustration.

I ask how her marriage held up with all that was happening and she tells me, "We argued a lot. Because if I happened to let Alex go with her and he came back smelling of smoke, he (Vincent) would say things like, 'You shouldn't have let him go.' And then I sort of resented that he could go to work every day. He didn't have to do the majority of it. Although if he was here now, he'd argue with you, saying, 'I gave up a lot too.' But if the baby was sick, I called in sick to my job, not him. I was the one, I felt, with more of the stress. I had to deal with Rose more. I was the one who went to court. But he went along with everything I said."

"So you were in agreement," I confirm. "And even though it was stressful, you were at least going in the same direction."

"Yes," she replies. "He was worried about the baby's safety. And he did have to share it while I worked. It was difficult."

Jeannie brings up her disappointment with the court system. "I felt like the court system didn't do anything. After a while, my lawyer said, 'Let's have a plan for the future.' So I said okay, let's have Rose work up to regular visitation. It was all done with mediators or through lawyers. The judge didn't ask anything." Alexander was never assigned a Guardian Ad Litem.

"Of course, Rose's lawyer was free. Every time we went to court or had to draw up papers, I had to pay. I guess she has the rights because she's the mother, but the first time we went to court she didn't even show up. And I thought, isn't this judge going to look and say, 'If this mother's so concerned that she wanted visitation, where is she?' But they never said anything about it, they just rescheduled."

Rose periodically petitioned the court for longer visitation and overnights, but she never managed to comply with the minimal requests Jeannie and Vincent made, like cleaning up the trash piled up outside the house she and her new boyfriend had rented and having the electricity turned on. Jeannie tells me that she felt in a way Rose actually liked the status quo. "She could use it to her advantage, she was used to it." Jeannie eventually told the court, "Before she gets the baby, I want her to have a job, to have a safe apartment, and to get counseling." Rose fulfilled those requirements sporadically at best. Meanwhile, whenever she had a personal setback or lost an apartment, she would move back in with her parents.

"As the years went by," Jeannie sighs and slumps, reliving her exhaustion, "she slowly made some changes." The Genarros fixed up a bedroom in her new apartment for Alex so that he could start to spend overnights. He was now nearly four years old. "Then one night around Christmas time, I went in the apartment and there were the people there she got arrested with. I picked him right up out of the bed, and I wrapped him up, and I took him out of the house.

"When I got home, she called and said, 'Did you see us divvying up our pot on the kitchen table?' I am so naive, I didn't even see that, but I said, 'Yeah, I did.' And I thought, all this time she's been fooling me! Me thinking she's doing better, and now she has those same friends there, and the baby's there, so how much is she thinking about him? But that really got to her, when I took the baby.

"How we worked it out, finally, was, she left that boyfriend, and came home to live again." Rose began to show a solid sense of responsibility, and the Genarros felt that she was straightening out and that it was time to place more trust in her. Also, Rose had received counseling on and off over the last few years, which, Jeannie felt, was finally beginning to pay off.

There are some wonderful prevention and early intervention programs for young mothers and families at risk, programs like the "Goodstart Initiative," sponsored by the Massachusetts Society for the Prevention of Cruelty to Children, and mentoring services such as Parent to Parent, and Visiting Moms. These programs are designed to offer emotional support, to teach young mothers the skills they need to care for their children, and to hook them up with a supportive network of peers in similar circumstances.

"My husband and I went on a vacation, and she was almost the main one responsible for the baby. Rose did a good job. When I came home the house was clean, and I felt really good. We started looking for an apartment for her."

"Did you help her out financially?" I ask.

"Every apartment that she got, I fixed up the baby's room." We both laugh in recognition of a fellow hypervigilant. "I had to make sure that he had everything he needed. Being the enabler that I was," she laughs at herself again, "I felt like I had to make a home for her. Bought her furniture. I thought it would help her." Most times Rose lost everything. This time at the age of 21 years old, after nearly five years of ups and downs, it finally stuck.

After Rose was settled once again, the Genarros allowed Alex overnights during the week. "We were still taking him on the weekends, but he got used to going back and forth. So by the time we did the custody thing, he was ready to go with her."

Jeannie stops to mention again that she felt abandoned by the court. They never "checked to make sure" Rose was fulfilling the requirements that had been set. "I guess they were too busy," Jeannie says generously, making excuses for them.

"I felt like she was doing well enough that he could go back with her. Besides I was so sick of dealing with all of this stuff. I didn't know that she was going to get any better. I didn't think that she was going to change that much more. And am I going to keep this child forever? Is that the plan? Am I going to fight with her, because now she wants custody? And she was crying a lot, looking back on all the things she missed. But when I gave custody over, I never really felt she had made all the changes that she needed to. It's just that he was sort of out of danger?" She says this as if she's trying to convince us both.

Alexander has been with Rose for two years. "It's been a struggle because I miss him wicked. I'm glad it worked out this way, because I like my freedom now. I never realized how much I missed it. I lost all my friends at that time. They were all at the point that I was, getting new jobs and working. They're going to hang around with somebody who has a baby? I never got back with them.

"Now I don't even know how I did it, because he's a handful when he stays over. And I am glad, looking at the future, that I am not raising teenagers. But I suppose, if I still had him, I just wouldn't think of that. ..."

"You would think about it," I interrupt, "and it would be horrible," I joke, "but you would do it."

"But it's been difficult, because I miss him wicked. He's my spirit! And I raised him till he was five, so it's something that I don't think I'll ever get over." Jeannie quotes a remark made by Margaret Walker-Jackson who appeared with me on a local television segment about raising grandchildren. "One thing that lady said and I'm hoping that it's going to be true, is if you have them until they're four or five, then they are sort of already what they're going to be. So I hope that that's going to be true, because today's world is so hard. I mean, my daughter has made a tremendous amount of change, but it's not how I would raise children, and it's not what I wanted for Alex.

"There are a lot of struggles between her and Alex, but my husband and I just step away from it." Jeannie tries to be supportive of Rose. Sometimes Rose calls her mother after an argument with her son, "I don't know how you ever did it Ma." Jeannie comforts her, "I know. You just have to try and get through it."

Vincent Genarro arrives home at this point. He is very Italian—black, curly hair, hawkish nose cutting through a weathered face, trim and fit-looking in his jeans and work shirt. Jeannie leaps up for introductions. After exchanging pleasantries, he sits down with us, pushes his chair away from the table, leans back, and folds his arms across his chest.

"Even now," Jeannie continues, "I have to not say things I really want to say. Sometimes my husband says them, and she'll hang up on him. It's very hard, it's like she's raising our child, and I don't know if that feeling is ever going to go."

> A mix of powerful emotions will continue to affect caregivers who, for one reason or another, relinquish custody of their grandchildren back to birth parents. The reality is that only one factor will help to resolve the pain and help to let go—time. I would advise grandparents to take each day as it comes, and face each bout of sadness with the satisfaction that they played an important role in their grandchild's life.

"I don't know what other people do, but if we want him to play baseball, we sign him up. We pay for his tuition at parochial school, so at least he'll get some good morals. Not that she's not a good person, but this generation is just ... different. She doesn't think like we do as far as what his needs are. Maybe because she didn't have him growing up. It's a struggle for her, and it's a struggle for us to let go. We still say too much I think, but I don't think that will change. I tell her, 'Even if you don't listen to me, let me say it, please.'"

"How does she take it?" I ask.

"I think she feels that we feel that she can't do a good job. Well, in some ways that's true. It's not that she can't do a good job, but it's not the job that I would do if I were raising him. Now she has a little girl, three months old, and I don't have the same issues with her as I do about Alex. And I think because she didn't have Alex, she's really close with this baby and is enjoying every minute of her, and I like to see that. We try really hard a lot of times to keep our mouths shut."

"I can't keep mine shut," Vincent confesses unrepentant. "She hung up on me the other day, but that's the first time she's hung up on me in a long time. She ended up calling me back, whereas before she would've never called back. I think she felt bad hanging up on me, maybe even thought a little bit about what I had said, and that's all I want to do is get her thinking.

"The issue was karate the other day. He's supposed to be there at four o'clock. She calls up at three and leaves a message, 'Alex is not going to go today, he's being punished.' She can punish him all she wants, but she shouldn't take away constructive things that he's doing. That's not punishment, that's destroying him, as far as I'm concerned. All that he's working for." Vincent tells me this, a hard edge of anger cutting into his voice.

Jeannie continues, "If we were his parents, that's how we should feel, but he shouldn't be our responsibility. It's hard to get away from that though. In a way, we're still raising him like he's ours." She is talking both to me and Vincent, weighing her feelings, her thoughts. She says quietly, almost in a whisper, almost to herself, "Maybe when he gets older, we'll ...," and trails off, lost in thought.

I point out to them that through it all, the ups and downs, the arguments, the tears and years of struggle, they were able to maintain that strong bond, the iron grip of family connectedness.

Vincent responds with a half smile curling up, breaking open his tough guy exterior, and I can see pride flickering around the edges.

"She's come back, let's put it that way. She was gone, she really was. I think she's done a good job. She made a comeback; she's come back to us." He stops for a moment and says finally, "We worked at it. We fought tooth and nail for it."

> Letting go means that the loss needs to be put in perspective, the loss needs to be understood, the loss needs to be felt, and most important, the loss needs to be accepted and resolved.

Certainly the feelings around the loss will come up over and over again, which is healthy and normal. A movie or similar situation on the evening news, or even a song on the radio could trigger memories and a strong emotional response. Sometimes people try to bury the sting of feelings. However, this denial often surfaces in the form of physical ailments, such as ulcers, later on. The other extreme is for the feelings of loss to loom so large that people find they are consumed by them. They may not be able to function in the present because they are stuck in the past.

Although we cannot always control what we feel, we can control what we do with those feelings. Grandparents should look for a healthy outlet for expressing their feelings as well as recognize that their care and commitment had a positive effect on their grandchild that will be a constant source of strength from which the child can draw always.

9

Grandchildren—
Having Their Say

"You be a good girl now. You hear? Don't you make people think I didn't raise you right. You hear?"
                    —Maya Angelou, *I Know Why the Caged Bird Sings*

President Bill Clinton, Maya Angelou, Carol Burnett, Jack Nicholson, Oprah Winfrey, Speaker Newt Gingrich, Mary Tyler Moore; what do these well-known individuals have in common? They were all raised by grandparents, each under different circumstances and for varying amounts of time. When I envisioned this last chapter, I saw a series of glowing, happily-ever-after reports from well-adjusted, successful individuals like these who happened to be raised by grandparents. That is not quite what I got.

What I encountered in the process of interviewing grandchildren for this last segment was relatively happy, healthy, but somewhat ambivalent young adults, still working to put the events of their childhoods into perspective. The stories they tell are full of loving anecdotes, secure foundations, and family connectedness, but they also contain elements of confusion, disappointments, and unresolved hurt.

What follows are the stories of four grandchildren, each at different stages of life: Kit, a Hispanic teenager; Linda, 21, a bi-racial college student from the inner city; David, a budding politician of 25; and Paul, 36, with a family of his own. They are a diverse group from different backgrounds and economic strata. They each grew up with various legal statuses, from informal arrangements to legal adoption. But for the most part, their stories unfold in similar ways. Because I give my interviewees the lead, usually letting them take me where they want to go, I often get something other than what I expect. But patterns and truths emerge from their unique, untampered-with perspectives. What becomes clear from these interviews is that the loss, absence, or failure of one's parents is a lifelong legacy that leaves an indelible imprint on even those who have been fortunate enough to have loving family replacements step up to the plate. These adult grandchildren demonstrate how important those replacements are to their development and how the way in which grandparents handle the ebb and flow of family relationships is critical to the health and stability of the children involved.

David's story is the one most unlike the others. I feel compelled to include his set of circumstances because they are so commonplace—the somewhat easier, often part-time versions of raising grandchildren. Also, I was talked into including such a story by my friend Ruth.

I sometimes share "The Ride" into Boston with my friend Ruth. Ruth is in her sixties and has multiple sclerosis. The Ride, a shuttle-bus service for the handicapped, allows her a companion and if I'm not running late, which is rare much to the consternation of Ruth who is a stickler for punctuality, I join her. I always enjoy this time with Ruth. She is an interesting, salty, "old pacifist" from the 1940's and 50's, when protesting violence and war were dangerously unpopular pursuits, and we have wonderful talks on our meandering way into town.

Ruth is a feisty, no-nonsense lady with a killer-diller smile which she flashes while zinging you with her straight-shooter retorts. She gets along very well thank you with her two aluminum canes decorated with yellow paper Stars of David Scotch taped to the handles by one of her grandchildren. One morning on The Ride, Ruth lambastes me. She asks me how work on my book is going, and when I tell her whom I'm interviewing she pulls me up short.

"What about us?" she challenges me. She thinks I should include the grandparents who are always there for their grandchildren, the ones called on constantly to be "parents in a pinch." They may not have custody of grandchildren, but they pick up the slack for the busy, overburdened, overwhelmed parents or run interference for the neglectful, irresponsible, hurtful ones. Grandparents whose way of life includes chauffeuring grandkids to school, dentist appointments, ballet lessons, and birthday parties. Grandparents who spend their weekdays playing nurse to sick children, and on weekends find themselves on damp, arthritis-inducing soccer fields, or risking heat stroke while sitting on fanny-numbing baseball bleachers. The countless, uncounted, underappreciated grandparents. The glue that quietly holds so many kids' lives, so many families, together.

"Ruth," I plead, "give me a break. That's a whole different book!" But I changed my mind when I found David.

David

David's parents were divorced when he was eight years old. But he had always spent most of his time with his grandparents. "It used to be me, my grandmother, and my dog Onyx. We used to drive all over town doing errands for my grandfather. He owned a grocery store. I used to hang out with them. And then when I started getting involved in sports, baseball, my grandfather was always at the games. We used to play father-son games out there, 60 years old running around the bases. I was his son. He had only one daughter, and now finally he had a son that he could go to the games with, talk sports, go fishing, and do all that. He used to go everywhere, driving an hour just to go see baseball tournaments and football games. I'd look out and see him in the stands."

His parents were 20 and in college when they got married and dropped out. His grandparents helped the young couple as much as they could. His father worked at the grocery store the grandfather owned. Once they were able to get back on their feet, they went back to school and completed their education. David was about four years old at the time and from that point on, his grandparents basically raised him.

"What happened was when my mother got divorced, I moved in with my grandparents just as a temporary thing," David explains. "It started off as temporary, but then after about a year, they ended up putting an addition onto the house and said, 'Move in with us.' It was partly for financial reasons and partly convenience.

"Well, my mother ... she's a school teacher, she'd be working. Our relationship is more like my mother is my sister almost, and my grandparents were my parents. That's the relationship that I have now with my mother."

I ask if he remembers the divorce and whether it was upsetting to him. "No, I don't remember it being upsetting. I think it was because I was happy where I was. It wasn't all that messy. To give credit to my dad, he understood what the situation was and didn't try to use me as a pawn. I guess that happens a lot. He probably figured my mother and my grandparents would do the best job raising me; he obviously knew he couldn't do that. He always sent me cards and would call and stuff like that. It's not like he was totally out of the loop."

David is adorable, from his teddy bear eyes, as round as buttons, to his wavy blonde hair and cleft chin. He is every mother's dream for her daughter; what a catch! Oy, if only I were a matchmaker! David works for Congressman Barney Frank and looks as if he fell out of the Brooks Brothers wagon, all oxford cloth—light blue to match his eyes—and penny loafers. He has a gee-whiz enthusiasm that's infectious. I always give David a kiss when I see him, he has that kind of face, the kind of cheeks you either want to kiss or pinch, like a Yenta.

His most endearing quality is that he is oh-so-careful to say good things about his mother. Each time he gets on a roll regarding his grandparents, he stops to say an alternately positive thing about his mother. I think it's both unconscious and conscious. I think his loyalties are just a little bit torn.

"My mother is my hero, the way she was able to go back to school and get her degree and now she's a school teacher. She always gave me everything I needed or I wanted. It was always me first. And when I look back on it, I am really thankful."

"What about your father?" I ask. David just shrugs, "Well. ... "

"You didn't keep in touch?" still probing.

"We did and we didn't, you know. We just ... for whatever reason ... I guess I was just a little too young to really know what happened when they got divorced. My mother kind of said, this is our family, me, you, and my grandmother and grandfather. And that was the strength right there.

"It's funny, I never really thought too much about it. I mean my grandparents were so great. The more I look back on it, I am sure at some point when I was a kid, I got upset about it. But I don't think it's affected me that much.

"I remember when it was Father's Day and I was about 12 or 13, and instead of saving my allowance for a gift I wrote my grandfather a note—it was all misspelled, it had all the x's where the a's should have been or whatever—basically thanking him, 'You've been a father to me,' and all that stuff. He still has it."

"I'm sure he does!" I tell him. "It's probably one of his treasures."

His mother never remarried. David says she "made a commitment to me, that I was the most important thing."

I ask if his grandparents had the main parenting role and he says diplomatically, "It was almost like parenting by committee." Although they had very different parenting styles—David's mother's was very laissez faire, his grandparent's was discipline-oriented—they did not clash openly about it. David recalls that his grandparents deferred to his mother for the final word.

David and I are chatting over pasta and salad at a little Italian restaurant near Congressman Frank's Massachusetts headquarters, with the clang of dishes and utensils and the noisy drone of lunch hour clamor competing for attention. David tells me, "I think we've gotten too nuclear. The sense of extended family isn't around anymore." Congressman Frank's mother, Elsie Frank, who is the president of MAOA (Massachusetts Association of Older Americans) has spoken to David about the value of programs that pair children with elders, for instance, reading to children at day-care or in the elementary schools, or rocking and holding infants at area hospitals. He agrees that elders have much to give.

"I go to the New Bedford 'Y,' and I love hanging out in the steam room and the sauna talking with the old-timers, the guys that have been going to the 'Y' for years. You learn so much just sitting there talking to the guys. It's funny, these guys are telling me about Ted Williams and all these other guys. I'm never afraid to ask them questions, because I like to learn from them."

"Well sure, because you've always had such a positive role model in your grandfather, you don't see them as these aliens with nothing to give," I agree.

A couple of years ago David's grandfather had a heart attack. "That was really tough. Going through the divorce or any of that stuff growing up was nothing compared to that, and here I was an adult. That was a lot tougher to handle than anything else, to see a guy who's been so strong all his life, to see him in the hospital like that. ... " David trails off shaking his head.

I ask David what he would say to other kids being raised by grandparents.

"Embrace your grandparents, embrace your family because some people don't have that. Growing up, looking back, I was royalty. And I consider myself so lucky to have that. Be happy for what you have."

Kit

Of all the grandchildren I interviewed, a girl I will call Kit was by far the most troubled. Her life had been a series of abusers, disasters, and heartbreaks. She was very fragile emotionally in spite of the safehaven her grandmother had provided for much of her life. She appeared to be vulnerable to repeating the cycle of self-destruction, traveling the same path her drug-addicted mother took. During the course of the interview, she regaled me with wild tales. I had trouble deciphering how much of it was true, how much fabrication, and how much embellishment on basic facts. She was eager to talk to me, so eager in fact, I found out later that she lied about her age. Ultimately, I was unable to use her interview because she was underage, and technically in the custody of her birth mother.

Kit was the first of the grandchildren I talked with and, oddly enough, she set the pattern I was to see in most of the other interviews. Kit enthusiastically embarked, in her adolescent way, on a litany of transgressions perpetrated by her grandmother: she was too possessive, too strict, not trusting, unappreciative, and didn't understand her, her music, her nose ring, or her need for leeway. And when she was done with this self-righteously indignant laundry list of wrongs, she then bowled me over with a sincere, if unexpected, declaration of love and appreciation for her. Once you scratched the brash surface and moved beyond her teenage swagger, she was clearly centered, at the core, by the knowledge that her grandmother was the one person that would always be there for her.

Like Kit, each grandchild had an agenda. They needed to get things off their chests, clear their individual air. They wanted to tell me about their struggles and grievances, and then once that was done, they moved on. It disturbed me at first, and then I realized that if you were to interview anyone about their childhood, they would do the same thing. They would tell you stories about the particularly hard row they had to hoe, the injustices they suffered, and the difficulties they had to overcome. Then they would wax poetic about how good it was, how green, as no other, was their personal childhood valley. The adult children profiled here are no different. Here is what they want you to know about themselves, what they wish to tell other grandchildren in similar situations, and what it meant to them to be raised by grandparents.

Paul

Traveling out to another far-flung valley, I pass lakes and hills with names like Mattawa and Monadnock, and swollen, rushing rivers with jagged, rocky beds that curl around hillside passes and race by cars like mine wending cautiously down the narrow roads. In the summer the rivers slow to an inviting gurgle, the killer rocks become stepping stones, skipping stones. But now, on the brink of spring, they are in a fury to get down the mountainous ridges—like reckless teenagers, impatient, thrilled with the wild ride, heedless of the end.

This area is hunters' heaven, acres of dense forest and natural springs, unbroken miles of ancient deer paths and sheltered pools, scarred only by incipient duck blinds. It is beautiful. This is where tourists come in the fall to worship foliage, to buy corn, pumpkins, jars of put-up relish and homemade wild blueberry jam. They come to pick apples with the kids— Macoun, Baldwin, Rome Beauty, Winesap—jostling down mowed paths in haywagons to bountiful, forgiving orchards. Some stay on for the peace, the pace, the endless, breathable space.

The Powickis have been here for generations, Paul Powicki nearly all his life. At 36, Paul is a serene and steady young man of medium height and build with dark, slightly receding hair, dark eyes, and skin the color of a late August tan. He is very soft-spoken and deliberate in his speech, visibly measuring everything he says, and it is obvious he has given everything he says long, exhaustive thought.

Paul was adopted at six months of age by his maternal grandparents. I ask him if he knows the circumstances surrounding his adoption and he replies, "I do *now*. It took a divorce, a lot of work, and dealing with who I consider to be my parents, in trying to find out what was going on.

"My birth mom was going to school at Harvard, and she met my father who was a Chilean citizen. I was a result of that. She wanted to get married at the time, and he didn't. She was 25. My grandmother, who has always been the dominant leader of the family, said, 'You are not going to give this baby up for adoption, we are going to raise him.' So what they did is they sent her to Ohio to get her out of the area, because they didn't want anybody to know about it. Because this is where all the Powickis and all the Guralniks were raised and it was a big, big, big family secret.

"She went to live with the person I always considered to be my brother, and his wife. And that's where I was born, and then about six or seven months after that, I was brought to Brooksborough."

"So your birth mom had you for six months," I confirm.

"Yes."

"Was it difficult for her?" I ask, thinking it must have been absolutely wrenching to give up a baby after caring for him for six months.

"I've tried to talk to her about this. She just really does not want to deal with any of the issues around that. It was interesting though, she was really kind of like a participant observer in my life for many, many years. I can remember being a very small boy and having her take me up to the pond behind the house. I can remember one time when she came home and we went for a walk up to the ledges, and she took a lot of pictures of me. I always looked at her as a sister. Everybody told me that."

"As you were growing up, did you sense that there was something else you weren't being told?" I ask, and he begins to unravel the threads of his childhood for me piece by piece.

"When I was nine years of age, I can remember getting off the bus. And there was a kid up the road, Billy, who I still know to this day, and he was teasing me, 'You're adopted, you're adopted!' And geez, I was really disturbed by this. I was like, 'What the hell's he talking about?' I didn't have any concept of that. After that, it felt that something was different. My mother and father always treated me as truly one of their own; there was never a question of that. But he started me wondering, and I really had a rocky relationship with Billy after that for the next 10 years. We were not good friends anymore.

"It wasn't until I was 12 years of age, I was sitting down with my mom—my father was working the swing shift—and we were having pirogies. I don't know if you know what pirogies are, they are a Polish food. They're kind of like a ravioli, only big, and they're filled with cheese and potato and mushrooms, and you sauté 'em a little bit in butter. They're really nice. And I was sitting at the table, I was sitting in my father's chair, and she says, 'Your father and I wanted to tell you something. We've been thinking about this for a while, and we wanted to let you know you're adopted.' I was like ... Oh? And it seemed like right after that she was asking me for the pepper to put on the pirogies—and that was it! I was just left with that. I was so shocked at the time, I, I could feel this coldness come over me. I was like, 'Oh my God, Billy was right after all these years.' "

"When she dropped that bomb on you, you didn't respond in any way?" I ask, while Paul shakes his head sadly, no. I continue while Paul continues to shake his head, "You probably had a million questions, but there was no way to ask?"

"I attributed it to be such a bad thing to be adopted. Because kids had been picking on me, like Billy, it wasn't a thing to be proud of in any sense. That's one of the things I learned from that situation. And you know, they kept it from me for so many years, I inferred it's not something to talk about, and I didn't talk about it, you know, to my friends or family members, for a long time.

"It's interesting that my parents were kind of on a little denial trip themselves. Because two years later, I was taken to a hospital in Boston to get some blood tests done. And when I asked, 'Why am I having these blood tests done?' my mother said, 'Well, you know your father has cancer, and we want to get you checked.' I knew it was odd, and I'm thinking why am I here? I was panicking!

"A couple of years after that, I discovered this letter. I can remember digging around my mother's drawers, and I found this letter that came from some attorney in Florida. And the letter said, 'This letter is in regards to the 14-year-old boy whose biological father is Miguel Cantera.' Miguel Cantera has a rare blood disorder and he almost died on the operating table because he had an allergic reaction to an anesthetic. So that's why I was tested."

"So your birth father initiated the testing for your sake," I confirm.

"Right."

"As time went on, I started to wonder, Who is my mother? And where is she? And why was there this secrecy about it? I started to rebel. Through years of psychotherapy about it, I've learned that my rebellion was related to the confusions and the wondering. I can remember one of the biggest ways I rebelled was to go into the service. All the other Powickis all went to college. When I told my mother, she cried and my father gave me what's known as a Polish wave."

"What's a Polish wave?" I ask.

"A Polish wave is. ... " He laughingly demonstrates a dismissive gesture of the hand that suggests, "Be gone with you then!"

After serving his tour in the service, he went on to college, got his master's degree and now works as a rehabilitation counselor. He talks about some rocky years between the time he went into the service and the time he finally sought therapy—years of difficulty making commitments, engaging in acting-out behaviors, broken relationships, and an inability to trust.

"For me to sit here and do this today, I consider it a milestone. In the past it was like, 'Thou shalt *never* speak of this' was my view.

"When I started to go to school, it was like, 'This isn't an issue; it's not a problem for me.' A couple of times I asked my mother about my biological parents, and she'd say, 'Well, you know, we're really not sure.' And then came the Santa Claus story, I call it. My mother said, 'We went to the orphanage and we saw this cute little monkey and we knew you were the one for us.' And I was like—Geez, that's it?"

"When I was about 26, I asked the same question, and they gave me the same answer. And that was the story I was given consistently throughout my twenties."

"So when did you start your detective work?" I ask.

"My detective work started around the same time that my divorce happened. I was sitting across from a client one day, the person was really struggling, I mean it was obvious this person was really having a hard time. And I said to him, 'It seems like you've really got to be honest with yourself, honest with what you feel, and honest about what you want for yourself.' And when I went home I realized, Wait a minute, what are you doing? How can I be prescribing this to a person, when I am not even doing it for myself?

"I remember it was in February of '90 I called my brother, and I said, 'Tom, I've got some questions for you about who is my biological mother.' He said, 'I don't know anything, you've got to talk to Ma.' I said, 'I've talked to Ma, she gives me this same damn Santa Claus story.' He said, 'Well, Ma knows all the details. I was really young at the time. I really don't remember much.' I mean, there's a 20-year difference between the two of us, so once again, I'm thinking he knows something.

"He just was giving me the impression that something else was there and he just wasn't sharing it. I happened to stop by home and my mother said, 'You've been doing a little detective work tonight I hear. I hear you've been checking up on who your mother is. Your father and I had a talk, and we're going to talk to you about this tomorrow.' There was a part of me that was excited, and there was a part of me that was as scared as all hell.

"Of course my father didn't want anything to do with it. My mother was sitting on the couch and said, 'We've talked to your mother, and she said that it's okay if you know this information.' She was tearful as she was telling me this and just very upset. Finally she told me that, 'Your sister Kay is your mother.'"

"My response at that point was, 'Oh thank God! Thank God I am a Powicki! Thank God she's alive! Thank God I know what my roots are!' Because, Deborah, that was the biggest thing, just that constant, constant wondering. It really felt like ... " Paul gives a huge, heaving sigh, "80 pounds was lifted of my back at that point.

"I went home after that, and I was talking to my wife, and she said, 'Did you find out?' And I said, 'Yeah.' And she said, 'I knew who it was.'"

"She knew?" I ask, shocked.

"She knew. I really felt deceived. Here was a person that I had just married, and I really felt like she was in collusion with this whole cast of characters. I could feel, as time went on from that point, I can't stay here anymore." Paul soon left his wife, began therapy, and, "started working on a lot of this stuff.

"I started picking up the self-help literature, books on psychology. I figured if I read enough, I could reduce the anxieties. That doesn't happen by just reading books. I think with a person getting into a therapeutic relationship, or having the family in a therapeutic relationship, and starting to see, 'Gee, this is really scary for me, this is uncomfortable for little Sue or little Johnny, this is hard for me to work on, or, I am unsure and I'm struggling,' to recognize those feelings and work on those feelings is a real benefit not only for them but for the child.

"In the process of therapy, I had my biological Mom come to therapy, which was really difficult for her."

But all the years of burying the truth had taken their toll, and Paul's birth mother was unable to come to terms with the past. Paul asked his adoptive mother into therapy as well, but unfortunately, she was uncomfortable with the whole idea of counseling and told him in no uncertain terms, "No, I don't want to do *that*."

"I think the biggest thing that (therapy) did was allow me to get in touch with how I was feeling. Not just about being adopted, about who I am, what I wanted." Because Paul had his masters in social work, he came into therapy with his own self-diagnosis. "Core identity issues, adjustment disorder with mixed emotional features ... this is what's going on for me," Paul told his therapist. "But after a while, I put the diagnosis aside and started to work on things like, how am I feeling toward my biological mother, as well as my grandmother, as well my wife? I think therapy for me in the beginning was, 'Okay, let's see if we can ground you here,' because there was part of me that just wanted to leave the area, there was part of me that just wanted to sweep it back under the rug and not deal with it, and there was also another part of me that didn't want anything to do with my wife.

"As soon as I found out about my (birth) mom, I was on this other quest, (to find his birth father) with all the similar feelings." When Paul tried to question his birth mother about his birth father, she was evasive. Fortunately Paul worked part-time at the police department. "There's a brotherhood and a sisterhood there." Paul tapped into information dug up by that invaluable resource, and subsequently found his birth father's address. He sent a card and a picture at Christmas of that year. "And the next thing I know he called me at work. Since then we developed a great relationship." Paul has siblings from his birth father's marriage, some of whom do not want to deal with having a half-brother under these circumstances. With others, "We're still in the building stage.

"What's interesting is that not only do I have Polish in me, but there is also Chilean as well as Austrian," he says this with wide-eyed wonder and pride.

"So you really have a rich heritage."

"Deborah, the moment I found out I was a Powicki, you can't imagine the amount of peace I felt in my life. In spite of the secrecy, there was a lot of consistency with the Powicki family. I deal with a lot of families today in my profession, and it's hurting to see the conditions that a lot of people are struggling with.

"I always knew the limits, and religion was a very big factor in our family, I have a hell of a work ethic, and that comes from Emily and Leo Powicki. My father is dead now, but I can remember many, many days that I'd be working with him, whether it was picking stones, driving the tractor, driving the truck, driving the car, or making something in the shop. I was truly part of the family, and loved and shown right from wrong. I love my mother immensely, and she is still a big part of my life. Finding out the truth was almost healing in a way, it was so much easier to accept.

"1990 was a hell of a year. It was the toughest year of my life, but at the same time, it's allowed me to become a much better husband (Paul has remarried), a much better friend. I'm much more open and honest with people. My Christianity has blossomed through this whole experience. I hate to use the term "born again," but I feel much more at peace. I am not in therapy now, but if I need to go back to therapy, I'm okay with that. So sitting here today, I feel extremely fortunate."

"Was there ever a rift within the family that occurred because of all that came out?"

"Not really. One of the offshoots of what happened is that we grew a lot closer. A lot of those resentments that I had on a deeper level seem to have abated. Because I was able to work through who my biological parents were and a lot of my relationship issues, and working out my feelings and stuff.

"If people learn one thing from this interview: secrecy is destructive.

When kids start asking questions, tell them the truth. Don't bullshit around with this stuff. This is somebody's physiological and psychological make-up here we're dealing with. I say physiological because I can remember having my stomach in knots just wondering."

I ask Paul what he'd like to say to other grandchildren, and he whispers reverentially, almost like a prayer, "Be thankful. Be thankful for being kept where you are desired and loved."

Linda

Linda was the last person I interviewed. She is a young woman who embodies everything grandparents hope for. She is successful, confident, gracious, and has come to appreciate the sacrifice her grandmother made. She remains solidly connected to her family. In some ways, however, she also reveals some aspects of what we grandparents hope against. Linda is a child divided. It seems that she remains in a struggle against the divisions of class, race, heritage, and loyalties. She combines the maturity to work through adolescent issues with her grandmother, with a blind spot pent-up anger has provided regarding the failings of her birth parents. She remains in denial over how deeply she has been wounded by her father's absence, and focuses heavily, almost exclusively, on her birth mother's lack of racial sensitivity.

Linda is still unfolding; like the flowers closed down tight on the early spring afternoon I visited her, she is on the verge of blossoming. She needs to do the hard work of sorting through her complicated family structure, and finding, identifying, examining, and putting to rest each of her feelings about her birth parents, one by one, before she can emerge unencumbered and bloom.

If Zeus walked among the mortals today, I am convinced he would be ensconced somewhere at Yale University; this place looks like it was built for the gods. Maybe he would borrow books from this library near where I am sitting, a structure that looks like an ancient Roman Cathedral. He would walk up to the megalithic, sinuous checkout desk, his mythic foot-falls echoing through the cool, indifferent halls overlooked by soaring, stained glass depictions of other more banal deities. He would stride along the bricked footpaths that lead past these majestic granite edifices. Zeus would feel at home among the domed, arched, turreted, spired castles that rise up in surreal side-by-side existence with students impossibly gliding by on rollerblades, toting lumpy bookbags and wearing shredded jeans. He would look right here; the rest of us look wrong, like shabby, inconsequential, intruding ants.

I have time to ruminate on these things ad nauseam because I am sitting in front of the Sterling Memorial Library at Yale University 30 minutes early for my one o'clock meeting with Linda Swan, who is a student here.

It is the first perfect spring day of the year, the kind of day that makes you doubt winter. This spring has been slow in coming, laboring to break through mean drizzle and raw winds. Today the trees wave at the stringy clouds that drift by, and baby leaves shudder with delight at the fine blue sky and the first firm gaze of sunlight. However this interview turns out, I think, even if she doesn't show, I'm glad to be sitting here on this cool stone bench hugging my knees with the sun on my face.

I forgot to ask Linda what she looks like so I play a private guessing game with every young black woman that passes, matching them up with the voice on the phone, the image I conjured. I check my watch, 12:55. I begin to think I am in the wrong place at the wrong time so I abandon the only shady bench under lacy trees that border the walkway to the library steps to have a look around. I scan the sweeping grounds dotted with students stretched out in the grass trying on the first real warmth of the season. I look all the way up and down first one walkway and than the other and slowly circle the sleek, black marble fountain—a refreshing antidote to the Greco-Roman glut—then I see her. She is striding with long, confident legs toward the library steps, black leather backpack slung over a bared shoulder, short, gauzy sundress the color of straw and stacked espadrilles. She looks around a bit, never breaking stride, and enters the library with me trying to catch up on my shorter legs and comparatively Minnie Mouse-like steps. I rush to catch her—my last interview.

When we meet up, we move along to a dreary basement cafeteria to talk, the hidden underbelly of the ornate book temple above us. Linda is tall and slender, but strong looking and solid, as opposed to willowy or lanky. She has a perfectly oval face and large, shining eyes under well-defined, jet black eyebrows, sharp as arrows. Her hair is a close cap of small black swirls, and her skin is the color of warm.

She is very formal with me, her answers to my questions are short and to the point. Oh no, I think at first, this is like pulling teeth. I ladle out questions one after the other to sustain the flow. "And so ... ," I keep saying, trying to draw her out. She is careful—friendly and pleasant, but guarded. I wonder what it is she holds so closely to herself. Her brown eyes, the same shade as mine, look ceilingward as she considers what she will say and how she will say it, exactly how much she will give me.

Linda has been with her grandmother since she was a baby. She tells me she sees both her birth parents regularly but says dryly, "They don't participate actively in my life as far as support, financial or emotional. My mom, she does try. However, considering the circumstances, um, that precipitated my being under my grandmother's guardianship, the need never arose for me to look to her for that support because I've never had it, so I never wanted it, and I don't care to have it now."

It takes my breath away, the force of her cool rationale. "So why don't we go back, if you want, and talk about what precipitated it," I suggest.

"Well, my mom is white. Italian American, third generation. My older brother was born out of wedlock, so at the time that wasn't the best thing to happen. My father's family was much more receptive to my mother, than my mother's family was to my father. So basically, she was disowned, had no money, nowhere to go, so she stayed with my grandmother. They got married later when I was born. She got really sick, ill, she was hospitalized for a couple of years, so my grandmother took us in. My father went into the Marines, and basically that was the end of their marriage."

She is rushing through this, not entirely comfortable, curt almost. I think she's wondering why the heck she ever agreed to do this interview. I ask her why her mother was hospitalized, and she replies coolly, "She had a breakdown."

"After she came back home, she didn't want to displace us again, so she just left us there." Her voice is smooth as cream but there is a rough overlay that winks in and out of her speech, surfacing only now and then, scraping hard over a telling phrase; it bears down when she says, "left us there." I think she is totally unaware of this revealing lapse, and would be mighty displeased with herself if she knew.

"And she wasn't able really to take care of kids, never mind two black kids." There it is again, that harsh dip in tone, pursed lips, and downward turn at the corners of the mouth. "Her dad finally came around and took her back in. And he was a little bit more receptive to us as well. He was never like, *Grandpa,* but he let us come over weekends, and he cooked us dinner, and he was nice as he could be considering the circumstances. And that's it in a nutshell."

"When you say, 'He was as nice as he could be considering the circumstances,' do you really think that's true?" I ask.

"I think that he had a lot of conflicting feelings. He was a very strong

Catholic, so I think that his religious upbringing and convictions sort of conflicted with how he was treating his daughter's selection for a mate. So I think that in a sense, that perhaps motivated him to be receptive. Because whenever we went over there he always got "God" with us." She says this sarcastically, bitterly. "I think that he was trying to come around, but it was hard. All these racialized ideas had been inbred. I think he was definitely trying to come around because he loved his daughter, and if his daughter had black children, he had to love them as well, as much as he could." And there it is again, like sandpaper, or something deeper, like the serrated edge of a saw.

"Did you feel love from him?"

"Hmmm ... ," she muses, looking away from me, gazing off into the homely interior of the cafeteria, with its bald fluorescent lighting, scarred, brown tables and cold, spindle-legged chairs. She reminds me a lot of my Tyra, with her intelligence and heads-up walk, her wide shoulders, and the curve of her slender arms, even the color and elegant consistency of her skin. Tyra tans easily and deeply, inheriting what I refer to as our "Italian skin;" I am half Italian, like Linda. My Italian heritage, though, has always brought me a wellspring of riches which I relish. I feel saddened that Linda feels only a negative connection there.

"Looking back now, I don't think so. Of course, he passed when I was 13. And when I came over, he was nice, he did all the superficial things, like he cooked us dinner and bought us Christmas presents. So of course I thought, 'Wow, he really cares for us.' But, looking back, he never went beyond that. But he never was an emotional man, he never went beyond that with my mom either."

"So until he passed away, do you think he was making an attempt to come to terms with his biases and make a peace with his daughter and his grandchildren?" I am pressing for an answer in the affirmative. It's something I need to hear.

"I think the only reason he was motivated to do that was out of love for his daughter. I think he was trying, but just basically to make things better for his daughter." The rough, sawing edge drags deeply over this, and she is just a little haughty. I think Tyra would behave the same way if she were the grandchild in these circumstances. She, too, would cover any sensitivities with a brave, brittle shell, daring anyone—with head held high and straight—to question her authority over the loose threads of her life.

"When you first went to live with your grandmother, did everyone think it was a temporary situation?"

"I don't think that was ever a concern, just because my grandmother's household has always been a very welcoming one. You know, relatives who come up from the south stay there, and when they get their finances going, they leave. It's sort of like, if you need a place, there's always a place there. It's just a very welcoming place. It's like family is family is family."

Linda was adopted at 10 years of age. Before that, Linda believes it was an informal arrangement.

"I never missed having a nuclear family because I just never had one, so I never knew what it was like. A lot of people ask me, 'Are you bitter that things turned out the way it did?' and I'd say, 'No, I don't know any other way.' And I'm just thankful that I did have someone there, so that never bothered me."

"Do you harbor any resentments for your birth mother?" I ask.

"No."

"Or your birth father?"

"My birth father, yes. My mother, I think I excuse just because of her mental incapacity. I understand she is just not able or equipped to raise a family. I have issues with her being white. My father, on the other hand, he remarried, and he takes care of his other kids. And while I never really wanted ... any, um," she pauses, reaching for accuracy, precision, "emotional support from him, it's been a struggle going to school and being independent from my grandmother, whose only source of income is Social Security. I would have liked some help. But I understand that he's not rich. Actually he remarried and has seven other kids with his new wife. But never anything, never even like 20 bucks here and there, never. And that bothers me." Interestingly, although she says this with righteous, static anger, that same low, dragging inflection that sometimes unintentionally surfaces is missing from her overtly angry remarks.

"And it also bothers me that he never helped my grandmother out with little things. She was raising us by herself, and he could have helped with groceries, not even pay for them, just come by, pick us up, take us to the store. Nothing. Nothing, ever.

"I don't think he has any great disdain or dislike for us, I just don't think he knows how to be a father. I don't think he is anymore of a father to the kids he's presently raising. I mean, he just doesn't know how to."

Author Jan Waldron's memoir, *Giving Away Simone*, depicts her experiences around giving her daughter up for adoption, their subsequent reunion, and the ongoing work of reconnecting. In the book, she works through many of the issues Linda has filtering through her own life. In a passage on absent birth fathers she tells us, "Abandoning fathers, though personae non gratae, are still woven seemlessly into our agenda of familial liabilities. When men leave their families, they are called, frivolously, dead-beats. A missing father's breach is financial. His emotional and psychological debts are not even implied."[1] It appears that Linda glosses over the emotional cost of her father's absence. She dismisses, too quickly, the effect on her life of the miserly way in which he gave of himself.

"My mother made more of an effort to visit. Every weekend we would go out, and that was fine. We'd go to the movies, or to her house for dinner. And that was always nice, but it was more like a friend, because she was never there changing diapers or helping with homework. It was kind of cool, having a friend on the weekend. And she knew that's how we viewed her, and there was nothing she could do about it."

"What did you call her?" I ask.

"Mummy," she says sweetly, just like a little girl.

"You say you have issues with her because she's white? Do you want to talk about that?"

"Sure. Initially I had a very warped view of my racial identity. I considered that because my mom was white and my dad was black, I enjoyed the best of both worlds. But society is not like that at all, and you really do have to choose. I grew up in a black neighborhood, I was treated as black, and I never really was accepted into the white world. There was just no way, no way. Just look at how my mother's family received us, my father. That was a big slap in the face."

I ask when she started to feel this way, and she answers, "I guess senior year in high school." Before that, "I was just very idealistic, and I just believed everyone could get along. And I finally realized that was not the case.

"Even little things that my mother says bothers me." Linda is holding a pen, flopping it from side to side and tapping it on the table for emphasis. "I think that if a woman could marry a black man (tap) and have black children (tap)—and I know she would die for me right now, I know how much she loves me—and if *she* still harbored racist views, it's really hard for me to believe any white person can be sincere (tap)."

"For instance, when I was applying to colleges I said, "Yeah Mummy, I'm applying to Yale and Princeton," and she's like, 'Well, are you sure you can get in?' And I was like, 'I'm pretty confident,' and she's like, 'Well are you sure? Maybe you shouldn't try, or aim as high.' All right, I let that alone. Then just recently I went to visit her with my niece. My niece is light-skinned with long hair. I don't know if you're aware of this, but in the black community they tend to give more privileges to black children that look white. Shauna's mom is very dark-skinned with short, kinky hair, so she looks very black in a sense. So my mother was talking to her boyfriend, and she said, 'Shauna has a beautiful skin complexion and she has really nice long hair even though her mother is *dark*.' And that really bothers me, but I never confront her with it, because I know she's not intellectually able to confront me with that. She has no awareness of that, and she's actually very bothered that I don't claim my Italian heritage, but I'm like, 'Mummy, it never claimed *me*.' But I never talk to her about racial issues because she's not really aware. I love her, but I just can't deal with her on a lot of different levels."

I offer her my two cents worth in regards to her mother's discomfort about Linda's choice of colleges. I tell her it sounds to me like a typical scenario in which a mother fears her daughter may get hurt or disappointed. I ask her if her mother would acknowledge any bias and she replies, "No! But I don't think that excuses it or makes it any less hurtful.

"I just became aware of it myself. I am sure there were numerous examples, but I was just too blind myself to see it. Lately I've kept my eyes open. But I tend not to talk to her about those things because I can't deal with it. She gets on my nerves. She thinks I'm crazy. She thinks *I'm* crazy." She laughs, but it is mirthless and dripping with irony.

"I think her racial views are very colored by her attraction to my father, because he was never much of a family man." She drags down heavily on these words too. "He was never much of a husband, of a father. So of course these ideas trickle down on how you treat other people of color (tap, tap). I think that has a lot to do with it."

I wonder how much of Linda's distress and focus on a perceived racial bias in her mother is really diverted anger over other less tangible issues. Jan Waldron has a lot to say about the mother-daughter rift in her book. There is one line that seems to me particularly fitting here, "All the language and behavior between my birth daughter and me is subject to a phantom translation, in our heads, by that awful spirit that presided over the day I walked away."[2] It would be understandable if Linda's buried abandonment issues influenced the way she reacts and interacts with her birth mother.

"Let's switch gears and talk about your grandmother. Tell me about her."

"She's a very industrious woman. She's very hard-working, and for her it's not really a choice, it's just how she grew up. Her dad was a sharecropper. Ever since she was young, she was out in the fields, and that work ethic has carried through. Even with all her kids, and however irresponsible they are with their parenting duties, she just takes it up. I don't know if I could be as strong. I don't know if I could do that, just seeing how much she struggled with raising me, my brother, my little cousin that she's raising now. I don't know if I could do it. I don't know if I'd want to do it.

"I understand that its not the children's fault *at all*. It really disgusts me how parents do not take their job seriously, and I understand that there are a lot of circumstances that enter into the equation—financial, sometimes drug addiction, a lot of different factors. But people take child bearing, or child raising ... they don't take it seriously anymore.

"For me, family has become so important just because I see how hard she has worked to preserve her family, even though it's not a family in the traditional sense. For me, I very much want a husband, I want "two-point-five" kids, I want a house. Those are very important things for me, and I'm willing to work hard for that. She has inspired me. However, I don't think I could raise a family like she has. I would be drained, I'd just be *gone*. She's in her seventies now, and she's still raising kids!"

Most of her grandmother's children got "caught up" in drugs. Linda grew up in Dorchester, but went to Tyndall, a private school in another part of Boston.

"I think that made all the difference. I really don't consider myself much different from the strain from which I emerged. I don't think I am much different from my family members who did get caught up. I think that my exposure to professional people, to achievement-oriented people, to the middle-class, gave me the leverage I needed to work harder to get myself out of a bad situation.

"I know that I am in a very privileged position, basically going between both worlds. And I do think both of them (mother and grandmother) do live vicariously through me. And that's hard, that's really hard. I feel added pressure; my degree is their degree. It bothers me when my grandmother boasts about me, because I feel like it creates a much deeper divide between me and my family. And I know that, in a sense, I have strayed just because I am at Yale. But I don't want my little cousins and nieces and nephews to think that they can't achieve the same thing. By revering me, she's (unintentionally) putting them down."

I ask her how she wound up going to a private school.

"Actually, in fifth grade I had a pretty committed teacher who encouraged me to go to a private school. I didn't want to go. I wanted to be with my friends. But he encouraged me, and my grandmother encouraged me, so I went, and I hated it. But I wouldn't trade it for the world now."

"You mean you hated it initially, but then you ... ," I begin.

"I always hated it. I went there seven years, and I appreciated it while I was hating it. It was a private, all-girls school. It was a big culture shock for me. For instance, I always thought that I had it made, like I had everything in the world. I would go to school with these girls and they'd be saying, 'I'm going skiing at Colorado this weekend,' or, 'My sister just got a new Volvo for her sixteenth birthday.' And then I'd be in class, I remember I was in Latin class and we were learning this new declension, and we were talking about dialects and my Latin teacher—there were two black girls in my class—my Latin teacher looked at both of us and said, 'Maybe Linda and Doreena can tell us a little bit about dialects.' That was hard because there was a race issue *and* there was a class issue. Even the black girls were very middle class. So it was hard to make friends, we lived in different places, our parents did different things. I had a totally different household than they did. And it was strange because I thought that it was normal to have 12 people living in your house. And then when I went to visit them, it was mom and dad and brother. I was like, 'Where's everybody else! Don't you have uncles and cousins?' And they were like, 'Well, yeah but they don't live here.' And it was that type of exposure that gave me the ability to see beyond my immediate surroundings, which a lot of my family members never had. I mean a lot of them have just never been out of Boston, as simple as that is. So I think, had I not gone to private school, I would not have had the exposure I needed to prosper academically.

"A lot of the reason I'm here is basically because of her (grandmother's) participation in my life. She worked up until I was in high school. Even when she wasn't working she was so resourceful that we never struggled. For instance, she always got us housing, and we were never hungry, and we never wanted much. And for that, I am really thankful. For a long time I thought we were pretty rich, until I went to Tyndall. But I never wanted anything; she was there."

I ask her how she got through her teenage years being raised by a grandmother. "Actually, I was a pretty good kid, but, of course, I'm a little biased." She laughs warmly, happily for the first time, and I'm relieved to hear it. "I stuck to my studies without any pushing from her, I was very self-motivated. But there came a time when she didn't like my friends, and she told me I couldn't hang out with my friends. That was a big struggle, I was about 15. She didn't like my music."

"How about your clothes?"

"She never had problems with it then. Now she does, my skirts are too short." She laughs again. "And now she loves all my friends. All my friends are either graduated, or working, or are presently in college. None of them have kids. We don't hang in the street or go to seedy clubs; we're just college kids. I think she appreciates my choice of friendships."

"I am sure she loves to see that," I say. "That must be such a pleasure to see you going off with friends like that.

"Did you butt heads while you were growing up?" I ask.

"Yeah. Yeah, we did. It was difficult because we'd have so many people in the house, and I always resented it because you'd have to share your room, you don't have personal space to grow. I really believe you need physical space of your own. It's nice to feel like you're part of something larger, but if that's always being invaded, that's really hard. I was always a little bit resentful because of that, but then I understood what she was doing. Basically, she had a bigger picture, and I was very self-focused and self-centered. That's what being a kid is about."

"What would you like to say to grandchildren being raised by grandparents?" I ask.

"It took me a long time to get to this point, but when I was an adolescent, I would always think in terms of my needs not being met, be it financial or emotional, what she could not do for me. Until recently, just a couple of years ago, I realized how hard it is for her. That was such a new thing for me to think about her feelings, and I am still embarrassed about that. That was a big epiphany for me.

"Basically, she was done mothering, and she had to start from scratch. I was two days old, I'm 21 now, and she's still mothering me. *Imagine* how hard it was for her considering the big generation gap, considering how hurtful it probably is for her to know that the children she raised can't raise their own. Even though we never discussed it, I know it must really bother her. Whenever I am upset about something she's said or something she's done, I stop to think how strong she was to raise us, and then I'm not so indignant as I was initially. What I'm trying to say is, you need to make yourself more aware of why your grandparent is doing what they're doing. Because they care."

Linda interjects that one of the most important things that grandparents can accomplish is to make sure that birth parents are somehow involved in the children's lives. Even though she has had her share of difficulties with her birth parents, she is glad they are a part of her life. "Access to biological parents should always be there," she urges.

"As I've grown, I've been able to understand more why she has done what she's done and it's only out of love and affection and wanting to preserve her family that she took me in. And if that's understood, you can get over the bumpy rides."

> The need to belong, to claim a heritage, the need for a past and an identity, these are all are critical and heartfelt themes demonstrated by, David, Kit, Paul, and Linda.
>
> In all my years working with children and adults who have been part of the foster care system, I do not recall hearing one state, "Boy, growing up in foster care was great!" And while I have heard countless foster children share their appreciation for some of the quality, loving care they did receive while in foster care, they do, however, long for family bonds and lifelong connections. Like many other grandchildren, David, Kit, Paul, and Linda were able, thanks to their grandparents, to maintain family connections and their roots.
>
> The grandchildren who have spoken in these last pages have provided us with valuable insights, leaving images that will last long after we have put this book down. We have the been given the opportunity to see with a certainty that it is in the best interest of the child to receive their care and love from a supportive family member. The grandchildren themselves have made this powerful point, loud and clear.
>
> Will it always be a gentle, easy experience? No, but with openness, honesty, and mutual respect for the truth, the potholes and cracks in the road won't stop you from staying on course.

As Linda and I part, I feel at a loss. Standing at the foot of the library steps in the softened afternoon sunlight together, I want, suddenly, to ask her more questions, get to know her better. I embrace her before she leaves, patting her back like she was my own, and hesitate, asking her what she's going to do with the rest of the afternoon, with the summer, with her life. I hang on her words as if they contain some magic information for me, as if she might be a gypsy looking into a crystal ball telling my future, my grandchild's life swimming before her in the glass globe. "My degree is their degree," she told me earlier. Your degree is *my* degree, I think, your success is our success, you represent the potential success of all our grandchildren, that it can be done. You are the reassurance that all will be well in the end. I want her to tell me something tangible and perfect as a jewel, something I can take with me like a talisman.

She is going to Princeton this summer, she says. She's interested in education reform, and they have programs there that will get her closer to her goal. I'm glad to hear it, and I'm happy for her, but that's not really what I want to know.

I want to hear that it was wonderful to be raised by grandparents. That children's hearts can grow without scars, healed clean by the burning devotion of loving caregivers. That family connections have so grounded them that they never feel shaky in their shoes. That what they missed by not having birth parents to care for them was more than made up for by the stalwart affection of grandparents. That grandparents are really not second best, just a lateral alternate, like a quick two-step to the side, never breaking the rhythm or disturbing the healthy momentum of childhood. I need reassurance from Linda, from all the grandchildren I interviewed. That's really what I wanted all along.

In my head, I know better, that there is no clear, happily-ever-after path, only the road well traveled. I know that the work of raising emotionally secure children is so very difficult, and grandparents must use every tool available to accomplish that goal. I know that working to preserve our families is a way of life, not a part-time job, and that forgiveness is the best route to healing. In my head, I know that this work is never truly finished.

But in my heart, I wish to hold comforting assurances that all that we work for will have a satisfying payment, that there is nothing I can do that is more important than keeping my family together, and that I am blessed to have my family intact and moving forward toward the future. There is room in my heart for all these things.

Epilogue

As I criss-crossed New England over this past year, conducting interviews, meeting families, getting to know grandparents, and talking with many others interested in the various issues involved when grandparents raise grandchildren, I very quickly realized that I could not play the objective journalist. This book became more than an exploration of an issue, more than a personally pertinent project; each step brought me closer to a kind of affirmation, and ultimately became an enlightening odyssey for me. In tapping into the stories and struggles, joys and heartaches of others, I was drawn into each family's story in a way in which I had not intended; the thread of my experiences was woven tightly into the tapestry of theirs. Walking with them as they relived their journeys, I reexperienced my own and was able to come home to a sense of peace and conviction that this was not merely an issue born out of individual failure, but one of triumph—of families who have faltered, rallied, and sustained.

When I began this book, my goal was to offer grandparents and grandchildren a look at what others have been through and survived. I hoped that through their example as well as the therapist's insights, grandparents would be better equipped to deal with challenges that might come their way. And I hoped to raise awareness in others who may not realize the depth and complexity of this growing trend while providing a common sense outlook onto the issues.

In addition, I hope that I dispel any complacent attitudes that may exist that would dismiss these problems as something on the periphery only, something that happens to "them" but not to "us." I hope the examples of

225

grandparents and adult children portrayed here will show that no one is immune to the destructive influence of drugs and alcohol, or the common vagaries of immaturity and irresponsibility. Lastly, I hope that in raising awareness, I might give a boost to the efforts of those involved in rewriting social service policy, encouraging judicial reform, legislating regulations, and shaping this country's attitudes toward child welfare and family preservation.

Organizations such as the American Association of Retired Persons, the Brookdale Grandparent Caregiver Project, and the American Bar Association's Center on Children and Law, as well as many others, are now focusing on the concerns of grandparents raising grandchildren. The Child Welfare League of America (CWLA) is currently exploring options regarding Kinship Care and Kinship Adoption. Systems in place that do not yet serve the specific needs of family helping family need to be rethought and reworked. Kinship Care and Kinship Adoption, as proposed by the CWLA, would leave room for birth parents in a legal reworking of custodial rights. In Kinship caregiving arrangements, the grandparent or other kin could become the legal parent, while keeping intact the important connection of the birth parent and providing each with a legal designation for inclusion in the child's life. A spokesperson for the CWLA recently explained, "Many current policies, and even some proposed policies, fail to allow for what Kinship care does best: support and affirm the extended family, without unnecessarily severing ties with the nuclear family."[1] The efforts of the CWLA represents a new, broader, more inclusive and critically necessary way of thinking about family and family preservation.

The lifelong opus of family relationships is like an elaborate tango, sometimes close to the skin, warm and embracing, sometimes spinning apart in separate, self-absorbed revelries, sometimes flung together in hard, hurting passion. We move always in sync with, or in contrast to, the other participants in the intricate dance we call family. Out of step or in perfect time— what we do, what we are, is defined by not only the steps we take, but also by the steps taken by those in closest proximity to us. Whether they exist for us in body or spirit; whether they are tangible or bind us only as an unshakable psychic pull, they remain our partners in life, for life.

We are all inexorably wound together as individuals, as families, as communities, and as a society. We must take care to value, accommodate, and, at times, assist the variety and diversity, each unique facet, in the noble work—the blessed art—of family.

Notes

Introduction

1. Meredith Minkler and Kathleen M. Roe, *Grandmothers as Caregivers: Raising Children of the Crack Cocaine Epidemic* (California: Sage Publications, 1993), 2.

2. "The Orphanage: Is it Time to Bring it Back?" *Newsweek,* 12 December, 1994, 28.

3. National Center for Health Statistics, 1992.

4. Daphne Muse. "Parenting From Prison," *Mothering Magazine,* September 1994, 98.

5. Carol Levine and Gary L. Stein. *Orphans of the HIV Epidemic: Unmet Needs in Six U.S. Cities* (New York: The Orphan Project, 1994).

6. "The Orphanage: Is it Time to Bring it Back?" *Newsweek,* 12 December, 1994, 30.

7. Child Welfare League of America, *Kinship Care: A Natural Bridge* (Washington, D.C.: Child Welfare League of America, 1994).

Chapter 4

1. *Kinship Care: A Natural Bridge,* Child Welfare League of America, (National Committee for the Prevention of Child Abuse 1993).

2. *Child Abuse,* A study by League of Women Voters of Massachusetts, 1990.

Chapter 7

1. Maya Angelou, *Wouldn't Take Nothing for My Journey Now,* (New York: Random House, 1993).

Chapter 8

1. *A Blueprint for Fostering Infants, Children and Youths in the 1990s,* Child Welfare League of America.

2. Hope Edelman, *Motherless Daughters: The Legacy of Loss* (New York: Addison-Wesley, 1994).

3. Joseph A. Califano Jr., "It's Drugs, Stupid," *The New York Times Magazine,* 29 January 1995.

4. Globe Staff, "Family Values II," *The Boston Sunday Globe,* 21 May 1995.

5. Edward, M. Hallowell, M.D., and John J. Ratey, M.D., *Driven to Distraction* (New York: Pantheon, 1994).

Chapter 9

1. Jan Waldron, *Giving Away Simone* (New York: Times Books, 1995).
2. Ibid.

Epilogue

1. *Brookdale Grandparent Caregiver Information Project Newsletter,* (Berkeley, Calif.: University of California, October 1992).

Glossary

AARP—American Association of Retired Persons
ADD—Attention Deficit Disorder
AFDC—Aid For Families with Dependent Children
Al-Anon—Support groups for family members of alcoholics
Alateen—Support groups for teenage family members of alcoholics
CHINS—Children in Need of Services
COA—Council On Aging
DSS—Department of Social Services
DYS—Department of Youth Services
EOEA—Executive Office of Elder Affairs
FAS—Fetal Alcohol Syndrome
GAL—Guardian Ad Litem
GED—General Equivalency Degree
HHS—Health and Human Services
OFC—Office For Children
PA—Parents Anonymous
PTSD—Posttraumatic Stress Disorder
SAIN—Sexual Abuse Investigation Network
SSI—Supplemental Security Income
WIC—Women, Infants and Children nutrition program

Bibliography

Publications for Adults

Abrams, Justice Ruth I., and Chief Justice John M. Greaney. *Gender Bias Study of The Court System in Massachusetts.* The Supreme Judicial Court, 1989.

Angelou, Maya. *I Know Why the Caged Bird Sings.* New York: Random House, 1970.

Angelou, Maya. *Wouldn't Take Nothing for My Journey Now.* New York: Random House, 1993.

Bolles, Richard. *What Color is Your Parachute?* Berkeley, Calif.: Ten Speed Press, 1992.

Califano Jr., Joseph A. "It's Drugs, Stupid." *The New York Times Magazine,* 29 January 1995, 40-41.

Carpenter, Liz. *Unplanned Parenthood: Confessions of a Seventysomething Surrogate Mother.* New York: Random House, 1994.

Chalfie, Deborah. *Going It Alone: A Closer Look at Grandparents Parenting Grandchildren.* Washington, D.C.: AARP Women's Initiative, 1994.

Chalfie, Deborah. *The Real Golden Girls: The Prevalence and Policy Treatment of Midlife and Older People Living in Nontraditional Households.* Washington, D.C.: AARP Woman's Initiative, 1995.

Child Welfare League of America. *A Blueprint for Fostering Infants, Children and Youths in the 1990s.* Washington, D.C.: Child Welfare League of America, 1994.

Creighton, Linda. "Silent Saviors." *U.S. News & World Report,* 16 December 1991, 80.

Donahue-King, Sheila, et al. *A Resource Guide for Massachusetts' Grandparents Raising Their Grandchildren.* Boston: Massachusetts Executive Office of Elder Affairs, 1995.

Globe Staff. "Family Values II." *The Boston Sunday Globe,* 21 May 1995.

Partnow, Elaine, ed. *The New Quotable Woman.* New York: Meridian, 1993.

Sewell, Marilyn, ed. *Cries of The Spirit.* Boston: Beacon Press, 1991.

Edelman, Hope. *Motherless Daughters.* New York: Addison-Wesley, 1994.

Hallowell, Edward M., M.D., and John J. Ratey, M.D. *Driven to Distraction.* New York: Pantheon Books, 1994.

Johnson, Ivory, et al. *Kinship Care: A Natural Bridge.* Washington, D.C.: Child Welfare League of America, 1994.

Levine, Carol, and Gary L. Stein. *Orphans of the HIV Epidemic: Unmet Needs in Six U.S. Cities.* New York: The Orphan Project, 1994.

Melina, Lois Ruskai. *Making Sense of Adoption: A Parent's Guide.* New York: Harper and Row, 1989.

Minkler, Meredith and Kathleen M. Roe. *Grandmothers as Caregivers: Raising Children of the Crack Cocaine Epidemic.* Newbury Park, Calif.: Sage Publications, 1993.

Morganthau, Tom, et al. "The Orphanage: Is it Time to Bring it Back?" *Newsweek. 12 December 1994, 28-35.

Muse, Daphne, "Parenting From Prison." *Mothering Magazine.* September 1994, 99-105.

Tannen, Deborah, Ph.D. *You Just Don't Understand: Women and Men in Conversation.* New York: Random House, 1990.

Van Biema, David. "The Storm Over Orphanages." *Time,* 12 December 1994, 58-62.

Waldron, Jan, L. *Giving Away Simone.* New York: Times Books, 1995.

Walker, Alice. *In Search of Our Mothers' Gardens: Womanist Prose.* New York: Harcourt Brace and Company, 1984.

White, Alexandra, et al. *Grandparents Raising the Next Generation.* Boston: Boston Aging Concerns—Young and Old United, 1994.

York, David, Phyllis York, and Ted Wachtel. *Toughlove.* New York: Bantam, 1990.

Books for Children

Fraser, Debra. *On the Day You Were Born.* New York: Harcourt Brace Jovanovich Publishers, 1991.

Hoberman, Mary Ann, ed., *My Song is Beautiful.* Boston: Little, Brown and Company, 1994.

Hopkins, Lee Bennett, ed., *Through Our Eyes.* Boston: Little, Brown and Company, 1992.

LaCure, Jeffrey R. *Adopted Like Me.* Franklin, Mass.: The Adoption Advocate Publishing Co., 1992.

Pellegrini, Nina. *Families Are Different.* New York: Holiday House, 1991.

Williams, Vera B. *More, More, More Said the Baby.* New York: Greenwillow Books, 1990.

Resources

American Association of Retired Persons (AARP)
and AARP Grandparent Information Center
601 E Street, N.W.
Washington, DC 20049
(202)434-2296
Parenting Grandchildren: A Voice for Grandparents—newsletter published by the AARP
Grandparent Information Center (GIC)

American Bar Association's Center on Children and Law
740 15th Street, N.W.
Washington, DC 20005
(202)662-1000

Cambridge Documentary Films (CDC)
P.O. Box 385
Cambridge, MA 02139
(617)354-3677
Defending Our Lives, produced by CDC and Peace at Home—an Academy Award-winning
documentary film that portrays the severity of domestic violence.

Child Find of America
1-800-IAM-LOST
National Hotline will assist in search for runaways and children who have been taken by a
non-custodial parent.

Child Welfare League of America (CWLA)
440 First Street, N.W.
Suite 310
Washington, DC 20001-2805
(202)638-2952

Morning Glory Press
6595 San Heroldo Way
Buena Park, CA 90620
(714)828-1998
Publishers of *Do I Have A Daddy?* by Jeanne Warren Lindsay, and *School-Age Parents: Three Generation Living.*

National Center on Women and Family Law, Inc.
799 Broadway, Room 402
New York, NY 10003
(212)674-8200

Peace At Home
95 Berkeley Street
Suite 107
Boston, MA 02116
(617)482-6504

The Guilford Press
72 Spring Street
New York, NY 10012
Publishers of *Grandparents As Parents: A Survival Guide for Raising a Second Family* by Sylvie de Toledo and Deborah Edler Brown

Index

235